WOMEN WRITERS AND
POETIC IDENTITY

MARGARET HOMANS

Women Writers and Poetic Identity

Dorothy Wordsworth, Emily Brontë,

and Emily Dickinson

PRINCETON UNIVERSITY PRESS

To the memory of
Thomas F. Weiskel

Contents

Acknowledgments

I would like to thank, for their generous interest and help during the conception and the writing of this book, Harold Bloom and J. Hillis Miller; and for their careful and imaginative criticism of later drafts, Margaret Ferguson and Stacy Pies. Mary Poovey has helped me to understand the larger issues that surround this book's concerns and has encouraged me greatly with this and related projects. Without the enthusiasm and sweet temper of Ethan Nadel, writing this book would not have been the pleasurable experience that it was.

In connection with the unpublished manuscripts of Dorothy Wordsworth I am grateful for the assistance of Stephen Parrish and of Susan Levin and for the use of the Dove Cottage Library and the Cornell University Library.

I would also like to thank the Whiting Foundation for a fellowship during the year 1977-1978, during which most of this book was written.

Grateful acknowledgment is extended to the following:

The Trustees of Dove Cottage for their very generous permission to quote from the unpublished poems of Dorothy Wordsworth in their keeping at the Dove Cottage Library, and from poems by Dorothy Wordsworth published in *The Wordsworth Circle*, copyright 1978.

Harvard University Press and the Trustees of Amherst College for permission to reprint lines from poems #12, 19, 25, 106, 124, 135, 668, 689, 811, 1036, in their entirety; portions of poems 2, 67, 85, 239, 632, 670, 683, 790, 812, 1400 and 1651, from *The Poems of Emily Dickinson*, edited by Thomas H. Johnson, Cambridge, Mass.: The Belknap Press of Harvard University Press, copyright © 1951, 1955 by the President and Fellows of Harvard College.

Little, Brown and Company for permission to reprint lines from the following poems from *The Poems of Emily Dickinson*,

WOMEN WRITERS AND
POETIC IDENTITY

Introduction

How does the consciousness of being a woman affect the workings of the poetic imagination? The nineteenth century provides an appropriate locus for addressing this question because the Romantic tradition makes it difficult for any writer to separate sexual identity from writing. Sexual identity by itself does not determine the nature of a poet's work, but where the poetic self represented in a text identifies itself as masculine or feminine, the reader must ask why it does so, and to what effect. In literature as in experience, sexual identification (or polarization, if it comes to that) is not static but rather develops dynamically out of interactions, being for the most part learned through imitation of figures of the same sex and in response to figures of the opposite sex. Where the major literary tradition normatively identifies the figure of the poet as masculine, and voice as a masculine property, women writers cannot see their minds as androgynous, or as sexless, but must take part in a self-definition by contraries. This book explores the ways in which three representative nineteenth-century women poets, textually conscious of their femininity, attempt to shape for themselves their own identities as poets in response to a literary tradition that depends on and reinforces the masculine orientation of language and of the poet. The book's purpose is to define the special challenges faced by women who aspired to be poets, and thereby to illuminate both their failures and their successes.

Critical interest in the relation between gender and literature has generated a large body of literary criticism in recent years, and I would like here to indicate how my approach differs from others and why a new approach might be useful for looking particularly at poetry.

Nothing in literature is simply or inherently feminine. Static definitions and symbols of femininity have had their place in culture for so long that it is sometimes difficult to

separate them from actual sexual differences, but only usage
and context create symbols; nature is not inherently Mother
Nature but only where Milton and Wordsworth and their
readers agree to see it that way. There is an apparently reac-
tionary tendency among some feminists today to designate
and celebrate "the feminine," taking cultural fictions for ac-
tuality. The French critic Hélène Cixous, arguing from female
characters created by male authors of the past, finds that there
are innate psychic as well as biological differences between the
sexes and that these differences are of primary importance in
the formation of two separate bodies of literature.[1] These in-
nately feminine characteristics are of course said to diverge
from traditional definitions of femininity; Cixous' essay be-
gins by decrying the standard associations of passivity and
corporeality with the feminine and activity and abstraction
with the masculine. But given that our language cannot be
remade in a moment, it is impossible for these terms not to
regain their old significations. Cixous writes of an ideally
bisexual woman who would erase traditional boundaries be-
tween masculine and feminine, but then goes on to grant her a
kind of writing that scarcely differs from the old notions of
women's capacities. The new writing will be an inscription in
the body, and the symbol for this writing will be her milk: a
white ink. Elaine Showalter concludes her otherwise extraor-
dinarily effective *A Literature of Their Own* with an exhorta-
tion to women writers to concentrate unflinchingly on "female
experience," by which she means primarily the experience of
the body.[2] Women writers who essay to transcend their sexu-
ality, she writes, are actually evading it. That transcendence
and abstraction may be the distinctive traits of patriarchy ac-
counts for a feminist reaction against them; but transcendence
is the major value term for poetry in the Romantic tradition,
and if it is an evasion, it is a splendid one. It would be a great
loss to believe that it is marred by its historical association
with an exclusively masculine system of value.

My purpose here is not to continue the battle for priority
between established values, but to see how this battle affects

the writers born into its midst. It is useful to describe the ways in which culture has defined women, if it is remembered that these definitions are historical fictions, not necessary truths. Although Freudian theory is often accused of perpetuating sexual stereotyping, it is acutely descriptive of nineteenth-century family patterns and it offers a dynamic rather than a static model of sexual identity; in reading nineteenth-century women writers it may be useful to examine an analogy—not a causal relation—between their works and psychoanalytic models of femininity.

Probably the most effective approach to delineating a feminine imagination has been to look at social pressures that affected all women, literary or not. These consisted mainly in the pressure to conform to certain patterns of ideal womanhood, none of which included the possibility of a poet's vocation. It was considered scandalous in the early nineteenth century for a woman to write publicly; if she did, she was judged not as a writer but as a woman. The conditions in which women found it difficult to become poets ranged from practical constraints such as the lack of "a room of her own and five hundred a year" to the more insidious cultural belief that women's minds were not capable of abstract thought.[3] Expectations about women's minds were self-fulfilling because women were denied formal education and the experience of public life and were confined within a domestic circle, whether married or not. The restrictions that frustrated Virginia Woolf's fictive Judith Shakespeare obtained with equal force in the nineteenth century. With very few exceptions, it was only by turning these restrictions to advantage, instead of battling them, that a woman could become a successful writer. Even so, none of the women poets of that era led what anyone would call an ordinary life. Emily Brontë and Emily Dickinson embraced the limitations of their circumstances, Brontë resenting every excursion outside her father's home and Dickinson cultivating an even greater seclusion. Christina Rossetti and Elizabeth Barrett Browning also spent most of their lives in deep seclusion. Dorothy

Wordsworth, who never quite acknowledged her poet's voca-
tion, most closely approximated one of the expected patterns
for women of her day; all the evidence suggests that she was
happy to let her brother's extensive family occupy her time
and care. Cultural patterns may help to determine sexual iden-
tity, but the powerful poet can, if she chooses, adapt these pat-
terns to her own purposes.

The major interpretive application of this historical ap-
proach is the examination of fictional characters for the degree
of their conformity to societal ideals and limitations. Because
the greatest differences between men and women are enacted
on a social stage, and because characters in nineteenth-century
novels obey and disobey the same rules of conduct that their
creators lived by, the novel is logically the first place to look
for signs of sexual identity in literature. Patricia Meyer
Spacks, for example, traces continuities among the figures of
women created by many different women novelists, whether
the author's self-presentations or her female characters; these
continuities are available and important because they are
grounded in the actual experience of women's lives.[4] But a
novelist's experience in society—certainly, at least, the docu-
mented experience available to critics—is likely to have far
more relevance to her work than would a poet's. Lyric poetry
lacks the novel's representational framework of character and
plot, and a theory of feminine imagination appropriate to
poetry cannot make use of historical material as effectively as
can theories appropriate to the novel.[5]

Few critics have acknowledged the special situation of
women poets or have widened their theories to include a less
accessible literature.[6] It may also be because there are fewer
women poets than women novelists that criticism about
women authors tends to ignore the poets or to assume that
the same principles may be applied equally well to poets and
to novelists. Rosalind Miles, for example, says bluntly,
"When we say 'women authors' . . . we mean women
novelists," casually explaining the scarcity of women poets as
an accident of history.[7] Woolf, too, decries a lack of recent

women poets that does an injustice at least to Emily Brontë, Elizabeth Barrett Browning, Emily Dickinson, and Christina Rossetti, and perhaps to others as well (*A Room*, p. 99). There may be fewer poets than novelists among nineteenth-century women, but not so many fewer as these comments suggest. The same literary atmosphere that made it difficult for women to become poets must have made it—and still makes it—difficult for readers to appreciate those who did succeed. This critical blindness to women poets, and to the difference between poetry and prose, demonstrates that the same conditions that originally restricted most women writers to the novel still obtain. If the novel was more available to women because those portions of society that women experienced formed appropriate subjects for prose fiction, then the novel is more readily available to critics of women's writing because the connections between the work and a measurable, describable "female experience" are so much more demonstrable than in poetry. Both the novels of the past and the present criticism of them are grounded in the practical rather than in the transcendent.

It is quite true that much poetry by women is available to the sort of interpretation that has illuminated women's novels in the past. Much of the work of Christina Rossetti and Elizabeth Barrett Browning, the major nineteenth-century women poets who are not considered here, is written from an explicitly feminine point of view. Barrett Browning's poetry contains many polemics about feminist issues and many characters who could be analyzed in the light of Victorian culture, especially in her "novel-poem" *Aurora Leigh*. Many of Rossetti's poems are about frustrated female sexuality, or take up conventional feminine stances, particularly that of an intensely humble religious devotion. "An Artist in His Studio" overtly criticizes a male artist for replacing a real woman with his dreams about her, but for Rossetti the issue appears to be more personal than aesthetic. Most love poems written by women differ unsurprisingly from love poems written by men, in having the voice or the point of view be a woman's.

But all these differences are thematic, with bearing on women's social roles. Ellen Moers extends her study of literary women to include poets as well as novelists, but because she encompasses them with the same techniques of thematic interpretation, she limits her discussion to poems and issues that reflect the poet's life and experience, with the result that many aspects of the poetry must be left out.[8] Poetry requires a theory of its own.

The problem that concerns this study is that Romantic poetry generally minimizes its connections with practical experience, so that women poets writing in this tradition elude a thematic interpretation based on that experience. If the poetical character transcends time and place, according to the Romantic ideal, then it should transcend gender as well. We should not expect Romantic poetry by women to bear very heavily the traces of sexual identity, socially experienced; and yet something often impedes this poetry from achieving what appears to be a desired Romantic transcendence.

If biographical and thematic interpretations only partly illuminate the works of these women poets, a different order of "female experience" does contribute in a major way to the shaping of poetry by women: literary experience, the experience of reading poetry written almost exclusively by men. Though poetry is ideally unconditioned by gender, the literary tradition inherited by nineteenth-century women poets has implicit male biases that are ordinarily not perceived as such by male readers. Even in a realm that the women poets might have sought in the hope of escaping society's restrictions, they would have found echoes of those restrictions. Wordsworth was burdened by the greatness of Milton's poetry; the women poets are burdened by the masculinity of both. Literary experience is the poet's equivalent to the novelist's societal experience, in that it is the primary formative experience in the development of her identity as a poet. In part, literary experience simply exaggerates the report of societal experience: the men are even bolder, the ladies even more beautiful and passive, in Byron than in life. But there are other and subtler ways in which the literary tradition betrays a masculine point of view that is oppressive to women and, even when the poet is able to proceed beyond her reaction to conventional stereotyping, there remain further inhibitions. The poems that confront the impediments from literary tradition are not necessarily marked by explicit feminism or by any theme or quality that has been traditionally defined as feminine, because that masculine bias manifests itself as much in structures of thought and of language as in overt discussions of gender roles.

This book, then, tests the hypothesis that it should be possible to read the poetical works of women writers primarily as literary texts and in a literary context, while at the same time finding a language for evaluating the literary effects of the author's femininity. The first chapter attempts to duplicate the way in which a nineteenth-century woman of literary talent might have read Romantic literature and its antecedents, and it traces selectively those aspects of literary tradition that made it difficult and even undesirable for such women to think of themselves as potential poets. The subsequent chapters examine the variously successful efforts of three women writers to overcome the impediments encountered in their experience of tradition: the works of Dorothy Wordsworth, Emily Brontë, and Emily Dickinson permit a sequential anatomization of the feminine Romantic response to the masculine tradition. Although it may seem unfair to compare the poetry of Dorothy Wordsworth and even of Emily Brontë to Dickinson's, I am comparing not so much achievement as what precedes achievement, the process that leads to a sense of poetic vocation or identity. That Dorothy Wordsworth and Brontë are not primarily known for their poetry, as Dickinson is, is part of their significance here. They were both potential poets who, for reasons that will be explored below, redirected their best energies towards other forms of writing and of activity. Dorothy Wordsworth and Brontë are better poets than many readers may now think, and I hope to show as far as possible that they might have been poets as brilliant as Dickinson. But they are as interesting for their failures as for their successes, because they show us the immensity of the difficulties to be confronted by any woman poet, and because they help us see just how extraordinary Dickinson's achievement is. The concluding chapter argues that recent poetry by women is still confronting many of the same challenges met by nineteenth-century women, and that it should be possible to bring a reading of the nineteenth century to bear on the present.

September 1978

SINCE THIS book was completed, Sandra M. Gilbert and Susan Gubar have published *The Madwoman in the Attic: The Woman Writer and the Nineteenth-Century Literary Imagination* (New Haven: Yale University Press, October 1979). This brilliant and inclusive work of feminist literary criticism takes as its subject the nineteenth-century woman writer's response to the patriarchal literary tradition, a starting-point that the present book generally shares, although with very different results; Gilbert and Gubar go far toward justifying this book's hypothesis, that it should be possible to synthesize a literary criticism that is both textual and feminist. Although it has not been possible to engage their argument in the body of my book, I hope that my discussion of women writers primarily as poets will complement their concentration on women novelists. Their wide-ranging introductory chapters on the patriarchal literary tradition and its constricting effects on all nineteenth-century women writers prepare for a major (though not exclusive) emphasis on character, theme, and story—the essentials of prose fiction—whereas my introductory reading of literary tradition aims more specifically at identifying what would have been especially salient for the formation of poetic voice and identity, the essentials of lyric poetry. Although the authors do discuss various reasons for the rarity of great women poets in the nineteenth century, they map the outlines of a territory that is still, I hope, worth exploring further; and that our approaches to Dickinson are so very different testifies to the richness of this extraordinary poet. Although I regret that I cannot here respond to this book in the depth that it demands and deserves, I am grateful to its appearance for creating a context for my book and for giving me the encouraging sense of being part of a shared enterprise.

CHAPTER I

The Masculine Tradition

In Romantic poetry the self and the imagination are primary. During and after the Romantic period it was difficult for women who aspired to become poets to share in this tradition, not for constitutional reasons but for reasons that women readers found within the literature itself.[1] Where the masculine self dominates and internalizes otherness, that other is frequently identified as feminine, whether she is nature, the representation of a human woman, or some phantom of desire. Although this tradition culminates in Romantic poetry, it originates in the Bible, which directly and through Milton's transmission reinforces the Romantic reading of gender.[2] To be for so long the other and the object made it difficult for nineteenth-century women to have their own subjectivity. To become a poet, given these conditions, required nothing less than battling a valued and loved literary tradition to forge a self out of the materials of otherness. It is not surprising that so few women succeeded at this effort; very few even conceived of the possibility of trying.

This chapter will concentrate on two major ways in which women readers must have found woman's otherness reinforced: her association with nature and her exclusion from a traditional identification of the speaking subject as male. Although for the purposes of analysis these topics will be considered separately, here and in the chapters on the three individual authors, they are in fact complementary aspects of one larger problem.

WILLIAM WORDSWORTH'S feminization of nature is the most obvious example of sexual polarization in the literary tradition that would have shaped women poets' conception of poetry. When nature is Mother Nature for Wordsworth, she is valued because she is what the poet is not. She stands for a lost memory, hovering just at the edge of consciousness, of a time before the fall into self-consciousness and into subject-object relations with nature, whether that original unity took place in earliest infancy or, fictively, before birth.[3] As the object of the poet's love, Mother Nature is the necessary complement to his imaginative project, the grounding of an imagination so powerful that it risks abstraction without her. But he views her with a son's mixture of devoted love and resistance to the constraints she would place on his imaginative freedom. She is no more than what he allows her to be. It has become customary for feminist theorists and historians to invoke the idea of a matriarchal society that predated the dualistic patriarchies of Egypt, Greece, and western culture thereafter. This matriarchy is generally described as originating in the worship of fertility, in which the earth is a mother goddess and all nature, including humanity, is her creation and her domain. Whether this matriarchal society is mythic or historical, that the memory of it should be kept alive demonstrates that some portion of the human mind likes the notion that women could be as powerful as men. But there is an important distinction to be made between women and the "feminine principle," and the myth emphasizes the latter over the former. The powers of Wordsworth's maternal nature or of this prehistoric matriarchy have no necessary bearing on the powers of real women. Whether as a cultural or political memory, or as personal myth transmitted into poetry, Mother Nature is not a helpful model for women aspiring to be poets. She is prolific biologically, not linguistically, and she is as destructive as she is creative.

There are many other models of femininity in literature, but Nature is doubly imposing. She has a special status not just as a figure of the mother but also as a mother figure in that, as the most powerful feminine figure in Romantic poetry, she dominates the consciousness of women entering the tradition as newcomers. She was there before them, as the mother precedes the daughters. For the male poets of the Romantic period, the poets of the past and the figures of the poet represented in their works constitute a father figure against whom the younger poet, picturing himself as a son, must define himself.[4] If the figure of the powerful poet of the past is the father, in this family romance, then the mother is surely the Mother Nature represented as the object of that poet's love. Freud tells us that it is the father-son conflict that provokes growth and creativity in the son. His view of the mother-daughter relation is somewhat different, but for the women poets this is surely the major formative conflict. The women poets must cast off their image of themselves as objects, as the other, in the manner of daughters refusing to become what their mothers have been. The difficulty is that the image of Mother Nature is so appealing. The women poets do not want to dissociate themselves either from Nature or from nature even though they know they must.

None of the poets treated here became mothers themselves. Two lost their mothers early, Dorothy Wordsworth at the age of six and Emily Brontë when she was three, and Dickinson's remarks about her shy and traditional mother suggest what the other poets might have felt about theirs had they lived.[5] "I never had a mother" signifies for Dickinson, perhaps, her sense of distance from her mother's life and concerns. Dorothy especially suffered from being an orphan, and yet literature may have benefited from her and Brontë's not having had images of compliant femininity to love and emulate. Carroll Smith-Rosenberg has shown from diaries and letters written by relatively ordinary nineteenth-century women how intensely close and untroubled relations normally were between mothers and daughters.[6] But these daughters had no other ambition than to become what their mothers were: good wives and mothers. Contemporary women are startled at these revelations because dissonant relations between mothers and daughters are now the rule rather than the exception, if the mother is a "mother-woman" like Madame Ratignolle in Kate Chopin's *The Awakening*, and if the daughter aspires to be anything more than that. Nineteenth-century women poets are more appropriately grouped, in this respect, with twentieth-century women than with their contemporaries. To be writers they cannot foster, as Wordsworth does, intimate relations with maternal nature. They cannot be docile daughters of Nature because they know it is all too possible to pass from continuity to identification and thence to a loss of their own identity. Lynn Sukenick uses the term "matrophobia" to refer to Martha Quest's fear of becoming too like her own mother in Doris Lessing's *Children of Violence*, but the term applies as well to nineteenth-century women poets' relations with Mother Nature.[7]

According to Freudian psychology, women both reject and then masochistically imitate their mothers. Seeing the world androcentrically, Freud insists that the oedipal theory apply to women as well as it does to men. Because girls must conform to the oedipal pattern they are obliged to reject the object of their first love, the mother, in order to redirect their love to masculine objects. They must take a circuitous route through pre-oedipal and oedipal stages whereas boys follow an undeviating path: "In the course of time . . . a girl has to change her erotogenic zone and her object—both of which a boy retains."[8] Freud's assertion that the girl not only redirects her love toward her father but also actively rejects her mother is based on his questionable definition of females as castrated males. The girl, discovering her "lack," holds her mother responsible. This theory of femininity may have been and may even still be descriptively accurate, but only because women have internalized their oppressors' negative view of femininity. If women reject maternal figures it is because they have been conditioned to do so by a masculine culture that held Freud's beliefs long before Freud articulated them.

Yet insofar as the mother has feelings of inferiority, or views herself as psychically castrated, the daughter has good reason for her matrophobia. Karen Horney examines cultural factors that may better account for what Freud took to be a biological matter.[9] Citing the "masculine character of our civilization," in which women are restricted to the narrowest of functions, Horney says that "a girl is exposed from birth onward to the suggestion—inevitable, whether conveyed brutally or delicately—of her inferiority, an experience that constantly stimulates her masculinity complex" (p. 69). The women held up as models of femininity to other women are those who, by their passivity and infantility, pose the least threat to the "superiority of the masculine principle." Clara Thompson interprets penis envy, the correlate in Freud's thinking to feminine "castration," as a symbol for women's quite rational envy of the power and privilege associated with being a man.[10] These interpretations make sense of the girl's rejection of her mother as herself "castrated" and as responsible for the daughter's cultural castration. It is the mother's cultural powerlessness that the daughter is rejecting, not the mother herself. She denies her love for and identification with her mother only insofar as the mother stands for a situation that the daughter wishes to rectify.

Mother Nature is hardly powerless, but, enormous as her powers are, they are not the ones that her daughters want if they are to become poets. A human mother's giving birth may be an extraordinarily active event, but as a model for the daughter's vocational ambitions it is simply not applicable, because it stems from what she is, not from what she does (Horney, p. 145). Milton's Mother Earth, giving birth to herself, is passive and requires the active agency of "Main Ocean" to complete the process, in the following passage from *Paradise Lost*:

> The Earth was form'd, but in the Womb as yet
> Of Waters, Embryon immature involv'd,
> Appear'd not: over all the face of Earth

Main Ocean flow'd, not idle, but with warm
Prolific humor soft'ning all her Globe,
Fermented the great Mother to conceive,
Satiate with genial moisture, . . .

(VII, 276–282)[11]

Mother Nature is also traditionally associated with death as much as with life. Even Wordsworth, who attributes to nature an active and beneficent love, retains the tradition of her amorality in his portrayal of her mixed ministries of fear and love. She has no consciousness, only materiality and an elusive presence; no center, only diffuseness. Writing poetry would seem to require of the writer everything that Mother Nature is not, and the first project of any poet who is also a daughter must be to keep herself from becoming her mother.

One critic of Freud, Luce Irigaray, finds that this somewhat involuntary rejection of the mother may be responsible for depriving the daughter of a strong sense of identity and therefore of subjectivity.[12] Without subjectivity, women are incapable of self-representation, the fundamental of masculine creativity. Irigaray suggests that a new feminine creativity, and a renovation of culture, would result from women's recovering the maternal origins from which masculine culture separates them. Returning to her proper origins, a woman will acquire so strong a sense of identity that she will not need to search for self in everything she sees; creativity will begin with an acknowledgment that the rest of the world is not to be possessed. (Cixous also praises women's potentially greater respect for otherness.) This original creativity would be free from the masculine trait of domination by the central self. But Freud's theory of femininity describes almost the same position, if negatively, since Freud uses it to deny creativity to women: cut off from origins, a woman has no central self by means of which to subjugate the objective world. But although Irigaray's formula would seem the more positive, the feminine self in the Wordsworthian tradition finds herself in a peculiar dilemma. To identify with the mother in this case would be to identify with nature, and to identify with nature would be to put an end to writing about nature.

The traditions surrounding Mother Nature in Romantic poetry affect Dorothy and Brontë more than Dickinson, because the British writers are more concerned with nature than are the Americans. The literary tradition in which Dickinson finds herself, as defined largely by Emerson, transcends Wordsworth's respectful view of nature. Emerson is as much or more self-centered than the British Romantics, but his exaggeration of this mode is helpful to Dickinson, his female successor. Because his self is so inclusive, he cares less for the specific characteristics of the "NOT ME," so that Dickinson is not confronted with the same relentless myth of female nature and female objects of desire that Brontë and Dorothy Wordsworth face. Enormous as Emerson's egotism is, it is more easily adapted by a woman, because it has no sexually defined objects. Dickinson's sense of her femininity is more evident in reference to rhetoric than to maternal nature, and this chapter will return to questions of rhetoric later on. But the two matters are not entirely separable, and Dickinson does write about Mother Nature, just as Dorothy and Brontë also encounter rhetorical problems.

Wordsworth's major characterizations of nature as maternal occur in *The Prelude*, published in 1850, two years after Brontë's death. But several poems by Wordsworth available to all early nineteenth-century readers characterize nature as maternal or feminine, most notably two central formulations of poetic project, the verse Prospectus to *The Excursion* and "Ode: Intimations of Immortality."[13] In the Prospectus to *The Excursion* Wordsworth's "spousal verse" for the marriage between the intellect and nature assumes a masculine "Mind of Man" for the poetic psyche, and it assumes the traditional feminine characterization of nature for his counterpart.

Paradise, and groves
Elysian, Fortunate Fields—like those of old

Sought in the Atlantic Main—why should they be
A history only of departed things,
Or a mere fiction of what never was?
For the discerning intellect of Man,
When wedded to this goodly universe
In love and holy passion, shall find these
A simple produce of the common day.
—I, long before the blissful hour arrives,
Would chant, in lonely peace, the spousal verse
Of this great consummation.

By invoking the idea of pagan paradises in this context, the poet images the communion between the mind and nature in the manner of Plato's primordial androgyne, so that the fall is like the separation of the sexes. Through the reference to Milton, here and elsewhere in the Preface, the poet relates his bridal "external world" to Milton's maternal nature of Book VII of *Paradise Lost*. First the "great Mother" emerges from the womb of waters; later,

>   the bare Earth, till then
> Desert and bare, unsightly, unadorn'd,
> Brought forth the tender Grass, whose verdure clad
> Her Universal Face with pleasant green,
> Then Herbs of every leaf, that sudden flow'r'd
> Op'ning thir various colors, and made gay
> Her bosom smelling sweet.
>
>   (VII, 313-319)

Wordsworth's image of the universal marriage is beautiful and convincing in itself and because it exalts as it typifies the rest of his project. But it depends on identifying matter and otherness as female and subjectivity as male.

Maternal nature in the Intimations Ode is less exalted than the bridal universe of the Prospectus to *The Excursion*. Man is here the child of heaven, but the foster-child of Earth, who is explicitly opposed to the memory of a primordial heaven.

Earth fills her lap with pleasures of her own;
Yearnings she hath in her own natural kind,
And, even with something of a Mother's mind,
    And no unworthy aim,
    The homely Nurse doth all she can
To make her Foster-child, her Inmate Man,
    Forget the glories he hath known,
And that imperial palace whence he came.

Self-involved, Mother Earth has no capacity for understanding her foster-child's infinite desires, and opposes transcendence. Only by transforming nature into a reminder of "What was so fugitive"—the infant's unconscious communion with heavenly things—does the poet cease to feel threatened by natural objects and find a renewed intimacy with them. Maternal nature is depersonalized into "ye Fountains, Meadows, Hills, and Groves," and the new relation that the poet prescribes means a shift from living "beneath your more habitual sway" to a less hierarchical love. The poet learns that he can still love nature without submitting to her control and without being like her. Similarly in "Tintern Abbey" the two stages of youth that the speaker has now passed are both characterized by a likeness between youth and nature. The "glad animal movements" "of my boyish days" give way only to the time "when like a roe / I bounded o'er the mountains." Growing up depends on being able to have a separate identity and to "look on nature" rather than seeing nature from within.

Although the poet values his own distance, most of the female figures depicted in his poetry are like nature or merged with nature. For some, like Dorothy in "Tintern Abbey" or in *The Prelude*, or his wife in "She was a Phantom of delight," being like nature is seen by the poet as felicitous. For others it is more sinister, because being like nature is a fatality. Lucy, Ruth, the Mad Mother, Martha Ray, several vagrant women, and Margaret in Book I of *The Excursion* undergo a dissolution of identity, either by literally dying or by entering a termless, semiconscious life-in-death as a part of natural process. Some of them are themselves mothers, inflicting on their hapless children what they themselves receive from nature. All are daughters of Nature. Young boys and old men are represented as sharing this experience of a vegetative or naturalized life. The Boy of Winander "Blew mimic hootings to the silent owls," and the old man of "Animal Tranquillity and Decay" "is insensibly subdued / To settled quiet." But the poet's own active subjectivity is almost the sole representative of adult man, and he assures us that his consciousness maintains a loving distance from nature. In these others, male and female, he represents a possibility for the self that he cannot consciously adopt for himself, a merging with nature that is at once desired and feared.

The Lucy poems image a feminine figure for whom there is no discontinuity between imaginative sympathy with nature and death, and a masculine speaker for whom Lucy's death is non-catastrophic, sanctifying nature as well as darkening it. In "Three years she grew in sun and shower" Lucy is most explicitly the daughter, or foster-daughter, of Mother Nature, who, self-involved as in the Intimations Ode, takes possession of Lucy in order to have a child of her own. The mother's purpose is to make her daughter be like herself. The Church Fathers interpreted Genesis to mean that only Adam was formed in God's image, leaving Eve open to interpretation. This new Eve is to be made in Nature's image, for Nature's beauty "shall pass into her face:"

> "She shall be sportive as the fawn
> That wild with glee across the lawn
> Or up the mountain springs;
> And her's shall be the breathing balm,
> And her's the silence and the calm
> Of mute insensate things.
>
> "The floating clouds their state shall lend
> To her; for her the willow bend;
> Nor shall she fail to see

> Even in the motions of the Storm
> Grace that shall mould the Maiden's form
> By silent sympathy."

Like God's creating Word, Nature's "shall" is immediately efficacious, although the reader is carefully kept from knowing whether Lucy's development into a natural creature preceded her death, or whether, more startlingly, her early death is the manner in which her naturalization is accomplished.

> Thus Nature spake—The work was done—
> How soon my Lucy's race was run!
> She died, . . .

Though Lucy leaves the speaker bereft, her legacy to him is synonymous with the natural world of which she herself has become a part:

> She died, and left to me
> This heath, this calm, and quiet scene.

In "I travelled among unknown men" England draws the speaker back from his travels not to a particular spot but to a region diffusely consecrated by Lucy's lingering memory.

> And she I cherished turned her wheel
> Beside an English fire.

> Thy mornings showed, thy nights concealed,
> The bowers where Lucy played;
> And thine too is the last green field
> That Lucy's eyes surveyed.

That wheel, though it seems to indicate a domestic image, is not quite specific enough to be representational, and projects instead Lucy's death in the last poem in the series, where she is "Rolled round in earth's diurnal course, / With rocks, and stones, and trees." Lucy, apparently complicitous in her own disappearance into nature, once turned the wheel that now turns her. Not only is she Mother Nature's daughter in appearance and bearing, her wheel-turning is the predecessor of nature's wheel-turning, so that the daughter is the mother of the mother in an ominous closed circling of their own.

Although from the point of view of the nineteenth-century woman reader the Lucy poems trace problematic distinctions between subject and object, to a modern reader they demonstrate Wordsworth's exceptionally tactful restraint about such distinctions. Frances Ferguson reads them as the poet's effort to school himself not to appropriate his poetic object, which he traces out of sight until in the last poem Lucy's having been at all is conjectural.[14] By repeating an experience of loss they curtail his usual tendency to dominate in subject-object relations. But these two readings are not irreconcilable. Although Lucy escapes his grasp as an object—it is nature instead that appropriates her—elusiveness is one of the qualities of otherness in a larger definition of appropriation, and Lucy's vanishing into nature contributes to nature's consistent otherness.

In the story of Margaret in *The Excursion*, the woman's decline is measured by and seen through a decline in the cultivated nature around her, particularly her garden. There are no discursive accounts of Margaret's state of mind; instead, descriptions of nature's encroachment on the house and garden represent her exclusively.[15] A few months after her husband has deserted her, in midsummer, the cottage is still cheerful, but natural growth is a little too lush. "The honeysuckle, crowding round the porch, / Hung down in heavier tufts," and another vine grows over the windows, "Blinding the lower panes." In the garden, flowers straggle beyond their boundaries and hang "their languid heads, wanting support"; and

> The cumbrous bind-weed, with its wreaths and bells,
> Had twined about her two small rows of peas,
> And dragged them to the earth.
>
> (I, 715-730)

On a subsequent visit, the Wanderer reads in the condition of the garden "that poverty and grief / Were now come nearer to her." The ground is hardened, and herbs and flowers and a young apple tree whose "bark was nibbled round by truant sheep" are all dying. Both woman and garden are returning to a state of nature: the garden by returning to an original wildness and the woman by dying and resting in the earth. Nature is thus more than a metaphor; its inexorable process is a secondary cause for her decline as well. Margaret's reaction to her husband's departure is the primary cause. He is no longer there to help fend off nature's encroachments, but, more important, Margaret now devotes all her thoughts and energies to her hope that he will return. She is betrayed by her imagination, but nature conspires with that betrayal.

The history of the poem's composition is emblematic of a different kind of encroachment. Beginning with an image of naturalization, the ruined cottage itself, Wordsworth wove around it the human story of Margaret, but after that, surrounded the story with his growing emphasis on the story teller, who is first the Pedlar, then the Wanderer. Partly because of the affinities between the Wanderer and the self speaking in *The Prelude*, the story of Margaret is read not for its own sake but for the sake of what it allows the Wanderer to reveal about himself. Margaret succumbs first to a misguided imagination, then, weakened, to nature, and finally to a narrative structure in which she becomes the object rather than the subject of the poem. Only with the addition of the Wanderer's concluding comments does the reader find Margaret's tragedy softened in any way. By finding in her return to the earth an image of peace and restored harmony, the Wanderer ends his tale on a cheerful note that is extrinsic to the story itself, because it depends on "faith." The weeds that, in the context of the woman's story, were a sign of her declining interest in life, are part of nature's undiscriminating loveliness in the conclusion.

> "She sleeps in the calm earth, and peace is here.
> I well remember that those very plumes,
> Those weeds, and the high spear-grass on that wall,
> By mist and silent rain-drops silvered o'er,

As once I passed, into my heart conveyed
So still an image of tranquillity,
So calm and still, and looked so beautiful
Amid the uneasy thoughts which filled my mind,
That what we feel of sorrow and despair
From ruin and from change, and all the grief
That passing shows of Being leave behind,
Appeared an idle dream, . . .

. . . .

                I turned away,
And walked along my road in happiness."
                            (I, 941-956)

The Wanderer seems a bit too consoled. This natural peace, exquisite as it is, is paid for by the woman's death. The speaker's reaction, prior to this passage, is more ambiguous, like the quiet sorrow of his response to Lucy's death. He "blessed her in the impotence of grief" and then, returning to the cottage, traces there "That secret spirit of humanity" that survives " 'mid the calm oblivious tendencies / Of nature." But whether the woman remains a ghostly and saddening presence, or whether her death eventually provides material for the "meditative sympathies" or for "meditation," the Wanderer and the speaker see and learn what it is not permitted Margaret to see and learn.[16] Each Wordsworthian landscape contains the buried presence of a maternal or feminine figure, whether she is a figurative maternal quality diffused through nature, or a more literal figure who once lived. The woman's death is lamented but made inevitable by the character of Wordsworth's project. He presses these figures to the boundary of nature and beyond because he searches for something that is hidden in nature. What is important for present purposes is that the object of the search, and its partial representations in figures like Lucy or Margaret, are definitively not figures for the poetic self.

Like the story of Margaret, the Lucy poems image an absorption of the woman into nature. The Lucy poems may or

may not refer to Dorothy, but Coleridge thought they did
and Dorothy probably concurred,[17] and when Wordsworth
writes explicitly about Dorothy in *The Prelude* he almost al-
ways identifies her with nature or with natural beneficence.
She is "Nature's inmate";

> Methought such charm
> Of sweetness did her presence breathe around
> That all the trees, and all the silent hills
> And everything she look'd on, should have had
> An intimation how she bore herself
> Towards them and to all creatures.
>
> (XI, 216-221)

Within nature, with faculties similar to nature's, she comes as
close as any living human can to a genuine reciprocity with
nature. This is a very different absorption from Margaret's or
Lucy's, being vital and felicitous. But it affords no better
paradigm for the subjectivity necessary to the woman poet,
especially for Dorothy herself, and is perhaps even harder to
cast off because it is so lovely. In "Tintern Abbey" the poet
identifies Dorothy as the sucessor to nature in ministering to
his spirits and as the inheritor of the period in his own life
when he was closer to an identity with nature.

> Nor perchance,
> If I were not thus taught, should I the more
> Suffer my genial spirits to decay:
> For thou art with me here upon the banks
> Of this fair river; thou my dearest Friend,
> My dear, dear Friend; and in thy voice I catch
> The language of my former heart, and read
> My former pleasures in the shooting lights
> Of thy wild eyes.

Later in the same passage he addresses Dorothy in the manner
of an address to nature, as if conflating her with nature:

> Therefore let the moon
> Shine on thee in thy solitary walk;
> And let the misty mountain-winds be free
> To blow against thee.

Yet when Dorothy herself writes and makes reference to her brother's works, she does not adopt this identification with nature or with naturalized beings, linking herself instead to a figure closer to her own position as writer. In *A Narrative Concerning George and Sarah Green*, a tale of pathos in a mode similar to that of Margaret's story, she borrows a quotation from *The Excursion* in order to compare her narrative fixation upon the suffering family to the Wanderer's fixation upon Margaret:

> I may say with the Pedlar in the "Recluse"
>
> "I feel
> The story linger in my heart, my memory
> Clings to this poor Woman and her Family,"
>
> and I fear I have spun out my narrative to a tedious
> length.[18]

Similarly, a verbal echo in Brontë's earliest poem explicitly on the imagination identifies the speaker with the Wanderer rather than with Margaret, even though the speaker's situation is desolate, like Margaret's, and, like Margaret, she is being encroached upon by nature. On his second visit, a few lines after the passage quoted by Dorothy, the Wanderer finds Margaret "self-occupied" and as they sit together by the fire

> sighs came on my ear,
> I knew not how, and hardly whence they came.
>   (I, 802–803)

Brontë's speaker is sighing from grief, in imitation of a storm outside,

> Sighed at first, but sighed not long—
> Sweet—How softly sweet it came!
> Wild words of an ancient song,
> Undefined, without a name.[19]

Margaret's sighs, emblems of the victim's woe, are here di-
vided into this speaker's similar sighs and a timely utterance
that, by making her a poet, rescues her from Margaret's fate.
This answer to a paradigm of feminine submergence may be
Brontë's talisman against nature's many encroachments on
her identity as a poet in subsequent poems.

The women poets were under no obligation to take their
self-images from Wordsworth's representations of feminin-
ity, but Wordsworth had behind him a range of models, from
"the figure of the youth as virile poet" of the poets of sensibil-
ity, whom Shelley and Keats in turn adapt for their personae
in their early romances of the self,[20] to the august intonations
of Milton and his predecessors in epic voice. Dorothy, read-
ing Byron and Shelley in her later years, and Brontë reading
them as a child, would have found there feminine figures less
fatal than Wordsworth's Mother Nature, but no more help-
ful. Shelley's Witch of Atlas is a feminine figure for creativity,
but her creation is sterile and flawed, much as, when Cole-
ridge pictures the mind as the passive and feminine Aeolian
harp, its product is "idle flitting phantasies" rather than imag-
ination. Both Byron and Shelley frequently create female
figures of imaginative desire. Like Blake's emanations, they
embody the object of the poet's quest, either narcissistically,
as in Manfred's guilty love for his sister Astarte, or as the per-
fect complement to the poet, as is the case with Asia in *Pro-
metheus Unbound* or Emilia in "Epipsychidion." Either way,
they mirror the poet or his protagonist, and bear no relation
to real women, as Shelley himself knew well, to his loss.
Though these ethereal females hardly seem classifiable as ob-
jects, in the manner of natural objects, they have no more sub-
jectivity than rocks or stones or trees. Wordsworth's maternal
nature or naturalized feminine figures like Lucy resemble

emanations, in that they are generated by the need of the powerful central consciousness for a beloved object. But these feminine figures also provide an image of what the poet's mind is not. Lucy is an admonitory image of the vegetation of the poet's mind that would take place if the poet were himself to come under the domination of Mother Nature.

THE LITERARY IMAGES available to women all demonstrate to women their unfitness for poetry. Equally responsible for negative models of feminine poethood is the patriarchal tradition of Christianity, which, unlike as it is to Wordsworthian paganistic reverence for Mother Nature, fosters an analogous view of femininity. The Judaeo-Christian tradition is notoriously misogynistic. The Church Fathers and later interpreters did a great deal to augment the identification of woman with sin, thereby justifying her religious and secular oppression, but there is ample evidence of misogyny in both Old and New Testaments. Brontë and Dickinson, raised in intensely religious households, attended church seldom or never but nonetheless read their Bibles, so that even though they avoided listening to sermons on the abject nature of woman, they were exposed to the Bible's calumnies. Biblical misogyny was not easily disregarded, as it was so deeply ingrained in culture, and because it is often so beautifully expressed. The women poets also read *Paradise Lost*, which magnifies religious misogyny while conveying it into literary tradition.[21]

The creation story, both in Genesis and in Milton's retelling, makes physical creation the power of a masculine deity, depriving the feminine figure of her one remaining prerogative. The story about Adam's rib comes as close as possible to saying that man can now give birth, along with all the other priorities given to him by Jehovah.[22] Eve is made to appear inferior to Adam in a variety of ways. Blamed for the fall, she is morally weak. Although the first creation story, in the first book of Genesis, offers a myth of original equality, it is the second one (Genesis 2), written earlier, that has been em-

phasized by later readers, as if it were an interpretation or ex-
pansion, rather than a contradiction, of the first. Milton's ac-
count of the creation in Book VII of *Paradise Lost* follows
Genesis 1, but for Adam's account of his own creation in
Book VIII Milton turns to Genesis 2, so that Adam is created
first and Eve as an afterthought, formed for Adam's use and
delight. Although it is clear that Eve was part of God's plan
from the beginning, the fact that we learn of her creation from
Adam's point of view emphasizes that she is as if Adam had
invented her. Only Adam is formed in God's image, and, in
the King James Version if not in the original (the translation is
what matters for the women poets of England and America),
Eve is Adam's "help meet," or, according to Milton,

> Thy likeness, thy fit help, thy other self,
> Thy wish, exactly to thy heart's desire.
> (*PL* VIII, 450–451)

As Adam is created in God's image, Eve is created in Adam's.
Even though both have "looks divine," "Hee for God only,
shee for God in him" makes plain their hierarchical relation-
ship.

In Genesis 2 and in *Paradise Lost*, the delay between Adam's
creation and Eve's permits Adam one other substantial advan-
tage over Eve: conversation with God. Adam receives di-
rectly from God the command not to eat from the tree of the
knowledge of good and evil, and in Milton Adam is able to
discuss with God his desire for a helpmate. Eve never hears
God's voice directly, but only through Adam's transmission.
The outstanding feature of the creation in Genesis 1 is that the
masculine deity creates with language. God's Word is what
supplants feminine fecundity, and when that Word is made
flesh it takes a masculine form. The Logos is a masculine pre-
rogative, handed down from Father to Son, and it is in words
of approximately the same language that God addresses
Adam and not Eve. God deprives Eve of her dignity by not
speaking to her directly, with the result that Milton can say
that she prefers to listen only to Adam, "not capable her

ear / Of what was high" (*PL* VIII, 49-50). The first human language act, naming the animals, is likewise Adam's. Synonymous with the things they name, his words have a portion of the power of God's own verbal powers, whereby words create the things they name: "and whatsoever Adam called every living creature, that *was* the name thereof" (Genesis 2:19). Though God empowers this naming, the names are original with Adam, who thus shares, in a limited way, in the creation itself. Excluded from the community of conversation shared by God and Adam, and deprived of an equal share in inventing human language, it is quite reasonable for Eve to respond more readily than Adam to the verbal appeal of another outsider. The first being who speaks to her is the serpent, and her first speech is, in reply to him, a recitation of the command not to eat from the tree. Adam participates in the invention of language, but Eve only repeats something that she has been told and that she perhaps does not fully believe.

The men poets who wrote at a time when the Bible still provided culture with its dominant metaphorical framework inherited and relied on this language tradition, whether they knew it or not. Though in 1821 Wordsworth accuses himself of blasphemy when his imagination presumes "To act the God among external things," his mind, at its most free, knows its own powers of divinity. Coleridge defines imagination so that the poet is the direct inheritor of God's self-asserting "I AM." The poet's creations are shadows of God's creation, because they ritually repeat the state of chaos that preceded the creation: the secondary imagination "dissolves, diffuses, dissipates, in order to recreate."[23] Emerson, even more powerfully than the British writers, makes the poet in the image of the Son, his speech Adamic, and poetry the inheritor of divinity:

The poet is the sayer, the namer, and represents beauty.
He is a sovereign, and stands on the center. For the world
is not painted or adorned, but is from the beginning

beautiful; and God has not made some beautiful things, but Beauty is the creator of the universe. Therefore the poet is not any permissive potentate, but is emperor in his own right.   (*CW*, III, 7)[24]

It is typical of the Judaeo-Christian tradition of language that his thoughts should run from poetry to centrality and rule. When he says "Words are also actions, and actions are a kind of words" (*CW*, III, 8), he is reaffirming the linkage between the Logos and the human poet.

Eve, and women after her, have been dislocated from the ability to feel that they are speaking their own language. They could not speak, with a right to personal usage, of the godlike powers of the mind. That Brontë and Dickinson always refused to be believers in orthodox religion, though Dorothy became more devout as she grew older, correlates with the degree of their imaginative freedom and poetic power. It seems that it was necessary, or at least helpful, to break free from the belief that a masculine divinity was the first and best speaker. Brontë and Dickinson were fortunate that their minister fathers respected their daughters' independence of mind. This tolerance saved the daughters the effort of personal rebellion and allowed them to direct their energies against the tradition instead.

Among St. Paul's many oppressive instructions about women is a specific injunction against speech, an injunction that contributed to the tradition that only men could be the transmitters of God's Word on earth:

> Let the woman learn in silence with all subjection.
> But I suffer not a woman to teach, not to usurp authority over the man, but to be in silence.
> For Adam was first formed, then Eve.
> And Adam was not deceived, but the woman being deceived was in the transgression.
>
> (1 Timothy 2:11-14)

That Paul (or the Pauline writer) goes back to Genesis for his authority shows how old and deep this prejudice is. Woman once spoke a lie, and she must be punished for it with perpetual silence. But note that this marginally logical reason is only his second reason: his first is simply that she is secondary.

In Romantic poetry, within the community of the Logos, the powerful self is inextricable from the use of efficacious language, since the powerful self is so often the poet, or a poet. He constructs the strong self from his own strong language. This centrism constituted of language is familiar to any reader of Romantic poetry.[25] Wordsworth and Coleridge both feared and combated tendencies of this kind in themselves, and it would be wrong to impute to them an unqualified egotism. Nonetheless, the typical Romantic subject is subjectivity itself, particularly in respect to the processes of imagining and writing, the word-centered activities that compose the subject in poetry. Wordsworth's imagination at its strongest shuts out the natural world, and although the poet sometimes recoils from this power and seeks to credit nature with the mind's own triumphs, in the closing lines of *The Prelude*—unaltered between 1805 and 1850—he finally calls on the "Prophets of Nature" to

> Instruct them how the mind of man becomes
> A thousand times more beautiful than the earth
> On which he dwells, . . .
>
> (XIII, 446-448)

Coleridge, apprenticing himself to what he felt was Wordsworth's belief in nature's wholly independent powers to converse with the mind and soften the heart, was much deceived. "The Nightingale" and "Frost at Midnight" attempt to argue against the possibility that what we see in nature is only a projection, but both poems turn to the speaker's child for displaced resolution, because the poet cannot deny projection for himself. "But *thou*, my babe! shalt wander like a breeze / By lakes and sandy shores." An ideal reciprocity, including such metaphoric relations among others, will exist between the child and nature. Yet the images of mirroring or reflection with which both poems end are ambiguous. "All

seasons shall be sweet to thee" precisely blurs the distinction
that the poet seems desirous of making, by suggesting both
"be gentle to" and "seem sweet to." For frost to be sweet in
either sense probably demands projection, and the image itself
contains two mirrors, in the reflection of the moonlight and in
the verbal repetition, both of which suggest an uncanny clo-
sure: "silent icicles, / Quietly shining to the quiet Moon."
Again, at the close of "The Nightingale" the child, crying, is
hushed by the sight of the moon, "While his fair eyes, that
swam with undropped tears, / Did glitter in the yellow
moon-beam!" Even in these imagined and ideal harmonies,
reciprocity may be only a generous name for nature mirror-
ing the mind.

The Dejection Ode makes overt the suppressed knowledge
that this reciprocity is a fragile fiction, now exposed. For
Emerson, this would have been an untroubling discovery. A
painful difficulty for the powerful, internalizing self in poetry
is that if it is pessimistic it cannot allow itself to find comfort
in externals. Subjectivity would have appeared to the women
poets as the necessary subject, just as Mother Nature or
another feminine figure would have impressed them as the
typical object, but Coleridge's fear of succumbing to solip-
sism must have stood as an admonition about potential dan-
gers. Dorothy did genuinely believe in nature's active minis-
tries and must have been hurt far more than William by the
lines "O Lady! we receive but what we give, / And in our life
alone does Nature live." Although addressing Dorothy indi-
rectly, Coleridge nonetheless hits an open nerve, as this pas-
sage from her journal indicates:

> Coleridge came to us and repeated the verses he wrote to
> Sara. I was affected with them and was on the whole, not
> being well, in miserable spirits. The sunshine—the green
> fields and the fair sky made me sadder; even the little
> happy sporting lambs seemed but sorrowful to me.[26]

Derrida's term "phallogocentrism" is useful here. The
human desire for a center and to be at the center manifests it-

self in this "enormous and old root" in which the center is
identified with the phallus and with the Word.[27] Derrida is
concerned to distinguish Logos as voice as opposed to writ-
ing, but the term is applicable even if we take Logos in the
more general sense of language. The speaker (or the writer) is
at the center, just as Freud believed that the possessor of the
male genital was at the center, and the female a deformity or
variant, an eccentric male. Writing should be just as suscepti-
ble to assimilation with phallocentrism as voice, because of
the connections Derrida demonstrates elsewhere between the
pen and the phallus. The written word distances its referent
while making it present, veiling while unveiling. The word
puts itself first, making meaning secondary. For Nietzsche,
the woman's "castration" causes her to stand for lack or ab-
sence, so that the woman is the absent and literal truth, the
absence to which the word refers.[28] But, as so often, the
figure of the woman, the woman as figure, invidiously be-
comes confused with real women, as Derrida points out in a
reading of Lacan, from whom he quotes at the close of the
following passage:

> Phallogocentrism is one thing. And what is called man
> and what is called woman might be subjected to it. . . .
> Androcentrism ought therefore to be something else.
> Yet what is going on? The entire phallogocentrism is
> articulated from the starting-point of a determinate *situa-
> tion* . . . in which the phallus *is* the mother's desire inas-
> much as she does not have it. . . . The sequel is familiar:
> phallogocentrism as androcentrism with the whole
> paradoxical logic and the reversals which it engenders:
> for example that "in the phallocentric dialectic, she [the
> woman] represents the absolute Other" [*Écrits*, p. 732].
>   (*Graphesis*, pp. 98-99)

Not everyone can occupy the center at once, and women, as
well as woman, tend to be scattered on the perimeter.

Deconstruction ought to help displace phallogocentrism.
Though the discrepancy between signifier and signified has

long been recognized, the model of the Logos and of Adamic speech, while it was still operative, made it the credible aim of words to have literal meanings, even if, paradoxically, that goal was known to be unreachable. But women writers, dislocated from the phallogocentric community, must have understood the subversive implications of this discrepancy with greater intensity, and may have consciously embraced them rather than attempting to deny them. Men were not in a position to see that their use of language was not a totality, but women could see how the Biblical tradition of language favors a particular bias. Dislocation from the phallogocentric community causes Dorothy Wordsworth great difficulty in creating a central sense of self in poetry. She embraces this difficulty because that centrism is as objectionable as it is difficult to imitate, and yet it is equally difficult for her to imagine other structures with which to replace that centrism, so completely does it occlude her view of the possibilities for writing. The same dislocation creates for Brontë an interminable struggle for possession of poetic power; it finally causes Dickinson to seek a different kind of language with which to constitute a different kind of self, but even for this more powerful poet the project is more a reaction against phallogocentrism than it is a positive construction. Dickinson reverses and undermines the usual meanings of words and questions some of the structures of language that had always seemed ordained, and that most support phallogocentrism.

The oppressive structure that Dickinson most effectively challenges is hierarchy in language, and her greater success as a poet may be due to her understanding that this hierarchy is at the heart of male supremacy. The desire to be at the center generates hierarchical thinking, but even the potentially neutral concept of opposition also turns into hierarchy, because it is impossible ever to be entirely disinterested and one element must be primary and the other secondary. This is true for both sexual and linguistic oppositions. In his discussion of Nietzsche's views on women, Derrida first shows that Nietzsche's "eternal war between the sexes" is "based on

what might be called a process of *propriation*," and then adds
that "propriation is all the more powerful since it is its process
that organized both the totality of language's process and
symbolic exchange in general" (*Spurs*, pp. 85, 87). Although
this passage serves as a useful locus for the connection be-
tween language and sexual difference, Derrida formulates a
cultural commonplace. Language's operation is to identify
otherness as self, to appropriate objects and transform them
into subject. Adamic language, theoretically ideal because its
words are synonymous with their meanings, is also the type
of appropriative language, since Adam understood language
to mean control over the beasts he named, and he named the
woman as well.

The larger structures of Romantic poetry repeat this aspect
of language's functioning. When Mother Nature and other
feminine figures are objectified as the other, they may then be
possessed or become the property of the subject. Explicitly
linking the two sexually charged aspects of literary tradition
sketched above, language and the theme of nature, appropria-
tion is the relationship between the self-centered Romantic
speaker or poet and the feminine objects about which he
writes. Emerson (like Rousseau and others) considers lan-
guage to have originated in the use of natural objects as sym-
bols for human thoughts, and he even calls this use a marriage
(see chapter IV). This marriage is also an appropriation:

> Nature is thoroughly mediate. It is made to serve. . . . It
> offers all its kingdoms to man as the raw material which
> he may mould into what is useful. . . . More and more,
> with every thought, does his kingdom stretch over all
> things, until the world becomes, at last, only a realized
> will,—the double of the man.   (*W*, I, 25)

Nature created in man's image is Eve again created for Adam,
"thy likeness, thy fit help, thy other self." In a passage from
"Literary Ethics" Emerson discusses how nature in poetry is a
cliché and an artifice constructed by men who know nothing
of nature. But even where he contrasts such usage with an os-

tensibly better kind, nature is still seen from the point of view of writing:

> But go into the forest, you shall find all new and unde-scribed. . . . any vegetation; any animation; any and all, are alike unattempted. . . . But when I see the daybreak I am not reminded of these Homeric, or Shakespearian, or Miltonic, or Chaucerian pictures. No; but I feel perhaps the pain of an alien world; a world not yet subdued by the thought; or, I am cheered by the moist, warm, glitter-ing, budding, melodious hour, that takes down the nar-row walls of my soul, and extends its life and pulsation to the very horizon.   (*W*, I, 106)

Whether nature defies or joins the human mind, its function is to serve ("not *yet* subdued"). From the phallogocentric point of view, appropriation works to make the world one; from the point of view of the appropriated other, the reverse is true. In the name of decreasing dualism or hierarchy, Romantic lit-erature augments it. Nature is servile in much of Emerson, but this servility becomes in other places a rebellious freedom. "For the infinite diffuseness refuses to be epigrammatized, the world to be shut in a word."[29]

The appropriative character of phallogocentric language may be invidious, but a non-dualistic language is unimagi-nable, and dualism without an order of priority seems almost as inconceivable. Two very different models for the origins of dualistic thinking involve the notion of control or possession of women or female figures. G. Rachel Levy, after describing the neolithic worship of fertility in the form of female po-tency, suggests that dualism entered primitive thought with the beginning of agriculture, which is control over the earth's fertility.[30] Controlling nature, to no matter how small a de-gree, demands the discovery of a sense of difference between the self and nature. The gatherer of wild foods is dependent on and part of natural process, whereas the farmer alters that process. Derrida, reading Rousseau's *Essay on the Origin of Languages*, says that writing originated with the prohibition of incest, for two reasons (*Of Grammatology*, pp. 255-68). Like

Levy's interpretation of agriculture, the incest prohibition implies a discovery of difference between nature and self, in this case through the resistance to a natural instinct. More important for present purposes, the prohibition of incest created a need for the concept of representation:

> The natural woman (nature, mother, or if one wishes, sister), is a represented or a signified replaced and supplanted, in desire, that is to say in social passion, beyond need. . . .
> The displacing of the relationship with the mother, with nature, with being as the fundamental signified, such indeed is the origin of society and languages.
>
> (p. 266)

Could we remember that it was just as important for a woman to find a substitute for her father or brother as it was for a man to displace mother or sister, this myth of origins might be more acceptable. But what matters about both Levy's and Derrida's formulations is that their assumption of male dominance in the structures of dualism and language reflects the present state of language usage. Such myths serve the present, not the past.

For the same reason that the women poets are ambivalent about rejecting the figure of Mother Nature, dualistic language and the hierarchy and enforced otherness that it includes are not casually discarded, because they appear so inevitable as perhaps to be necessary structures of language. There would be a gain in freedom, although the risk is unintelligibility, or even silence, in the manner of Hélène Cixous' white ink. Feminist poets and critics are encouraging a general discarding of hierarchies and all traditional forms and themes that are tainted with phallogocentrism. Two anthologists of women's writing, for example, have taken up Muriel Rukeyser's "The Poem as Mask" as prescriptive of the route that they feel women's poetry should take from now on. Concluding her selections with this poem and referring to it in this exhortatory way, one anthologist asks that women cease writing in a "disguised way" and instead "turn to an art based not on 'masks' nor on 'mythologies,' but on the real experience of their lives."[31] The poem also supplies both the epigraph and the title of *No More Masks! An Anthology of Poems by Women*; paraphrasing and decontextualizing the poem's closing lines, the introduction announces that "a new poetry is in the making. No more masks! No more mythologies! *And the fragments will join in us with their own music.*"[32] But we do not know what "their own music" is. A poetry that claims to be without masks claims that it can exorcize hierarchy simply by omitting one half of the traditional dualism. This unitary strategy wastes the freedom it intends to gain by making itself both obscure and banal. Lines like Rukeyser's and the expressions of faith derived from them are always exhortatory, never descriptive, because to speak without a mask is an impossibility, for men and for women, where all language is a mask.

The muses, coquettish in a man's world, refuse to help their "friend" Ardelia, who invokes their assistance in a poem by Anne Finch, Countess of Winchilsea, "To Mr. F., now Earl of W." (1689). Making the best of this refusal, Ardelia discovers that instead of invoking "Foreign Aid," she may "dictate from the Heart."

> Consulting now her Breast,
> Perceiv'd that ev'ry tender Thought,
> Which from abroad she'd vainly sought,
> Did there in Silence rest.[33]

The poet decides that, rather than write these tender thoughts into a poem, she will speak them so that "Her *Flavio* them alone might hear." A poem does get written, but as it is about substituting spoken endearments for enduring verse, it could very well be the poem to end all her poems. "Foreign Aid," whether it be from the muses or from a sense of otherness, may be necessary to writing of any kind. But hierarchy in language might be undone in other ways than by denying otherness, and both the means and the motive to do so rest, if anywhere, with the feminine imagination.

CHAPTER II

Dorothy Wordsworth

Dorothy Wordsworth wrote fewer than twenty poems, and only five were published in her lifetime, incorporated in the works of her brother. Yet a reading of her works forms an appropriate prologue to reading the works of more prolific poets, because the manner of her resistance to poethood demonstrates most effectively the difficulties challenging all women poets. There are implicit risks in studying the poetry of a writer who did not become a poet. To speak of a resistance to poethood is to assume what can never be finally verified, that she could have been a poet simply by choosing. But poetic power does not originate solely in the accident of individual temperament, and at every point Dorothy causes her readers to wonder why she never became a competent or ready poet, at the very least, if not a great poet. In letters written during her late teens and early twenties (1787-1793) she creates visions of the future to which, if they were the work of someone who later became a poet, we would surely trace the origins of poetic sensibility, as in the case of Dickinson's early letters. Dorothy's early journals, *Alfoxden* (1798) and *Grasmere* (1800-1803), contain passages of extraordinary beauty that at least partly fulfill Romantic definitions of the poetic imagination. Her potential for language and vision appears to have been just as great as her brother's, as far as such faculties can be measured. She may also have entertained the possibility of identifying herself as a writer. During the childhood of her nieces and nephews in the early 1800's she wrote poems and at least one story for their entertainment, and *A Narrative Con-*

cerning George and Sarah Green (1808), if not intended for pub-
lication, was written to be part of the public record of Gras-
mere Vale. She was willing to have the journals from her
travels circulated among family and friends. In poems from
all periods of her life, but particularly in poems written during
her later years (under self-deprecatory titles like "A Frag-
ment," "Irregular Verses," or "Irregular Stanzas") she con-
fronts, directly and indirectly, the question of why she did not
become a poet. At once suggesting and evading poetic iden-
tity, these poems derive their energy from the tension be-
tween her desire to be a poet and her resistance to this desire. [1]

If it is reasonable to speculate that Dorothy might have be-
come a poet, to the degree that poethood is subject to will and
choice, there remains the question of whether this curious re-
sistance to poethood originates in sexual difference. It may be
that two questions—why did she not become a poet? and how
does the consciousness of being a woman affect writing?—
converge in a single investigation. The circumstance of
Dorothy's close relation to her brother provides the best pos-
sible locus for beginning a fair examination of sexual differ-
ence in poetry, since there are otherwise such great similarities
between her and William in family experience, sensibility, and
adult environment. William's primary concentration on the
self and on subjectivity in poetry make Dorothy's contrasting
evasions of poetic identity especially salient, and especially
available to an interpretation based on sexual difference.

Differences of experience determined by custom rather
than by sexual difference *per se* certainly contributed a great
deal to the differences between brother and sister. While Wil-
liam was traveling widely and acquiring a classical education,
Dorothy remained at home in the relatively cloistered atmos-
phere of her foster home. Her formal education ended at the
age of sixteen, and even that was rudimentary, apparently
having consisted mainly in the art of "plain sewing." She read
widely in English literature but her reading lacked the struc-
ture that her brother's education provided. Important as these
cultural differences must have been in shaping sexual identity,

external factors of this kind cannot be ultimate causes, since the powerful poet can reinvent his or her past. Other women writers have overcome or ameliorated similar disadvantages. It could also be said that Dorothy renounced the ambition to be a poet in order not to compete with her beloved brother, but this argument, persuasive as it is when we look at Wordsworth's addresses to Dorothy in his poems, does not touch those earliest experiences that occurred before Wordsworth chose his vocation. Although both these possibilities are worth pursuing, this chapter will investigate a different kind of cause.

The first chapter, above, sketched the normative Freudian pattern of feminine development in which the girl, mirroring the Oedipal pattern, must turn from her mother to her father as the object of her love, through finding a "lack" both in herself and in her mother. This turn entails a repudiation of origins, which males never perform, and a consequent debasing of identity. Much of Dorothy's writing follows this conventional psychic pattern of femininity, faulty or not. Where the feminine psychology exhibited in Dorothy's writing is Freudian or conventional, mirroring masculine patterns, it is appropriate to consider her textual femininity as a response to the Romantic tradition.

Although it would be tempting to speculate about Dorothy's actual feelings about her family, what these really were can never be determined. What may be usefully compared to the Freudian model are the family relations that occur at the textual level, where we can fairly examine her representations of her mother and William. Our necessary ignorance about her actual experience can be supplemented by tracing her difficulties with the idea of the mother to her textual encounters with the variety of maternal figures created by William and also found elsewhere in literary tradition. Although the letters and journals that form the bulk of Dorothy's writing are informal and might seem to be transparent expressions of lived experience rather than literary texts, any writer selects what to write and what to leave un-

written, and anything represented in words has to some de-
gree, however small, departed from experience and entered
the realm of the imaginative. This discussion will include only
those passages which themselves suggest that they be read as
works of the imagination: passages in which she takes up a
traditional poetic project such as the construction of a myth of
origins, or the identification of a self, creative or not, in rela-
tion to the phenomenal world. Large sections of the letters
and journals concern family news and domestic details, and
her way of mingling imaginative passages with domestic ones
is part of her evasion of traditional poetic powers.

The initial rejection of maternal origins described by Freud
establishes a psychic pattern of evasion and divisiveness. It
first demands the construction of a new and preferred origin,
which, however, can never be a complete substitute, as the
prior origin returns to haunt the woman later. Dorothy's first
writing shows her to be engaged in a turn away from mater-
nal origins and in the textual construction of a secondary ori-
gin, both retrospectively and projectively. Although all the
Wordsworth children were orphans by 1783 when their father
died, Dorothy alone had been sent from home at the age of six
after her mother's death in 1778, so that she was, in effect, or-
phaned earlier than her brothers and deprived of the consoling
sense of family that they retained after the mother's death.
Her adolescent letters to her friend Jane Pollard concentrate
on her love for her brothers, and home is regretted chiefly be-
cause its loss separated her from them. In 1787, having left her
foster-home with her mother's cousin Elizabeth Threlkeld in
Halifax, where she knew Jane, she enjoyed a brief reunion
with her brothers during their holidays at their grandparents'
house in Penrith, where Dorothy was to remain. She sent her
first letter to Jane later than the promised date because she had
so few hours "to pass with my Brothers that I could not leave
them. You know how happy I am in their company. . . ."[2]
The second, similarly, was late because her brothers had just
departed and she was too disturbed to write.

She gives her brothers a parental role in sheltering her from

an alien setting, even though they are all close in age, for
when they are gone she feels vulnerable beyond the loss of
their companionship. "For a few hours I was absolutely mis-
erable, a thousand tormenting fears rushed upon me, the ap-
proaching Winter, the ill-nature of my Grandfather and Uncle
Chrisr., the little probability there is of my soon again seeing
my younger Brother . . ." (*EY*, 6, 6 Aug. 1787). In her fifth
letter she moves so rapidly from the thought of losing one's
parents to the separation of the siblings as to suggest that this
is the usual channel of her thoughts: "Oh Jane you cannot
sufficiently prize your kind parents. My Brother John has set
sail for Barbadoes. . . . How we are squandered abroad!" (*EY*,
16, 27 Jan. 1788). She describes herself as "a very skilful ar-
chitect" for building a "Castle" that is always the dream of a
restored home, and later she outlines her plan for the "little
Parsonage," to which she will welcome Jane as one of the
family:

> I have laid the particular scheme of happiness for each
> Season. When I think of Winter I hasten to furnish our
> little Parlour, I close the Shutters, set out the Tea-table,
> brighten the Fire. When our refreshment is ended I pro-
> duce our Work, and William brings his book to our
> Table and contributes at once to our Instruction and
> amusement, and at Intervals we lay aside the Book and
> each hazard our observations upon what has been read
> without the fear of Ridicule or Censure.
>
> (*EY*, 88, 16 Feb. 1793)

It is a home particularly without parents or authority of any
kind. Conversation is democratic and the poet is pictured as
contributing to the pleasure of the domestic workers. She
seeks not parental figures for her ideal home, but a brother
and a sister. At the same time, she transfers to William's affec-
tion for her some vaguely parental characteristics. Earlier in
the letter quoted above she describes "a sort of restless watch-
fulness which I know not how to describe, a Tenderness that
never sleeps" (p. 87). In a further letter of the same year she

equates the "Day of my Felicity" with "the Day in which I am once more to find a Home under the same Roof with my Brother" (*EY*, 93, 16 June 1793).

The home that Dorothy regrets losing and hopes to re-create is always defined by brothers, not by parents. It would hardly be surprising for a young woman to aim for a home of her own, but as long as her aims are retrospective, the selectivity of her nostalgia is curious. In forming her fanciful plans she would naturally wish for the possible, but it is striking that when regretting her lost home it is the unity of the siblings that she misses, far more and more specifically than parents. After her beautiful description of her ideal "little Parsonage" with William and Jane and herself reading around the tea-table, she reverts to the nostalgia that gave rise to the dream:

> I cannot help heaving many a Sigh at the Reflection that I have passed one and twenty years of my Life, and that the first six years only of this Time was spent in the Enjoyment of the same Pleasures that were enjoyed by my Brothers, and that I was then too young to be sensible of the Blessing. We have been endeared to each other by early misfortune.   (*EY*, 88, 16 Feb. 1793)

The "Blessing" clearly refers to having shared these pleasures with her brothers, not to the pleasures themselves. This is to say that her nostalgia is more than selective: it is creative, since, in any case, as she herself points out, she was too young to have retained many conscious memories of the period. Selectively reconstructing her infancy (to the age of six), she chooses to see her love for her brothers as the relationship in which her life originated. Wordsworth speaks of his childhood as if it were spent alone and in the company of nature, and of early childhood with his mother; Dorothy enters as the rediscovered sister of 1789 in *The Prelude*. Dorothy refers to her childhood as if mother and father and the home they created were a frame for the intense companionship of the siblings.

Desire for reunion with William is the motive energy of her writing and of her life during this period. When in 1795 she begins to realize her dream of making a home with William, her letters show that the new home merges in her mind with the idea of an original home, "a blessing which I so early lost" (*EY*, 146, 2 Sept. 1795). Racedown, she says retrospectively, "is the place dearest to my recollections upon the whole surface of the island; it was the first home I had . . ." (*EY*, 281, date unknown, 1799). Nature occurs to her now as a topic of interest, a new element in her writing. Dorothy associates their solitude in nature with the period of early childhood out of which their foster-child, Basil Montague, is just passing:

> Till a child is four years old he needs no other companions, than the flowers, the grass, the cattle, the sheep that scamper away from him when he makes a vain unexpecting chase after them, the pebbles upon the road, &c. &c. After the age of about four years he begins to want some other stimulus than the mere life that is in him; his efforts would be greater but he must have an object, . . .
>
> (*EY*, 222, 13 June 1798)

Basil may in some sense be a figure for Dorothy's and William's own childhood, since, as a semi-orphan, he permits Dorothy to correct the past by doing for others what was poorly done for her and her brothers. Dorothy has always been fond of the comparable solitude available to adults, the retired life. When living at Forncett she writes to Jane Pollard that the family's projected stay in London and Windsor does not in itself fill her with enthusiasm, but rather that "I look beyond the Pleasures of London and Windsor, to the Joy of returning again to the Quiet of Forncett better fitted to relish it's Enjoyments" (*EY*, 73, 8 May 1792). In the same letter in which she describes Basil's infant solitude (in a continuation of three weeks later, written at Bristol) she describes her own painful feeling of contrast between the busy city and their prior life of retirement:

I am writing in a front room, in one of the most busy
streets of Bristol. You can scarcely conceive how the jar-
ring contrast between the sounds which are now for ever
ringing in my ears and the sweet sounds of Allfoxden
makes me long for the country again. After three years
residence in retirement a city in feeling, sound, and pros-
pect is hateful.   (*EY*, 223, 3 July 1798)

The retired country life is the closest adult approximation of
the experiences of earliest infancy. The idea of home means
recreating the earliest stages of childhood by returning to the
object of her childhood affections and to the uncomplicated
solitude of childhood in nature.

This new home does not successfully replace genuine ori-
gins, because it does not fulfill its purpose of helping her to
grow up. It is not clear to which generation she sees herself
belonging. William is both fraternal and parental, and while
she acts as a parent to Basil, she also identifies with him as an
orphan. Similarly in *A Narrative Concerning George and Sarah
Green*[3] there is an implicit sympathy with the Green children
that must have arisen from her having shared their experience
of being orphaned, and yet at the beginning of the narrative
she establishes a different basis for her interest in the story.
"Recollecting my own dreadful situation" when, years ago,
she had come close to falling over the same precipice, she
links herself to the mother, Sarah Green (p. 46). A poem of
1826 opens with her fancying that she can play like a child.
She remains in a childish position because of the inadequacy
or incompleteness of her evasion. Most of the poems that she
and William must have considered her most successful, on the
evidence that he printed them among his own poems, are ad-
dressed to children: "The Cottager to Her Infant," "Address
to a Child, During a Boisterous Winter Evening," "The
Mother's Return," and "Loving and Liking: Irregular Verses,
Addressed to a Child." Although in each case the speaker is
adult, writing for children freed Dorothy from the anxiety of
being judged as an adult. In a letter of 1806 denying poetic

ambitions or powers, she says she never expected to write for "grown persons" but that "Descriptions, Sentiments, or little stories for children was all I could be ambitious of doing."[4]

Wordsworth, too, connects nature and childhood, but the connection he makes differs greatly from Dorothy's. Where in Dorothy's letters it is he who mediates and softens reality for her, in Wordsworth it is the mother whose original continuity with nature gives the child a stable sense of his relation to the objects of his love. In the "Bless'd the infant Babe" passage in Book II of *The Prelude* the child learns to love nature by gradually extending his love for his mother, and nature takes on a maternal configuration. It is "The gravitation and the filial bond / Of nature, that connect him with the world" (II, 263-264). The borders between nature and mother are permeable: the "one beloved Presence" is one manifestation of the "Presences of Nature." The opening of Book V describes "the speaking face of earth and heaven" as the "prime Teacher" of the boy's mind in the preceding books. Following his mother's death he was "entrusted to the care / Of that sweet Valley" and, "Seeking I knew not what," he finds the sight of a natural death that does not shock him (V, 12-13, 451-456). Growing up involves making the transition from seeing nature maternally to seeing her as a bride. The inauguration of a new kind of poetry is the "spousal verse" of the marriage between the intellect and nature. The scheme sketched above follows in its largest outlines Freud's scheme.[5] The boy must learn to separate himself from his mother, but he need not cease, as the girl must, to look for her representation in the later objects of his love.

Nature, which is later to become the major subject of both her journals and her poems, first enters Dorothy's writing in connection with William and their restored home. Her first extended description of nature is in a letter written from Windy Brow, where they had settled during their walking tour of the Lakes after a three year separation (*EY*, 114-115, 21 April, 1794). Love for nature and love for her brother ought to consecrate each other, but she cannot call nature fraternal

or masculine, for the very reason that she might wish to. If
her purpose is to consecrate accord with William, then she
must not contradict his view of nature as feminine. William
can portray his mother as the original for his relations with
nature, but Dorothy, seeing her brothers as her first relation-
ship, must find a discontinuity between love of brothers and
love of nature. The objects of her love are divided, and for the
purposes of writing they detract from rather than augment
each other. She cannot celebrate nature as maternal, either,
however, since this would oblige her to compete with yet
another female figure for William's love. Rejecting maternal
origins, she nonetheless cannot share William's attitude to-
ward nature.

"A Winter's Ramble in Grasmere Vale," a poem that
Dorothy wrote after she and William had been living together
for some time in the Lake District,[6] indicates the adverse psy-
chic effects of encountering a feminized or maternal nature,
and it seems in some respects to be a reading of "Nutting,"
one of her brother's poems that traces the inviolable con-
tinuity between mother, nature, and the object of a more ma-
ture love. The poem commemorates Dorothy's arrival with
William in their "chosen vale" in late December 1799, a mo-
ment obviously important in the history of her reinvented
sense of home, and its immediate subject is the first walk she
took by herself after they arrived. If William's initiatory rela-
tionship is with the maternal figure, and poetry is provoked
by a desire to recover that figure, and if Dorothy's corre-
sponding relationship is with William, then the reader would
expect from her a parallel gesture of separation and reunion.
She ventures into nature, but instead of finding versions of
her beloved, she finds his. The poem opens with her depar-
ture from William, structurally comparable to the boy's de-
parture from the maternal "frugal dame" at the opening of
"Nutting," though far less cheerful in tone:

> A Stranger, Grasmere, in thy Vale,
> All faces then to me unknown,

I left my sole Companion-friend
To wander out alone.

But instead of effecting a reunion with him, the poem is about
an entirely different figure, consistent with the split in her at-
tention, and instead of provoking poetry, this new figure
seems to arrest it.

To summarize very briefly the elements of "Nutting" im-
portant to Dorothy's poem, after leaving the "frugal dame"
the boy ventures alone into a "virgin scene" of natural loveli-
ness and fruitfulness, which he at length ravages. This act ex-
tends the implications of his original separation from the ma-
ternal figure, and it pains him in a way that causes him to
grow: he now turns and lovingly addresses a moral to a
"dearest Maiden," and he has acquired the poet's conscious-
ness that allows him to close, "there is a spirit in the woods."
That the "one dear nook" bears its violation without protest
shows him that he cannot break the continuity between him-
self and nature, and it forges a continuity between the frugal
dame and the maiden as the objects of early and later love.[7]

In "Nutting" all the female figures exist to let the boy make
his discovery, and, making it himself, to mature. Where in
"Nutting" the speaker is seen "O'er path-less rocks, / . . .
Forcing my way," in "A Winter's Ramble" it is the speaker
who is passive relative to a preternaturally active landscape.
She is "lured" and "led" by "a little winding path." What she
meets in nature collects the diffuse and submerged eroticism
of the boy's "virgin scene," in which he lies "with my cheek
on one of those green stones / That, fleeced with moss, under
the shady trees, / Lay round me," into a single, imposing,
feminized figure:

> . . . I reach'd a stately rock
> With velvet moss o'ergrown.
>
> With russet oak, and tufts of fern
> Its top was richly garlanded;

> Its sides adorned with eglantine,
> Bedropp'd with hips of glossy red.
>
> .   .   .   .
>
> Beneath that Rock my course I stayed,
> And, looking to its summit high,
> "Thou wear'st," said I, "a splendid garb, . . ."

This rock is never "she," but it is "thou," and the consistent metaphor of clothing, made overt in the final line of this passage, is sufficient to suggest a human shape: "velvet moss," "garlanded," "Its sides." Though the "hips of glossy red" refer actually to rose-hips, they contribute to the sense of corporeality, and the line, "Bedropp'd with hips of glossy red," is positively erotic. But nature retains its power by putting off revelation, by not permitting itself to be simplified by human terms.

While the "virgin scene" in "Nutting" is part of a progressive sequence of feminine figures, and the account of the scene's passive loveliness is prelude to the central action, the natural scene here is a static amalgam of aspects of the three figures in "Nutting," and the encounter arrests the action altogether. The boy asserts his own desires violently against what he must sense to be appropriate to the bower, but Dorothy's rock does not permit the speaker even to have her own thoughts of anything besides itself: "What need of flowers? The splendid moss / Is gayer than an April mead." The occasion for an initiatory act of violence having passed, there is now in place of the boy's pain an excess of cheeriness, and in place of the boy's earning through his pain the right to address his moral wisdom to a listening female figure, here the speaker is silenced and becomes a listener to a moral addressed to her by nature:

> —Beside that gay and lovely Rock
> There came with merry voice
> A foaming Streamlet glancing by:
> It seemed to say "Rejoice!"

Since it only "seemed to say," nature keeps us and the speaker from imputing to it any kind of overt threat, but the command is not a response to the speaker's conversational advances, and it seems to put an end to the speaker's interest in description. The poem is over as the speaker finds that there is a precise equilibrium between herself and reality, both between her expectations and what has happened and between what she has to say and what nature says:

> My youthful wishes all fulfill'd—
> Wishes matured by thoughtful choice,
> I stood an *Inmate* of this Vale,
> How *could* I but rejoice?

In "Nutting" the function of the encounter with nature is to return the boy to the human world, but with greater maturity, so that he may progress not just beyond nature but also beyond the frugal dame to the dearest maiden. The speaker here seems to sense that there are possibilities beyond present contentment, and beyond doing nature's bidding, but she never allows this tentative feeling to be openly articulated. What is for William a story of initiation and continuous growth is in Dorothy's revision a story of personal happiness set against poetic stultification. The gorgeous and domineering rock that blocks Dorothy's speaker's spiritual and physical progress is a female figure who, especially because she is located so particularly in Grasmere, may well represent Dorothy's reading of the effect on her of her brother's experience of nature and of maternal origins. That this maternal figure causes Dorothy so precisely to reverse the pattern of envoicing that closes "Nutting" may be Dorothy's way of accounting for her difficulties in sustaining poetic voice.

This inter-reading of "A Winter's Ramble" and "Nutting" is complicated by the fact that "Nutting" originally began with a passage in which a female figure named Lucy had shared the boy's initiatory experience of ravaging the grove.[8] This Lucy, unlike the Lucy of the Lucy poems, is quite human and even more likely to have been modeled after Dorothy;

whether Dorothy was the original for either or both of these Lucys, what matters is that she probably thought she was, since all the poems in question were written when she and William were living together in relative solitude. The probable reference to Dorothy in the early version of the poem increases the already strong likelihood that she would have understood herself to be the "dearest Maiden" addressed at the end of the poem (regardless, as in the case of the Lucy poems themselves, of whether or not a twentieth-century interpretation would yield this reading). Dorothy would thus have seen her active presence in the poem canceled out and replaced by a passive one. The cancellation shows Wordsworth in the process of understanding that he must shift from an actual memory of Dorothy as a child, who was just as aggressive as he, to the characterization of her necessary for his poetic project here and perhaps also a few months later in the Lucy poems. The point of the moral is for the maiden to gain the benefits of the speaker's experience without having to share its pain, but in sheltering her and in interpreting these benefits for her (an understanding of the need for being gentle to nature) he also keeps to himself what he knows to be the true gain. Dorothy is being asked in the final version to bypass the experience that the poem identifies as necessary to becoming a poet.

This comparison of William and Dorothy has emphasized the shared femininity of all the objects of his love, and the relative ease of his passage from childhood to adulthood. That transition is marked by a series of non-permanent separations, beginning with the growing child's discovery that nature, like the mother, is not a part of the self, but wholly other. To risk a large generalization, Wordsworth gets his start as a poet from losing his infant immediacy with nature. Enlarging the miniature pattern of "Nutting" in his major accounts of growing up, in *The Prelude*, "Tintern Abbey," and the Intimations Ode, what replaces the lost gleam of childhood is the poetic imagination or the ability to write poetry. There is always an imbalance of power between the mind and nature, in favor of the mind, as when at the end of the ode a natural ob-

ject, "the meanest flower that blows," has an effect dispropor-
tionate to the thing itself, stirring in the mind "Thoughts that
do often lie too deep for tears." The "something far more
deeply interfused" of "Tintern Abbey" only dwells in the
light of setting suns, and is not entirely explained by them.
This felt imbalance gives rise to poetry because of the need to
account for the surplus, and because of the need to remake the
bridge between the mind and nature that was implicit in
childhood. The "Bless'd the infant Babe" passage in Book II
of *The Prelude* exists to demonstrate the persistent continuity
between child and adult, but the pained tone of the argumen-
tative passage preceding it suggests a residual doubt. Some-
what too vehemently, he distinguishes the origin he is about
to describe from "that false secondary power, by which, / In
weakness, we create distinctions" (II, 221-222). By over-
criticizing discontinuity of another kind, "our puny bound-
aries," he exhibits defensiveness about a continuity too in-
vested to be openly doubted. In the ode Wordsworth converts
what might have been an alienation from nature into an
affirmation of continuity ("the primal sympathy / Which hav-
ing been must ever be"), but one way to minimize the break
with nature is to find positive value in that break:

> I only have relinquished one delight
> To live beneath your more habitual sway.
> I love the Brooks which down their channels fret,
> Even more than when I tripped lightly as they.

To relinquish nature's habitual sway is to acquire freedom,
and to cease to fret in a channel can be no great sacrifice. Po-
etic power comes from these separations, axiomatically.
When he says in "Tintern Abbey" of the time "when like a
roe / I bounded o'er the mountains" that "I cannot paint what
then I was," he means not that he cannot remember but that
poetry cannot result from such an identity with nature. From
his earliest recognition that the visionary power arises when
"the faculties . . . yet / Have something to pursue," sublimity
is in the beyond.

Wordsworth's filial relations with nature allow him to grow up. The separation from nature that is like the separation from the mother is gradual and is encouraged by nature herself. Nature teaches him to look beyond nature. This is the pattern of sublimation: cut off from his mother's love, the boy searches for it everywhere else. For Dorothy there are two potentially creative separations, both of which she either refuses or is prevented from making. Fatally, her wishes are all fulfilled, and her faculties have nothing to pursue. A poetry of sublimation with origins analogous to Wordsworth's might be provoked by a separation from William himself, but she retreats to a childlike position because she can continually assure herself of his actual love, and because the natural world in which she might seek his presence gives her images colored by his desire, images perhaps even of herself, as at the close of "Nutting." Similarly, although she is separated from origins, she avoids the risk of an overt break with nature by not explicitly naming nature as maternal, by never entertaining a mode of abstraction that would invite such an identification. This refusal to risk that break with nature prevents her from being a poet, at least from being a poet in her brother's mode.

Dorothy's project in *The Grasmere Journal* is in many ways congruous with the prelapsarian dream of an undivided world, which is traditionally identified with the experience or memory of earliest childhood. Her faith is that her language can and should do no more than name the individual objects of perception. She aspires to an absolute transparency of language. She draws back from the possibility that nature's appearance is altered by the viewer's feelings, even though she clearly knows that these alterations not only occur but also form the basis of ordinary perception. Her naivety is not quite believable when, at the opening of *Grasmere*, having wept for William's departure, she says "The lake looked to me I knew not why dull and melancholy."[9] She excludes from her vocabulary any language that would permit symbolic readings of nature.[10] This Edenic state brings reunion with William and reunion with (maternal) nature into alignment, because the idea of a world prior to division excludes all subject-object divisions, sexual division as well as separation between the mind and nature. The two early journals, written in this state of restoration, are continuous with the letters in that they are the textual confirmation of the sought reunion. She speaks in the letters of recollecting and imagining and projecting, all manifestly divided states of mind; *Alfoxden* and *Grasmere* omit memory and imagination and projection because of their confidence that the division has been closed. Transposing her reunion with her brother into a reunion with nature, she appeases maternal origins, writing as Wordsworth would write had he never left his mother's knee. The result is not poetry, but it avoids conflicts.

For Dorothy to make that break with nature would not be to open up a creative space of yearning, but would be instead a Freudian rejection of the maternal figure. *A Narrative Concerning George and Sarah Green*, the self-conscious work of art about orphans, is so cautious in its treatment of the mother that what it represses resurfaces later on. Freud's remarks about a girl's turn away from her mother apply here. "The turning away from the mother is accompanied by hostility. . . . A hate of that kind may become very striking and last all through life; it may be carefully over-compensated later on . . ." (*SE*, XXII, 121). The story begins with an apparently catastrophic break—the accidental death of the Greens and the abandonment of their eight impoverished children—and then devotes itself to making this break seem less severe. Dorothy seems to be writing in her brother's manner when she makes "their native Vale" implicitly the foster-mother for the orphans. The vale is literally one great family: one foster-parent shows "how closely the bonds of family connection are held together in these retired vallies" (*Narrative*, p. 65). The vale is also parental in bearing the traces of the love and labor of the parents and of more distant ancestors. "The love of their few fields and their ancient home was a salutary passion, and no doubt something of this must have spread itself to the Children" (p. 75). The children would take part in their parents'

work on the land "with a depth of interest which cannot be
felt, even in rural life, where people are only transitory occu-
pants of the soil on which they live" (p. 75), while she speaks
of their having to make money by selling peats "which they
dug out of their own hearts' heart, their Land" (p. 49).

The reader begins to feel too comforted, however. The
foster-parents assigned to the children are so adequate as to
make the original parents seem superfluous. The multiplica-
tion of mothers might be Dorothy's cautious way to limit the
power of the maternal figure, because it looks like adulation.
In *The Grasmere Journal* Dorothy chooses to recount at length
a conversation between Mary Wordsworth and Coleridge's
son Hartley, demonstrating a blindness peculiar to those who,
like Dorothy and Mary, grew up with a variety of foster-
parents:

> Mary said to Hartley, Shall I take Derwent with me? No
> says H. I cannot spare my little Brother in the sweetest
> tone possible and he can't do without his Mama. Well
> says Mary, why cannot I be his Mama. Can't he have
> more Mamas than one? No says H. What for? Because
> they do not love as Mothers do.
>
> (AG, 67, 7 Dec. 1801)

Hartley cannot prove why this is so, and it is just as much a
mystery to Dorothy. In *A Narrative* she emphasizes the ease
and rapidity with which the orphans adjust to their condition
and adapt to their new families. The eldest daughter, Jane,
"was as a Mother to her Brothers and Sisters when they were
fatherless and motherless, not knowing of their loss" (p. 66).
The infant, which all the vale has agreed not to separate from
Jane, "continues to call out 'Mam!' and 'Dad!' but seems not
to fret for the loss of either: she has already transferred all her
affections to her Sister" (p. 65). One woman in the vale, hav-
ing lost a son, cares for two of the boys as if they could replace
her own, and "They, poor Things! are perfectly contented"
(p. 69).

The death of the parents is made so uncatastrophic as to ap-

pear by the end to have been a blessing. The parents were so
poor, and, implicitly, so inadequate as parents, that both they
and the children are better off for the accident. Dead, the par-
ents may make the children "wiser and better," through the
recollection of their "awful end," than they could have done if
they had survived. Here is the story's final paragraph:

> There is at least this consolation, that the Father and
> Mother have been preserved by their untimely end from
> that dependence which they dreaded. The Children are
> likely to be better instructed in reading and writing, and
> may acquire knowledge which their Parents' poverty
> would have kept them out of the way of attaining; and
> perhaps, after the Land had been sold, the happy chear-
> fulness of George and Sarah Green might have forsaken
> them, and their latter days have been tedious and melan-
> choly.   (p. 87)

A consolation so positively framed exceeds neighborly op-
timism and raises questions about its motivation.

In context, this ending is also very abrupt. Long before this
ending Dorothy finishes her meandering account of the Green
children, and then begins a story about the children of
George's first marriage. Her narrative is without natural
limits; like the interconnected families in the vale, one story
leads to another. This structureless structure mimics the con-
tinuousness of life itself, but in this self-conscious work of lit-
erature she checks herself, apologizing for "having spun out
my narrative to a tedious length." Her manner of apologizing
is to (mis)quote from *The Excursion* the Wanderer's lines
about the way his "spirit clings" to the story of Margaret.
Beyond informing us that the story obsesses her, Dorothy's
reliance on a quotation also suggests that ending a story must
be an alien enterprise for her. It is following this that she hur-
riedly closes with her hope that the Greens have not died in
vain.

That the story has an artificial ending is borne out by the
fact that Dorothy keeps returning to it. She appends two

notes after the end. The first explains, in relatively proper footnote fashion, the name of a place she mentions in the text. The second simply extends her account: an incident mentioned in the text reminds her of a paragraph's worth of further description of the family's poverty and frugality, and a second paragraph simply opens "I ought to have mentioned that . . . ," followed by trivial details of the sale of the household. She keeps remembering things and these details, though interesting and part of the record, are not important enough to make their inclusion self-explanatory. Following these notes, her post-textual text meanders even further. She tells a story about Mrs. Green's natural daughter, which reminds her of an occurrence involving one Mary Watson, which provokes her to a detailed account of Mary Watson's son. This moves her, returning to the manuscript long after its completion (on the evidence of handwriting) to give an account of Mary Watson's own death (she was murdered by another son), which suggests, finally, an account of the grim fate of Mary Watson's grandson, to whom her estate came when she died (pp. 90-91).

What are we to make of all these extraneous additions? As in "A Winter's Ramble," she is lured on by a winding path but stops before she shows us the way back, and there may be no way back. It may be simply that she is indiscriminate and does not know when to stop, but her meandering thought does arrive at a track that it stays with, the grim life of Mary Watson. Overtly related to the plot of the Greens' story only by analogy (between Mrs. Green's daughter's and Mary Watson's reactions to hearing of the deaths of mother and son), the Mary Watson story must have some other connection to the Green story, in order for it to keep occurring to her as it does. The arbitrary cruelty inflicted on Mary Watson by circumstances is a corrective to the saccharine ending with which Dorothy felt compelled to close her narrative; the Greens' story is tidily symmetrical but the Watsons' is ominously open-ended. The last paragraph of the story, with the excessive optimism that leads up to it, now appears to have been the expression of an effort to repress certain elements that, after the formal ending of the story, now take their opportunity to return.

Mary Watson suffers as a mother. Her beloved son's death "caused universal regret in the Vale of Grasmere," while another son goes mad and survives to murder her. As if she had not been punished sufficiently during her life, her grandson wastes his inheritance, "took to dishonest practices, and is now under sentence of transportation." The quotation from *The Excursion* suggests a comparison between the story of the Greens and the story of Margaret. Each involves a negligent mother who is herself swallowed up and killed by nature. The ostensible reason for coming to Mary Watson's story is that when her son was drowned she insisted that she would have a special ability to find his body, and pleaded to go out in the boats to search, just as Mrs. Green's daughter is just barely prevented from endangering her life by searching the mountains herself as the night is coming on, so sure is she that "*she* should surely find them." (The Greens disappeared in the mist and snow on their way back from a "Sale" held in the valley next to theirs.) Mary Watson's special claim to being able to find her son is implicitly based on her desire to fulfill one last time the responsibilities of motherhood, to go to her child when he needs her. The breaking of that privileged link is the result of the son's death in this case, but Mary Watson is punished anyway, textually, as if that break had been the cause. The reason for this attribution of guilt may be that in Mrs. Green's story the breaking of that same privileged link was the cause of her death and of her children's abandonment. Mrs. Green's guilt is only hinted at in passing in the story, and usually it is disguised as praise:

> (. . . . it was well known that if the Mother had been *alive* she would have returned to her sucking Babe). . . . perhaps formerly it might be said, and with truth, the Woman had better been at home; but who shall assert that this same spirit which led her to come at times

among her Neighbours . . . did not assist greatly in pre-
serving her in chearful independance of mind through
the many hardships and privations of extreme poverty?
                                        (pp. 47-48, 50)

With her many cares and fears for her helpless Family she
must at that time [the time of her death] have mingled
some bitter self-reproaches for her boldness in venturing
over the Mountains.   (pp. 83-84)

The guilt that Dorothy does not like to assign to Mrs. Green
is transferred to Mary Watson, who suffers in her place. Mrs.
Green's crime, of dying and abandoning her children, is the
one of which Mrs. Wordsworth was also guilty, and it may be
that Dorothy is careful in the story not to accuse Mrs. Green
directly, because to do so would be to articulate, no matter
how circuitously, a more intimate accusation. The resentment
against the mother is repressed and only returns later after the
story proper is over. Sacrificing realism in favor of an impos-
sibly happy future for the orphans, the story exists to show
that natural parents can be of negligible importance, but it
ends by demonstrating the opposite. Dorothy cannot accuse
the mother, but neither can she acquit her.

In the Wordsworthian myth the sources of creativity are
hidden and found in earliest childhood, but for Dorothy the
route back to this source is blocked. In a poem of 1826, "Ir-
regular Stanzas: Holiday at Gwerndwffnant," she tries to
forge such a continuity, but again her ambiguous attitude
about the idea of home prevents her.[11] The speaker describes
her efforts to determine her relation to a group of children on
holiday in nature. Her fancy, deceiving her into imitating
them, mocks her lack of a genuine imaginative continuity
with them. At first she makes a frantic effort to join these
children by entertaining them. Her metaphors for nature are
hyperbolic, in imitation of what she supposes to be their play-
ful vision:

> Our carpet is her verdant sod;
> A richer one was never trod
>   In prince's proud saloon.

The pronouns in the first few stanzas are "we" and "ours," despite the opening qualification that "forty years have roll'd away / Since we were young as you." Her sense of community with the children is reduced to a pose by the revelation that these verses are self-quotation—"Thus spake I . . ."—and to a false pose by the contrast with reality: "Thus spake I, while with sober pace . . . ." The children then become "like a flock of vigorous lambs, / That leave their steady slow-paced dams / To gambol o'er the mead." As in previous texts, the speaker is not certain to which generation she belongs. "Recalled to consciousness," recognizing that "*we*, whose heads are grey" cannot possibly join in the children's play, the speaker severely curtails her fancy's promptings:

> So vanishes my idle dream
> . . . .
>
> Thought is not needed to suppress
> Those images of wild delight
> That flash'd before my dazzled sight
>   Upon that joy-devoted morn.

At the end of the day the children "retire / With no unsatisfied desire," and the morning of their departure brings no more than the slightest sorrow because their holiday has fully matched their expectations. Returning at the close of the poem to the "dear paternal roof," they receive an admonition from the speaker:

> Ah! Children, happy is your lot,
> Still bound together in one knot
> Beneath your tender Mother's eye!
> —Too soon these blessed days shall fly
> And Brothers must from Sisters part;

> And, trust me, whatsoe'er your doom,
> Whate'er betide through years to come,
> The punctual pleasures of your home
>   Shall linger in your thoughts—
> More prized than any future hope
> Though Fancy have her freest scope.
> And Ah! too soon your hearts shall own
> The *Past* is all that is your own.

The children's capacity for happiness originates beyond the happiness of that particular holiday. They are capable of leaving nature because they have mothers and families to whom they return, and because they are accustomed to being satisfied. Each holiday should be a "resting-place / For memory" not for its own sake but for the sake of the happy home from which it is a departure. Fancy or projection is a poor substitute for memory. Childhood should furnish a store of memories of contentment, so that at the time and later on the child will have a steady expectation of contentment, and will not need to turn to the inventions of fancy. If the speaker mocks her own "idle dream" at the beginning of the poem it must be because it, too, is a poor substitute for memory. Her admonition here accounts retrospectively for her opening curtailment of fancy: if she had untroubled memories like these children's, she would not now be obliged to pretend absurdly that she is young and agile. Her "idle dream" of childish activity in the present arose to replace some lack in childhood.

When Wordsworth talks about childhood it is usually to demonstrate the continuity between his childhood and his adult life. In Book I of *The Prelude* these references to childhood show that as a boy he experienced sublimity, unknown to him, in a guise that he could then comprehend:

>   . . . even then,
> A Child, I held unconscious intercourse
> With the eternal Beauty, drinking in

A pure organic pleasure . . . .

. . . .

   Thus, often in those fits of vulgar joy
Which, through all seasons, on a child's pursuits
Are prompt attendants, 'mid that giddy bliss
Which, like a tempest, works along the blood
And is forgotten; even then I felt
Gleams like the flashing of a shield; the earth
And common face of Nature spake to me
Remembrable things. . . .
               (I, 588-591, 609-616)

The poet here derives continuity with his childhood from these memories of the natural sublime, confirming his adult belief in the sublime by showing that it was once so natural, even if it is less so now. Although Wordsworth elsewhere qualifies this assertion of continuity, in Dorothy's poem there is nothing but discontinuity between child and adult. The children must be representations of herself, since to watch them play is to "read, as in a book, / A history of years gone by, / Recalled to Memory's fading eye . . . ," yet by describing other children, rather than her own memories, she dramatizes her sense of discontinuity from her own childhood.

   Entering into a dialogue with William's references to childhood, the poem suggests a reason for this discontinuity. For William, child and man are linked by the continuity of what is now recognized as imaginative power. The children in Dorothy's poem experience "fits of vulgar joy" without the "gleams." All that can interrupt their "unbridled course" is hunger, and after lunch "Again begins the emulous race, / Again succeeds the sportive chase" until "twilight check'd the noisy play: / Then did they feel a languor spread / Over their limbs," but it is the languor of fatigue, not of "calm delight." William occasionally refers to those moments in early childhood, rare for him, when the imagination was not active, and it is the language of these moments that Dorothy chooses to echo in her account of the children. Their sole pleasure is in running races:

> —Girl and Boy
> In gamesome race, with agile bound
> Beat merrily the grassy ground,
>   As if in motion perfect joy.

William uses the metaphor of the race to indicate a time prior to that which "brought with it a regular desire / For calmer pleasures:" "We ran a boisterous course; the year span round / With giddy motion. But the time approach'd . . ." (II, 48-51). In the passage that follows, the discovery that there are greater pleasures than being the winner of a race is associated with growing into "a quiet independence of the heart" (II, 55-78). In "Tintern Abbey," "glad animal movements" and, later, bounding like a roe, fulfilled only the desires of the eye.

Dorothy's chastisement of her fancy, directly following the account of these unimaginative children, entertains and reverses an echo of Wordsworth's grandest passage about imaginative continuity from the Intimations Ode. Because "those obstinate questionings" felt in childhood are the source of present sublimity,

> Our Souls have sight of that immortal sea
>   Which brought us hither,
>   Can in a moment travel thither,
> And see the Children sport upon the shore,
> And hear the mighty waters rolling evermore.

Aligning her metaphor with his, Dorothy denies what William asserts:

> So vanishes my idle dream
> That we through this long vernal day,
> Associates in their youthful play
> With them might travel in one stream.

It is the action of the irresponsible fancy, Dorothy says, that would lead her, at this point, to believe that she could "travel in one stream" with the unreflective play of these children, and their unimaginativeness is the projection of her feeling cut off from childhood. The imagination appears to be both cause and result of the continuity between William's past and present selves: cause, because it is present at all times; result, because it is based on strong memories of childhood. Dorothy's fancy tries to supply the place of genuine memories of childhood (by causing her to dream of playing like a child), but it fails to create a link between child and adult because it is not the imagination. Imaginative power must come from a continuity between childhood and adulthood, in order, paradoxically, to create that continuity. Dorothy sees herself excluded from a hermetic system.

A disruption of the relation between childhood and adulthood is again responsible for a lack of imaginative power, demonstrated as before by letting the fancy usurp the imagination's place, in a poem of a year later, "Irregular Verses" (titled, in a canceled draft, "To Julia Marshall—A Fragment").[12] Julia Marshall, the daughter of Dorothy's girlhood friend Jane Pollard, has asked for a Christmas poem, and Dorothy responds by telling why she did not write poetry at an earlier time: when she might have been writing she was instead spending her creative energies on plans for the future. Like the Countess of Winchilsea's Ardelia, she told these plans to her friend instead of turning them into poetry. This is the same kind of creativity as the "future hope" that the children of "Holiday" are warned not to place above memory, "Though Fancy have her freest scope," and the ancestor of the "idle dream" she entertains as an adult. Fully aware of the Coleridgean value-distinction between fancy and imagination, Dorothy presents a personal genealogy of fancy that parodies the Intimations Ode's continuity between the poet's birthright and his adult imagination. By limiting her definition of the poetic impulse to adolescent fantasy about the future, she excludes the possibility of poetry's coming naturally at any other period or for any other reason, so that she can never be accused of daring to be a poet, even in the present modestly titled irregular verses. By calling fancy the exclusive source of poetry she arranges a false opposition between poetry and truth: to write poetry would be "to decorate the truth," whereas she was "Contented to lay bare my heart" to her friend. Poetry is "jingling rhyme," as opposed to the "pleasant guileless dreams" that issued in the "simple prose" of her spoken narration and that, in an earlier version of the poem, were explicitly free from art:

> No costly work of studious art
> Did in those visions bear a part.

She is uneasy, clearly, about thus maligning poetry, because next she contradicts herself—"I *reverenced* the Poet's skill"—and offers a second explanation for not writing poetry, this time a passive one. She might have written,

> But bashfulness, a struggling shame
> A fear that elder heads might blame
> —Or something worse—a lurking pride
> Whispering my playmates would deride
> Stifled ambition, checked the aim
> If e'er by chance "the numbers came."

So far the poem's mood follows the pattern of "Holiday," in which an initial brave assertion is deflated by the acknowledgement of its groundlessness. It is "future hope" that is deceitful, not poetry, especially when she must say of that hope, "Alas! the cottage fled in air." Again as in "Holiday" the deflation is associated with a look at childhood. The passage continues:

> —Nay even the mild maternal smile,
> That oft-times would repress, beguile
> The over-confidence of youth,
> Even that dear smile, to own the truth,
> Was dreaded by a fond self-love;
> " 'Twill glance on me—and to reprove
> Or," (sorest wrong in childhood's school)
> " 'Twill *point* the sting of ridicule."[13]

If the poem refers only to the period when she knew Jane Pol-
lard, this "maternal smile" would have to belong to a foster
mother, either Elizabeth Threlkeld or, later, Dorothy's
grandmother. But it is more likely that the passage describes a
relic of an earlier time, because it represents so well the kind
of thing six-year-olds remember: not the whole person, but a
fragment. This does not mean that Dorothy's own mother
did or did not repress actual precocious creativity. Dorothy is
establishing a myth of earliest childhood in order to explain
how deeply ingrained is her habit of not trying her powers.
Whether fictional or real, this ambiguous smile remained in
her memory and participated in damping later endeavors.

In "Holiday," the children are happy to go home after their
exhilarating day, while the speaker, perpetually dissatisfied,
looks mistakenly to fancy to keep her in nature, because she
has no memory of another home to turn to. Both poems
exclude the imagination, discounting it as a compensation for
lost nature or lost memory. Mothers and nature acquire a
monopoly on the power to satisfy human wishes, because
Dorothy valorizes literal memory over everything else.

If in "Irregular Verses" Dorothy is creating the myth that
her mother's presence blocked her childish ambitions, and
that that memory prevented her later from being a poet, she is
contradicting the affect of "Holiday." There she laments not
having a mother; here she laments having one. In "Holiday"
fancy is diminished by comparison with the absent memory;
when she does confess to a maternal memory, those fancies
are now magnified into a lost power of poetry. Either way,
with or without the mother, creativity is blocked. Youthful
dreams of "future hopes" are nurtured in both myths: having
had a mother who restrained ambition she turned her creative
energies to dreams of the future; having lacked a mother and a
home she also turned her energies to dreams of the future.
That two stories written a year apart so openly contradict
each other suggests that she does not have a logical polemic in
mind, but rather that the self-contradiction is itself important.
That she can adopt either myth, and take up either position,

betrays a deep confusion about the self. Like the circularity of her implicit argument about the origins and effects of imagination, her illogic here exposes her outsider's feeling of loss.

Wordsworth tells us in Book II of *The Prelude* how he discovered, somewhat against his will, that both he and the natural world could exist independently of his mother after her death. He tells us how nature then carried this work of instruction one step further, teaching him gradually to separate himself from her. Identity must come from differentiating the self from the external world, and the child first discovers that his mother is not an extension of himself before he can discover his separateness from the rest of the world. "Nutting" demonstrates that a momentary painful separation from feminine nature is essential for writing, but that that separation is never final. Whereas Wordsworth makes separation and continuity indivisible parts of a unified myth, Dorothy's alternate myths of origins, in which the memory of the maternal can be either lamentably absent or oppressively present, preclude the possibility of a unified identity. Accepting William's myth that imagination originates in the past, yet lacking the requisite confidence in the continuity between childhood and adulthood, Dorothy leaves herself out of every center she proposes, whether in nature because she is too old to romp, or in the image of the integral family because her literal memory provides her with none of her own. She experiences an imposed separation from origins that her brother does not experience in the same way and that deprives her of the strong sense of identity necessary to writing Romantic poetry.

DEFINING IMAGINATION, Coleridge says that

> The poet . . . diffuses a tone and spirit of unity, that blends, and (as it were) *fuses*, each into each, by that synthetic and magical power, to which we have exclusively appropriated the name of imagination.
>
> (*Biographia Literaria*, XIV)

In Dorothy's writing there is often a spirit of fusion, but it is not the same as Coleridge's Imagination. Dorothy's habitual fragmentation of identity, resulting from division and evasion of origins, is reflected in the diffuseness of whatever imaginative or visionary passages she does achieve. To return to the beginnings of her history as a writer, the first entry of *The Alfoxden Journal* shows that what she finds worth recording are places where nature demonstrates metamorphic capacities, or moments when the mind supplies the same dimension: "The green paths down the hillsides are channels for streams." Metaphor then mimics this invisible interfusion: "After the wet dark days, the country seems more populous. It peoples itself in the sunbeams. . . . the shafts of the trees show in the light like the columns of a ruin" (*AG*, 1, 20 Jan. 1798). Imaginative though this passage is, the metaphors are whimsically selected and disjunctive with one another, so that the final effect is of a tension between minor unities and greater separations. Coleridge's definition of Imagination opens:

> The primary IMAGINATION I hold to be the living Power and prime Agent of all human Perception, and as a repetition in the finite mind of the eternal act of creation in the infinite I AM. (*Biographia Literaria*, XIII)

If the Imagination is a creative power modeled on the divine original, and if divine creation takes place by the assertion of a single unifying principle, then the human Imagination, in finite terms, must be an assertion of personal identity. If Dorothy's imagination "dissolves, diffuses, dissipates, in order to recreate," it does not also repeat "the eternal act of creation in the infinite I AM." The emphasis is on diffusion, rather than on either re-creation or the assertion of identity.

It may be a natural consequence of writing quickly, but Dorothy's omission of the "I" in many parts of many journal entries is symptomatic of a more central fact about her writing. The first entry, quoted above, is all observation about other things. The use of metaphor suggests the presence of a seeing "I," but we never observe it directly, and the whimsicality of her metaphors prevents a unified point of view. This odd omission begins in the second entry: "Walked on the hill-tops—a warm day. Sate under the firs in the park" (*AG*, 1, 21 Jan. 1798). It might have been trivially interesting to know if she were alone or accompanied, but beyond that we wonder where the self is located, if it so avoids direct mention of itself. A personal pronoun is at last called into use in the fourth entry, necessitated by recording an act of analysis:

> The sound of the sea distinctly heard on the tops of the hills, which we could never hear in summer. We attribute this partly to the bareness of the trees, but chiefly to the absence of the singing of birds, the hum of insects, that noiseless noise which lives in the summer air.
>
> (*AG*, 2, 23 Jan. 1798)

Her usual descriptive powers, as of that "noiseless noise," are unchanged. What is unusual is the analytical act of mind involved in saying, "We attribute this . . . ."

Consider the difference between these two sequential sentences:

> In the morning when I arose the mists were hanging over the opposite hills and the tops of the highest hills were covered with snow. There was a most lovely combination at the head of the vale—of the yellow autumnal hills wrapped in sunshine, and overhung with partial mists, the green and yellow trees and the distant snow-topped mountains.   (*AG*, 44, 10 Oct. 1800)

The first sentence makes a unity of the landscape, the same visual pattern appearing in the mist over the hills and in the snow on the highest hills. The second sentence, which gives a similar description of a slightly different view, is very differently constructed. There are four descriptive elements instead of two and they do not adhere to create the same kind of unified vision as before; she can only gather them loosely as "a most lovely combination." The hills wrapped in sunshine might be a repetition of the pattern of mist and snow on the hills, but the sentence goes on too long, and her addition of "the green and yellow trees" indicates that she is more faithful

to observed detail than to pattern. Furthermore, that she re-
peats the same elements of description (hills with mist and
snow-topped mountains) for two different views or angles of
vision undoes the illusion of unity that she could so easily
create. Instead of perceiving it as one landscape she sees it as
two separate sights that happen to be similar.

In the first sentence she has used one of her rare "I"'s, un-
necessarily as far as detail goes, because normally she is not
concerned to say where she was when she saw what she de-
scribes. "When I arose" tells us that it was early, and it may
possibly confer upon the scene a special quality of Edenic
priority, but chiefly it is a signal that there is a creative self in
this sentence rarely present elsewhere. In seeing that unified
vision she felt a stronger sense of self than in seeing other
things, whether she was aware of the difference or not, and
whether that sense of self is cause or effect of the more unified
vision. The sense of self is diverted into a passing remark
which does not in itself overtly exhibit its significance; she
says "when I arose" because she does not say "I saw."

Dorothy's tendency to omit a central or prominent self in
her journals becomes much more apparent when compared to
William's habitual concentration on the self. William's custom
of mining Dorothy's journals for descriptive passages to
transform into poems permits some close comparisons of this
kind. Dorothy's omission of self and William's emphasis on
self make the major difference between one of her *Alfoxden*
entries and the poem he wrote based on it.[14] Her account be-
gins and ends with practical specifics: where they were when
they encountered this vision, "Went to Poole's after tea," and
a closing detail, "(half-moon)," which, like "the green and
yellow trees" above, slants the description towards the topo-
graphical (*AG*, 2, 25 Jan. 1798). It is as if she wished literally
to bound or enclose her vision, to domesticate it by putting
the eternal in the context of the daily.

Went to Poole's after tea. The sky spread over with
one continuous cloud, whitened by the light of the

moon, which, though her dim shape was seen, did not
throw forth so strong a light as to chequer the earth with
shadows. At once the clouds seemed to cleave asunder,
and left her in the centre of a black-blue vault. She sailed
along, followed by multitudes of stars, small, and bright,
and sharp. Their brightness seemed concentrated,
(half-moon).

William's poem "A Night-Piece" begins with her second sen-
tence, and follows it, rendering it more elegant but not sig-
nificantly different. The substantive change begins half way
through Dorothy's entry. Where she writes "At once the
clouds seemed to cleave asunder," William has

> At length a pleasant instantaneous gleam
> Startles the pensive traveller while he treads
> His lonesome path, with unobserving eye
> Bent earthwards; he looks up—the clouds are split
> Asunder, . . .

Introducing this observing self so precisely between two ele-
ments of her description, William places the self beyond na-
ture. Similarly, after her description ends, William returns to
his pensive traveller:

> At length the Vision closes; and the mind,
> Not undisturbed by the delight it feels,
> Which slowly settles into peaceful calm,
> Is left to muse upon the solemn scene.

A schematic comparison between the two writers could
be made on the basis of these two passages. William looks at
nature for the sake of the mind, whereas Dorothy, unwilling
even to call it a vision, looks at nature for its own sake. Yet
the distinction cannot be so easily made, because one part of
Dorothy's description contains the germ of a self in its im-
plicit reliance on perspective. When she writes of the moon,
"She sailed along, followed by multitudes of stars, small, and
bright, and sharp," it is the motion of the clouds that makes

the moon appear to be in motion, but only to particularly imaginative eyes. Among Dorothy's descriptive details, William chooses to expand only this one, because it suggests an imaginative view:

> she sails along,
> Followed by multitudes of stars, that, small
> And sharp, and bright, along the dark abyss
> Drive as she drives: how fast they wheel away,
> Yet vanish not!—the wind is in the tree,
> But they are silent;—still they roll along
> Immeasurably distant.

The addition of his "pensive traveller" makes that imaginative point of view central to the poem, where for Dorothy it is marginal. In Dorothy's entry the eye's importance is acknowledged, but it is minimized in favor of a belief in nature's power to create illusions of its own. She turns the possibility of a creating self back toward nature.

In her poetry, Dorothy writes with this same exclusion of self, and since by writing in verse she implicitly compares herself to William, her selflessness almost seems to be a deliberate refutation of Wordsworthian egotism. When Wordsworth abstracts his mind from natural objects his mind becomes the center, and when he mourns a lost Presence it is imaginatively an absence, because the power of his imagination centers his world. That absence may be conjectured to have once been central, but where it was, the mind is now.[15] The absence Dorothy invokes in these eccentric poems is a genuinely empty center, filled by no self, outside which she writes.

In another late poem, "Thoughts on My Sick-Bed,"[16] Dorothy gives an account of her discovery, parallel to Wordsworth's, of the benefit to poetry of being distanced from nature, but the difference from his account is instructive. Hers is a programmatic explication of the idea that beauty recollected is more affecting than beauty seen. She describes first her "youthful days" in which nature produced an immediate joy in the senses. Then, in a movement not unlike that of the Intimations Ode or "Tintern Abbey," she goes on to claim a deeper joy for the more sober present:

> No—then I never felt a bliss
> That might with *that* compare
> Which, piercing to my couch of rest
> Came on the vernal air, . . .

The present bliss comes from her response to a gift of flowers brought by friends. She speaks of a "hidden life" to which these flowers have brought joy, but as if rejecting that term as obscurantist, she reveals that joy to be merely the experience of a powerful literal memory: "It bore me to the Terrace walk / I trod the Hills again." Wordsworth's memory, where it is most helpful to him, is of his impressions of a place rather than of the place itself, as when in "Tintern Abbey" he says "The picture of the mind revives again." He remembers his own mind more than he remembers the landscape. Dorothy seeks relief from her mind, and memory is valued most when it is entirely of the landscape.

> I *saw* the green Banks of the Wye,
> Recalling thy prophetic words,
> Bard, Brother, Friend from infancy!

The prophetic words that she means to fulfill here are those at the close of "Tintern Abbey" in which the bard predicts the time when memory will be as soothing to her as it is to him:

> when thy mind
> Shall be a mansion for all lovely forms,
> Thy memory be as a dwelling-place
> For all sweet sounds and harmonies; oh! then
> If solitude, or fear, or pain, or grief,
> Should be thy portion, with what healing thoughts
> Of tender joy wilt thou remember . . . .

In Dorothy's memory the final words must be, incorrectly, "this scene" or "nature," because the restoratives she continues to invoke are simple illusions of transportation: "—I thought of Nature's loveliest scenes; / And with Memory I was there." The passage actually continues, of course, with the words "me, / And these my exhortations!" Where for William memory means memory of the self, and all healing thoughts must involve the self, Dorothy turns his prophecy outward, to approve a loss of self in the enjoyment of nature. If she valorizes self-forgetfulness in the recollection of nature then she must consider the self to be pure selfhood, perhaps her uncomfortable body ill in bed, certainly not the poetic "I AM." Either she lacks this concept, or she deliberately refuses it.

Wordsworth's vision of sublimity achieved through recollections of "these beauteous forms" involves a similar loss of selfhood, but the selfhood is carefully distinguished from a higher part of the self:

> Until, the breath of this corporeal frame
> And even the motion of our human blood
> Almost suspended, we are laid asleep
> In body, and become a living soul.

Dorothy's self-forgetfulness resembles his—

> No need of motion, or of strength,
> Or even the breathing air—

but it sounds even more like Lucy's: "No motion has she now, no force." Not only does this echo propose in the present speaker a deathlike unconsciousness analogous to Lucy's, but also, because it is an echo, it indicates an even greater dissolution of self. The "I" of this poem becomes the "she" of another, and though any quotation denotes a suspension of identity, this one causes the "I" to abdicate altogether. In these last four verses the poem conceals the proposed "hidden life" and then offers two unsatisfactory substitutes: a photographic recapitulation of nature, or another's internal life that is as impenetrable as that recapitulation is superficial. Neither leads to an identifiable self. (These vectors away from identity might be aligned roughly with the conflicting attitudes that we saw earlier as Dorothy's options. Writing out of love for nature, she merges with nature and forgets her self; writing out of love for William she takes on the persona he designs for her and adopts a "hidden life" that is his, not hers, and therefore one that is as mystifying to her as it is to us.)

"A Winter's Ramble in Grasmere Vale" is the last of a sequence of three poems about Grasmere, the first two of which are titled "A Cottage in Grasmere Vale" and "After-recollections at the sight of the same cottage"; the sequence was originally written as one long poem and it is preceded by a poem on the same subject, "A Sketch," that stands as a sort of preface.[17] None of these poems comes any closer to describing a cottage than does "A Winter's Ramble," which opens with a departure from all human traces. Most of William's poems also involve a movement away, but the speaker in "Tintern Abbey" or in "Nutting" moves through and away from nature toward himself, whereas the speaker of "A Winter's Ramble" allows the streamlet to usurp all powers of future speech. Back home, if that were possibly an alternate center, there is a conjectural "What if William be dead?" These Cottage poems circle around their ostensible subject, but without the compensatory sense of an alternate center in the mind of the poet. The voice is all eye, apparently mindless in its inability to focus on its subject, lured everywhere. As in "Thoughts on My Sick-Bed," literal nature rises up to block what appears to be the poem's original intent, here by diverting her line of sight and obscuring the view of the cottage. Each poem reiterates the same vacancy: the house is the center of subjectivity, and since it cannot be entered, there is no subject anywhere.[18]

"A Sketch" invites an expectation of descriptive focus by announcing in the first line that "There is one Cottage in our Dale," but the second line immediately begins the process of submersion. The cottage is "In naught distinguish'd from the rest." The third line buries it even further: it is not distinguished "Save by a tuft of flourishing trees." In the fourth line we see the cottage for the last time, already concealed behind a metaphor, as a "little nest" sheltered by those trees. The remaining two verses take an even more distant perspective and concern the road that goes past the cottage, and particularly the fact that it is "hidden by the trees." Three times she repeats that it is lost in the trees:

> You lose it there—its serpent line
> Is lost in that close household grove
> —A moment lost—

The first time, the observer's eye is still involved in the scene, but in the second and third lines it is not just a visual illusion but a real loss or absence of the road. The road escapes, in the last line and a half, but only to mount to "The craggy hills above." She loses each potential subject in turn, first the cottage, then the "you" observer, then the road. All are consumed by the trees.

"A Cottage in Grasmere Vale", the first section of the original long poem, represents another attempt at describing the cottage. It begins, as does "A Sketch," with a view of the cottage's position in the dale:

> Peaceful our Valley, fair and green
> And beautiful her cottages,
> Each in its nook, its sheltered Hold
> Or guarded by its tuft of trees
>
> Many and beautiful they are
> But there is One that I love best,
> A lowly shed, in truth, it is,
> A Brother of the rest.
>
> Yet when I sit on rock or hill
> Down-looking on the valley fair
> That cottage with its clustering Trees
> Summons my heart: it settles there.

This seems a more promising start. Although she is not describing the cottage itself, her attention is drawn to it. There seems to be, furthermore, a fairly definite viewing self in the poem, an "I" that has both eye and heart. Yet the sense of exile in this poem is even stronger than in the first. "When I sit on rock or hill" suggests an uncannily mobile "I" that flits from one vantage point to another, defined not by who or even where it is but by what it gazes at. This diffuse self is then split into parts: the heart "settles there" but the eye does not follow.

The first two lines of the second verse echo "—But there's a Tree, of many, one," the line that announces the Intimations Ode's change of mood from exhilaration to loss. By alluding to this moment of contraction in her poem's most celebratory line Dorothy establishes the poem's ambiguous mood. The one cottage exerts a powerful centripetal attraction—it "summons my heart" and a few lines later it is compared to other cottages that "intice a *Wanderer's* mind"—yet the cottage prohibits the speaker's gaze as much as it invites it. Up to now, the central image is of "That cottage with its clustering Trees," with the cottage as subject and the trees syntactically subordinate, but just as before these encircling trees now proceed to replace the cottage as the focus of the poem, making the cottage itself unavailable, an absent center. The speaker describes a storm from which the trees protect the cottage, but because she shares the storm's exclusion and because she is in fact like the storm—"My Fancy is unfettered—wild"— her viewpoint and her sympathies lie more with the storm than with the enclosure.

> And when the storm comes from the North
> It lingers near that pastoral spot,
> And, piping through the mossy walls,
> It seems delighted with its lot.

She describes the storm for another verse and then breaks off abruptly—"—It may not enter there"—as if to suggest that if the storm may not enter the grove, neither may her verses or her fancy. The last two stanzas remain focused on the outside of the grove, with the cottage seen only to the extent that it is sheltered by the trees or touched by the sun:

A green unfading Grove it is,
Skirted with many a lesser tree
Hazel and holly, beech and oak,
A bright and flourishing company!

Precious the shelter of those trees;
They screen the Cottage that I love;
The sunshine pierces to the roof
And the tall pine-trees tower above!

The self is divided in this poem between an unseeing and silent heart inside the enclosure and an eye and a speaking voice that are kept out. Identifying eye and voice with fancy, she limits herself just as in "Holiday at Gwerndwffnant" and "Irregular Verses," forbidding herself the poetic imagination while also devaluing fancy. Coleridge, defining fancy as contrary and inferior to imagination, places it among the "essentially fixed and dead" objects opposed to the "essentially vital" imagination; it is a peripheral faculty that engages with externals, the "Drapery" of poetic genius of which the imagination is the soul. Dorothy, identifying poetic voice as fancy, defines her position as outside and secondary. To note that she calls the cottage, the inaccessible center, "A Brother of the rest" may help to particularize what her distance from the cottage signifies. She turns that home into a figure for the centralizing imagination that her brother possesses and that she lacks and can hardly dare to appropriate. The subjectivity that she requires in order to have the poetic imagination is inaccessible, and the subjectivity that she has is the devalued fancy that flits from one vantage point to the next, "a mode of memory emancipated from the order of time and space." That she identifies voice with the storm that threatens the cottage expresses her ambivalence about the centralizing "I" she desires and cannot have, but that she also does not want. The storm's goal ought to be to penetrate into the enclosure, but the speaker says that it is happy to remain peripheral; she preempts her being excluded by calling it her own reluctance to trespass into her brother's territory.

After the two-stanza "After-recollections at the sight of the same cottage," in which the poet again describes not the cottage but the spring-like weather of her first day there, the poem sequence ends with "A Winter's Ramble in Grasmere Vale." Separated in the preceding poems from the center of subjectivity that she identifies with her brother's house, she now leaves "my sole Companion-friend / To wander out alone," and she finds in that wandering a natural object that, reinforcing the lesson of the natural enclosure in preceding poems, stops her from returning as a poet to her brother or to the cottage. A poem written a few years after the last version of the Cottage poems, "Lines intended for my Niece's Album," repeats with an explicitly literary signification the Cottage poems' pattern of a natural enclosure barring imaginative entrance to a center that she identifies with her brother and with poetic speech.[19] The poem begins with the conceit that the album is like nature because Dora, godlike, has commanded that " 'My book shall appear in green array,' " and green is nature's "favored hue." Like nature, the album preserves divine works in the form of "Memorials of the Good and Wise." Dorothy describes the white pages of the album as an enclosure bounded by nature's green, like the one she portrays in the Cottage poems, and her difficulty here as before is that within these precincts lie the words of formidable poets—not just her brother, but his brothers as well:

> Perennial green enfolds these leaves;
> They lie enclosed in glossy sheath
> As spotless as the lily flower,
> Till touched by a quickening breath
>
> And it *has* touched them:—yes, dear Girl,
> In reverence of thy "gifted Sire"
> A wreath for thee is here entwined
> By his Brothers of the Lyre
>
> .   .   .   .
>
> But why should *I* inscribe my name,
> No Poet I—no longer young?

The ambition of a loving heart
Makes garrulous the tongue.

Made acutely aware of her inadequacies as a poet by what she sees "enclosed in glossy sheath," in selecting the verses to be copied into the album she excludes both those that connect the album's green to nature's and those that suggest competition with the "Brothers of the Lyre." When the album is no longer seen as being like the cottage, to enter it is no longer to trespass.

What blocks the reunion of parts of the self in the Cottage poems is the natural enclosure. "Floating Island," a poem with a somewhat less emotionally charged subject, emphasizes even more explicitly nature's role in the dissolution of self. Composed at an unknown date, though probably contemporary with "Lines intended for my Niece's Album" and "Thoughts on My Sick-Bed," the poem was published by Wordsworth in 1842 among his own poems.[20] Although he credits Dorothy's authorship of this and other poems, that he incorporates them in the sequence of his own poems subordinates her identity to his in a most practical way—even though she would have been flattered to have been included, and would never have published on her own. (When Knight prints more of her poems in his edition of Wordsworth, he is simply following Wordsworth's own practice.) This poem's subject, "a slip of earth," is "Loosed from its hold," floats free on the lake, still populated by flowers, trees, birds and insects, and then disappears or dissolves, literally a submerged object. This island is a latent figure for the dissolving self, but the poem ostensibly asks to be read not in reference to the self, but as a parable about nature. The first and last verses propose a diversionary moral about nature's creative and destructive powers all working to one beneficent end. Itself submerged, the island's operation as a figure is also submerged. The "I" in the poem casts loose, like the island, and becomes similarly diffuse, though it is unclear which causes the other to dissolve, because by the end they have collapsed into each other.

The poem begins relatively firmly: "Once did I see a slip of earth. . . ." This "I"'s sight is verifiable: "all might see it float." The next verse begins, "Might see it, from the mossy shore / Dissevered." As the island is dissevered from the shore, so is the verb "Might see" dissevered from its subject "all," which is left behind in the previous verse. The stanza itself is cast loose. The eye now embarks with the traveling island and describes its flora and fauna, but as in the Cottage poems it is an eye without an I.

That "might" in stanzas two and three is in the past tense, referring to a certainty. The poem now shifts into conjecture, but it does so in a beautifully imperceptible manner because all it need do is go from "might" to "may:" "through many seasons' space / This little Island may survive." Without our knowing it, another ground has shifted. With the disappearance of certainty in time the potential "I" dissolves, too. That the reader can logically attribute this disappearance to the speaker's having seen the island while traveling does not diminish the poem's eerie baselessness. The only self in the poem now is a conjectural "you," and even that "you" is on the verge of dispersal.

> Perchance when you are wandering forth
> Upon some vacant sunny day,
> Without an object, hope, or fear,
> Thither your eyes may turn; the Isle is passed away.

The "you" may not know that it is looking at a lost presence, rather than simply at a blank; it may not even be there at all. This tangible vacancy is shared equally by the "you," by the day ("some vacant sunny day"), and by the island. When in Book V of *The Prelude* the boy walks in nature "Seeking I knew not what" (V, 456) the image of death that he finds consoles him for his mother's death by assuring him of her continued, though diffuse, presence. The "you" of this poem, "wandering . . . / Without an object," finds an image of death, too, and tries to find consolation in the positive values of diffusion:

Buried beneath the glittering Lake,
Its place no longer to be found;
Yet the lost fragments shall remain
To fertilise some other ground.

The verbs are suddenly certain again, not conjectural: "is passed away . . . [is] Buried . . . shall remain." These certainties are piled precariously upon the foregoing conjectures and vacancies, and the positive tone they project is not altogether convincing. So much more is asked of the diffusion here than in the passage from *The Prelude*. There it is the (m)other who is dispersed into nature, while here it is that vanished self. Both subject and object disappear, and that groundless assertiveness in the last stanza can be spoken only from the point of view of an impersonal nature, because only nature derives power from centerlessness.

THE PLACE OF the chosen object is usurped by nature in "Floating Island," and, as in "Thoughts on My Sick-Bed" and the Cottage poems, the self dissolves in the face of literal nature. In the Cottage poems those clustering trees prevent the speaker from following her heart inside the enclosure, a situation that is restated in "Lines intended for my Niece's Album," whereas in "Thoughts" literal memory obscures the "hidden life" even to itself. The trouble that generates these poems and charges them with their energy has its origins in a quarrel that the feminine self has with the structure of language. Nature blocks the speaker's sight and subdues self because she lets it. The language Dorothy inherits descends from the performative Logos of a paternal deity, by way of a history of usage in which language aspires to subject the object world in the manner of Adam's control over the creatures he named. Language operates by what Derrida calls a process of propriation, and the object of propriation is normatively feminine, making the subjection of women and of feminized nature integral to any process involving language (see chapter I). Dorothy, identified with nature by her brother and by her friend Coleridge, may have had a special knowledge of the violation of identity experienced by all such objects of propriation, but as a woman she would know it in any case, and she extends her sympathy to nature. The lack or diffusion of self in the Cottage poems, "Thoughts on My Sick-Bed," and "Floating Island" may be augmented by a positive effort not to appropriate nature. In the selfless style of *Grasmere* and *Alfoxden*, nature is chief among those objects not to be subjugated, and all the journals tend to offer a view of nature not dominated by the viewer's consciousness. Implicit in her use of language in the journals is the belief that description should allow the natural world to retain its integrity while being named. She is trying to use language not to augment her own power but as a vehicle of her respect for the other.

The poems' disturbances usually occur because her selflessness contradicts what she has learned about writing poetry from her brother and from literary tradition, that poetry demands a central self. A journal is also highly personal in conception, presenting the thoughts and impressions of a single person, but traditional usage and the assumption of a wider audience make poetry claim a universality for the self that is lacking in journal writing. This is especially true for Dorothy's journals because of her insistence on restricting her audience to the immediate family and friends—those who would take an interest in the "I" in her writing because they cared for her herself, not because she could attempt to instruct them in any way. The journals are able to restrain the appropriativeness of language more happily than the poems because they are free of an appropriating self.

In her prose, suspicious of the operations of fancy, Dorothy often denies her participation in visionary or poetic moments. Visions of the interfusion of contrasting elements in nature appeal to her repeatedly, but she is always scrupulous to be the observer, not the maker, and to insist that these harmonies do not depend on orchestration by the human mind. Walking the hills in *Alfoxden*, Dorothy describes a complex series of interfusions performed by nature.

The sea at first obscured by vapour; that vapour afterwards slid in one mighty mass along the sea-shore; the islands and one point of land clear beyond it. The distant country (which was purple in the clear dull air), overhung by straggling clouds that sailed over it, appeared like the darker clouds, which are often seen at a great distance apparently motionless, while the nearer ones pass quickly over them, driven by the lower winds. I never saw such a union of earth, sky, and sea. The clouds beneath our feet spread themselves to the water, and the clouds of the sky almost joined them.

(AG, 4–5, 3 Feb. 1798)

The illusion that the distant country looks like dark clouds is one kind of union, the apparent overlay of near and far is another, and the actual near convergence of lower and higher clouds is yet another. This variegated "union of earth, sky, and sea" depends on point of view, yet she acts only as a spectator, guaranteeing her impartiality by her emphasis on the topographical and atmospheric clarity of the scene.

In the Coleridgean tradition, she identifies poetry with "a tone and spirit of unity." The occasion in *Grasmere* that "made me more than half a poet" involves a vision of interconnection in nature. Seeing a sublime contrast she waxes sublime—"O the unutterable darkness of the sky and the earth below the moon! and the glorious brightness of the moon itself!"—but she is not "made . . . more than half a poet" until nature unifies these picturesque elements: "when I saw this lowly Building in the waters among the Dark and lofty hills, with that bright soft light upon it, it made me more than half a poet" (*AG*, 104, 18 March 1802). Yet she is only partly a poet. The mode of this passage, and of the *Alfoxden* passage, is close to that of the first verse paragraph of "Tintern Abbey," where we recognize a synthetic power in the vision of the interfusion in nature:

Once again
Do I behold these steep and lofty cliffs,

That on a wild secluded scene impress
Thoughts of a more deep seclusion; and connect
The landscape with the quiet of the sky.

But though Dorothy's interfusions are strictly observed in nature, William's involve the mind as well by using the language of the mind ("impress / Thoughts . . . connect"). Though these mental actions are metaphors for natural events, they show the passage to be on the verge of turning away from nature. The mind here is compromising its impulse to dominate the landscape by imaging itself as part of the landscape. This powerful mind is the part of a poet that Dorothy lacks. To be fully a poet requires that an active agency of mind engage in creating visions of interfusion, not just observe them. That part of a poet that she does become, she is "made," characteristically directing attention away from herself. Nature is respected by not supposing that language can or should grasp it, while at the same time Dorothy eschews investigations or assertions of the self. She prefers to have nature be the poet, if the poet is the one who diffuses a spirit of unity. It may be that it is this complete deference to nature that is responsible for the unevenness of her success as a writer, yet in a few passages of extraordinary beauty she succeeds in matching her insistence on removing herself from the scene with a vision of a genuinely autonomous harmony in nature.

The description of Loch Lomond in *Recollections of a Tour Made in Scotland, 1803* is surely of these passages.[21] William, Coleridge, and Dorothy had taken a boat to an island in the middle of the lake and were climbing the island's hill. The following are excerpts from a much longer account:

We had not climbed far before we were stopped by a sudden burst of prospect, so singular and beautiful that it was like a flash of images from another world. . . . We looked towards the foot of the lake, scattered over with islands without beginning and without end. The sun shone, and the distant hills were visible, some through

sunny mists, others in gloom with patches of sunshine;
the lake was lost under the low and distant hills, and the
islands lost in the lake, which was all in motion with
travelling fields of light, or dark shadows under rainy
clouds. There are many hills, but no commanding emi-
nence at a distance to confine the prospect, so that the
land seemed endless as the water.   (*J*, I, 251-252)

She gives detailed descriptions of two islands lying immedi-
ately next to the island on which they are standing. These two
islands

were intermingled with the water, I might say interbed-
ded and interveined with it, in a manner that was exquis-
itely pleasing. There were bays innumerable, straits or
passages like calm rivers, landlocked lakes, and, to the
main water, stormy promontories. . . . Near to these is a
miniature, an islet covered with trees, on which stands a
small ruin that looks like the remains of a religious house;
it is overgrown with ivy, and were it not that the arch of
a window or gateway may be distinctly seen, it would be
difficult to believe that it was not a tuft of trees growing
in the shape of a ruin, rather than a ruin overshadowed
by trees.   (*J*, I, 252)

These visions of interfusion in nature in no way depend on
"swimming sense" or on a subduing of the bodily eye. They
achieve their effect by means of a steady attention to descrip-
tive detail.

Carrying Wordsworth's project to naturalize the imagina-
tion even further than he does, Dorothy continually natu-
ralizes his apocalyptic vocabulary. The view of Loch Lomond
"was like a flash of images from another world." In 1804
Wordsworth uses this language in Book VI of *The Prelude* to
describe the mind breaking away from nature, "when the
light of sense / Goes out in flashes that have shewn to us / The
invisible world" (VI, 534-536), but he also uses a visible
"flash" of moonlight to open the vision of naturalized imagi-

nation on Mt. Snowdon at the close of *The Prelude*, making mental operations into metaphors for natural events. Dorothy's similar usage prefigures the distance he crosses in the final arrangement of these two passages (as opposed to their compositional sequence)[22] and suggests a model for his curtailing and naturalizing the self-conscious imagination. Dorothy also naturalizes "beyond," a conventional term for sublimity. When she says "wherever we looked, it was a delightful feeling that there was something beyond" (*J*, I, 253), it is ambiguous whether she means physically or spiritually beyond, since the scene includes "islands without beginning and without end," and "the land seemed endless as the water." Although endlessness is a property of eternity, as in the "great Apocalypse" passage in Book VI of *The Prelude*, we do not know just where, if ever, Dorothy's topographical endlessness crosses a boundary to become an infinitude of the mind.

In a similar passage from the *Recollections of . . . Scotland* she begins and ends with the qualification that nature exceeds the various powers of the mind. "We beheld one of the most delightful prospects that, even when we dream of fairer worlds than this, it is impossible for us to conceive in our hearts" (*J*, I, 320). Writing retrospectively, she explores her memory of the scene to determine just what it was that made it so extraordinary, but her sense that she may have failed to do so is, to her, a tribute to its beauty. "My description must needs be languid; for the sight itself was too fair to be remembered" (*J*, I, 321). By "must needs be" she must mean to strike a note of prescriptive self-restraint (i.e., should be) because the description that precedes this disclaimer is not only gorgeous but also engages a mythical dimension:

> Green islands lay on the calm water, islands far greener, for so it seemed, than the grass of other places; and from their excessive beauty, their unearthly softness, and the great distance of many of them, they made us think of the islands of the Blessed in the *Vision of Mirza*—. . . . the

emerald islands without a bush or tree, the celestial col-
our and brightness of the calm sea, and the innumerable
creeks and bays, the communion of land and water as far
as the eye could travel. (*J*, I, 321)

The description hardly deserves to be called "languid," but
Dorothy is afraid of not recognizing the boundary between
observation and invention, and checks herself in order not to
risk crossing it.

Dorothy is usually an ascetic of the imagination, despite
passages such as these from the *Recollections of . . . Scotland.* In
Journal of a Tour on the Continent, 1820 she rarely risks visions
of interfusion that would in any way implicate her mind's
power at work. Starting to offer such visions, twice, she re-
treats to the position that the scene is indescribable, in order
not to take linguistic possession of it. Contemporary travel
writers turned the notion of indescribability into a cliché for
grandeur or sublimity. Like them, Dorothy uses it occasion-
ally for scenes of vast size, as when the view from a mountain
top temporarily daunts her descriptive courage, but she also
uses it for scenes that the other travel writers would probably
not have noticed. From the top of Rigi, in the Alps, a "trans-
formation" in nature characteristically attracts her eye.
Masses of clouds, mist, and vapors rush and recede, conceal
and then rapidly reveal the ground below. What she finds dif-
ficult to describe is the addition of another sensory element to
this visual interplay: "—yet I cannot express the quietness of
the valley sounds of matin bells, alike ascending to our ears
through dense or light vapours—or in their partial clearing
away, when houses and churches were descried, how far be-
low!" (*J*, II, 161). The confusion of the syntax here confirms
her disclaimer. Quiet sound is an interfusion that is perhaps
beyond the bounds of descriptive language, and the combina-
tion of one interfusion (aural) with another (visual) would de-
pend too much on the governing presence of mind.

At Chamonix, at the scene of Wordsworth's "Proces-
sions,"[23] her tone is apologetic when she describes the re-

semblance between the white-robed figures in the procession and the similarly shaped pyramids of the glacier under which they slowly pace. "It was impossible to look at one and the other without fancifully connecting them together" (*J*, II, 291). Her apology takes the form of implying that if the reader had been there, he would have seen as she did. "Imagine the *moving* Figures, like a stream of pyramids . . . ! and remember that these objects were seen at the base of those enormous mountains . . . ." By making her vision common, she defuses the possibilities of private visionary power. What is in Wordsworth's poem the abrupt curtailing of a "licentious craving in the mind / To act the God among external things" is for Dorothy a habit of mind. It seems to cost her no pain to acknowledge the separation of her mind from nature, whereas for him such a separation means, he now believes, to overpower nature by returning to it in an alien shape.

Dorothy rarely ventures connections between nature and the mind's importations, but when she does, they are immediately and radically checked. At the Mer de Glace a single gesture of thought encompasses a fanciful notion and its retraction. Fields of snow ascend to

> the fantastic or sublime masses of granite, which cannot be looked at without sometimes recalling images of castles, spires, towers, ancient cities, and fragments in the desarts of the East, though their bulk, their number, their sublime stations, forbid all but *transient* thoughts unconnected with lonely Nature, and the first mysterious Cause of whatever we behold.   (*J*, II, 285)

The sentence avoids admitting to a self, through the re-use of the apologetic expression, "cannot be looked at without . . . ," and through a deliberate confusion in the syntax: there is no one in the sentence to take responsibility for the "recalling." "Masses," the object of "ascend to" and the passive subject of "looked at," may do the recalling, but "sometimes" implies a personal subject, and in that case, the expression is subjectless. She ought to say, "which I cannot look at without . . . ," but that assignment of subjectivity to an "I" is just what she wishes to avoid. Further, she extends the sentence until she can unload her unwanted subjectivity on a legitimate subject, "the first mysterious Cause," a pious ending to a sentence that risked impiety.

Dorothy's respect for the objects in the landscape does not mean that she favors topographical description. The travel writers of her day and earlier were the masters of this style, an enumeration of the minutiae of the picturesque. At the falls of the Rhine at Schaffhausen Dorothy mentions that "Coxe and other travellers" have written such full accounts that she need not do so as well. "I took no description of the Falls at the time" (*J*, II, 89). The word may be adventitious, but "taking" is just what William Coxe does in his picturesque travelogue.[24] The description that Dorothy does write is impressionistic and partial (both in supplementing "whole" descriptions, and in being biased):

> It is impossible even to *remember* . . . the power of the dashing, and of the sounds—the breezes—the dancing dizzy sensations—and the exquisite beauty of the colours! The whole stream falls like liquid emeralds—a solid mass of translucent green hue—. . . . We walked upon the platform as dizzy as if we had been on the deck of a ship in a storm.   (*J*, II, 89-90)

By attempting completeness and claiming objectivity, Coxe takes more from the scene than Dorothy's awed venture does. He is very concerned with the exact height of the falls. He arranges the scene into a "picture, which I enjoyed at my leisure, as I sat . . ." and calmly makes a list of "the most striking objects." Where Coxe says he stood so close to the falls that "I could almost have touched it with my hand," Dorothy puts herself in the passive and makes the falls the active part of the sentence: "we were gloriously wetted and stunned and deafened by the waters of the Rhine." At another of the occasions on which she "cannot describe" a scene, she vouches only for her own astonishment, whereas at the same spot

Coxe makes the claim that he speaks for all writers, and for all artists too: "These are sublime scenes of horror, of which those who have not been spectators, can form no idea: neither the powers of painting nor poetry can give an adequate image of them" (*Sketches*, p. 160).

It may appear paradoxical that Dorothy, who constantly curtails the freedom of her imagination, should, by writing of her highly personal experiences and impressions, insert her personality into her descriptions, as when in the passage quoted above about the falls of the Rhine she includes her feeling of dizziness among other details descriptive of the falls. This sounds like the self-centered style she so carefully avoids. The difference is that though her personality enters into her description, it never imposes on what she describes. Keeping mental operations separate from nature, what she curtails is the possibility of affecting the landscape itself. The admission of subjectivity proclaims the limits of her view. She insists on the transience of her impression, always writing in the past tense of when she was there rather than in the absolute present. She acknowledges that weather, mood, light, and time of day condition and even control her vision of the landscape she describes, as a permanent apology for incompleteness of description. At Loch Etive, in the *Recollections of . . . Scotland*, she says "it must be remembered that mountains are often so much dignified by clouds, mists, and other accidents of weather, that one could not know them again in the full sunshine of a summer's noon" (*J*, I, 312). She is careful to delineate the object from its transient conditions, or to recognize that this delineation should be made. Despite the glamor conferred on these mountains by the clouds, she is scrupulously fair: "Whatever the mountains may be in their own shapes, the farm-house with its pastoral grounds and corn fields won from the mountain . . . must at all times be interesting objects."

In the vision of Loch Lomond, excerpted above, she gives first responsibility to the weather for one of the chief dynamics of the scene, its mobility. The scene was

a new world in its great permanent outline and composi-
tion, and changing at every moment in every part of it by
the effect of sun and wind, and mist and shower and
cloud, and the blending lights and deep shades which
took the place of each other, traversing the lake in every
direction. The whole was indeed a strange mixture of
soothing and restless images.   (*J*, I, 253)

Surely this contrast between permanent and transient attracts
her notice because it presents an image of her ideal seeing. It is
an ideal image, further, because nature provides it gratui-
tously. Her language does not take possession of the scene for
a metaphor, but rather brushes against it, as transiently as
does the kind of vision she may be referring to, as transiently
as do these lights and winds.

Dorothy often demonstrates her respect for nature's free-
dom from poetic appropriation in a very different way, by
emphasizing nature's very real power and capacity for vio-
lence. In *Tour on the Continent* she has numerous opportunities
for observations of this kind, dwelling morbidly on tales of
avalanches, the hardships of the inhabitants of the Alps, and
thoughts of her own exposure to danger. Nature's visual vio-
lence in the "Characters of the great Apocalypse" passage in
Book VI of *The Prelude* is terrifying to the poet because,
thinking of nature's beneficence, he expects her to help him
renaturalize his vision of imagination, not to show him a
mode even more apocalyptic than that from which he had
turned away. This passage exemplifies the masculine vision of
the world as mirror for the self, despite Wordsworth's belief
that nature is functioning independently from the mind at that
point. Because she respects nature's otherness, Dorothy is in-
terested in nature's violence for the sake of its real effects on
human life, hers and others', not because of its relation to the
imagination. She scoffs at a crude young German who, on the
precarious top of Rigi, in imitation of Faust or Manfred,
"wished aloud for thunder and lightning." Her sense of the
real dangers guards her from parodic romanticism. "*We*

should have been contented to form less sublime wishes—a clear sky—the splendour of a common sunset—and a long lingering on the mountain-top" (*J*, II, 159). The storm prevents long lingering: nature's violence is a rebuff to human interest, but it is not, as in the Apocalypse passage or in the view of the young German, a response to it.

Beginning with a distant view from the top of Rigi, she takes a recurrent interest in the Rossberg, the "fractured mountain" whose fall destroyed a valley, killing five hundred people and burying three villages. She walks with Crabb Robinson to the brink of a precipice of Rigi and observes that it is made of the same fragile materials that must have composed the Rossberg: " 'If the spot where we now sit should give way!' . . .—words that broke from us with a thought which made us shudder" (*J*, II, 163). Descending from Rigi, they pass through the trail of devastation left by the fracture. A few houses have been built where the town of Goldau was, now buried, but "masses of barren rubbish lie close to the houses, where, but a few years past, nothing was seen but fruitful fields" (*J*, II, 165). She never toys with an attraction to the devastation. What she notices most is the barrenness of the place and the patient, but largely futile, efforts the survivors have made to restore it. She sees "awe and melancholy" in the face of a poor woman who tells her about the fatal day, but "most of all when . . . she told me that the whole of this vale was formerly the greenest, and most beautiful and fertile of all the vales that we might see."

Language is better fitted to describe speaking subjects than inhuman ones. When she turns from the human results of the disaster to the natural event itself, her language becomes disturbed. When she refers to a little boy's narrative of the event as "a dream of horrors" it is syntactically difficult to tell whether she means the event itself or his use of language or some combination of the two. He tells his story "in a torrent of words with infinite energy of action and fire of countenance, interlarding the jargon (to me but a dream of horrors) with many intelligible exclamations, 'es war schrecklich!

mein Gott!' and the like . . ." (*J*, II, 166). Her language breaks down over an overconstructiveness in his language. By "jargon" she means unintelligible speech, although not understanding foreign speech is no new experience for her. What may be "a dream of horrors" is the boy's imitation of the disaster in his speech. He relishes the tale, and she is horrified that, as for the German on the top of Rigi, disasters of this kind can be fruitful to the imagination when they are so destructive to real fruitfulness. Language cannot, and should not, try to encompass nature's violence. The confusion of realms, language and catastrophe, is itself a dream of horrors, beyond the original disaster. Wordsworth is shocked when nature imitates the imagination; Dorothy is horrified by the mind's imitating nature. Observing the falls of Reichenbach, she is impressed by "the tremendous powers of nature." She says that her feeling was not pleasure, "it was astonishment, and awe—an overwhelming sense of the powers of nature for the destruction of all things, of the helplessness of man—of the weakness of his will, if prompted to make a momentary effort against such a force" (*J*, II, 128). Although she has written an impressive and personal account of the falls, she demonstrates her feeling of the difficulties, or perhaps the undesirability, of matching language to such a scene, by the apparent irrelevance of what she says next. "To bear away a memorial of that noisy shelter, I purchased a ladle and a paper-cutter . . . ." A ladle may do as well as a word, in making a memorial of such a spot, so reluctantly does her language grasp its objects. But these scenes of nature's violence only accentuate her usual linguistic response: she respects nature at all times, not just when it exhibits its capacity for violence.

THE PRINCIPLE OF not appropriating nature applies nowhere better than to the maternal characterization of nature in the poems. Not only is it in accord with Dorothy's scrupulous respect for nature not to characterize nature in any way, but also not to call nature maternal should release her from the particular problem associated with that traditional usage. Wherever nature becomes associated with a maternal image, as in "A Winter's Ramble in Grasmere Vale," it becomes inordinately powerful and antagonistic to the woman writing poetry. Where the mother's memory is invoked as a lost good, as in "Holiday at Gwerndwffnant," maternal power suffuses nature in a disadvantageous way. But where the maternal figure is openly said to be oppressive, as in "Irregular Verses" ("To Julia Marshall—A Fragment"), her presence can be separated from nature, and she can be challenged without harming the poet's relations with nature, and perhaps even improving them.

In the manuscript of "Holiday" nature is underscored, capitalized, and referred to as "she," and nature's function is to house and guard the children:

> 'Twas *Nature* built this Hall of ours
> *She* shaped the banks, she framed the bowers
>> That close it all around
> From her we hold our precious right
> And she, through live-long day and night
>> Is guardian of this happy ground.

An earlier version of the poem has instead of these last two lines, "And here through live-long day and night / She rules with mildest sway." This change from ruling to guarding makes nature parental as well as feminine, and the poem reinforces this parental function when it later defines the children's happiness as "that term of life / Which governed by your Parent's love, / Is free from sorrow and from strife," and when the poem ends with the notion that holidays in nature should be remembered for the sake of home. Thus invested with maternal power, nature is potentially threatening: earlier in the poem, it is nature, or physical reality, that defeats the poet's fancy, reprimanding her "idle dream": "recalled to consciousness, / With weight of years of changed estate, / Thought is not needed to suppress . . . ." Nature refuses her the dignity of thinking. In "Lines intended for my Niece's Album" the "perennial green" that excludes the poet from the pages it encloses is modeled on an image of nature that has the same guardian power present in "Holiday:" "She, careful Warder, duly guards / The works of Gods Almighty power." And what the album in its analogical capacity guards shares some of the oppressive connotations of nature's action in "Holiday:" it preserves for all time "Kind counsels, mild reproofs that bind / The Dead to the Living by holy ties."

Like the ambiguous grove of trees in the Cottage poems, this powerful guardian nature oppresses while it protects. The "mild maternal smile" in "Irregular Verses," which is a "dear smile" and yet represses, evokes the same ambivalent response, but with the difference that the maternal figure is purely human, and nature, dissociated from maternal power, is not stifling. Nature is permitted to be simply itself through the introduction into the poem of a human mother, the friend who betrayed a youthful pact by growing up and marrying and having children. The visionary cottage described at the outset was to have housed the two of them and no one else: "There with my one dear Friend would dwell / Nor wish for aught beyond the dell." But this idyllic project dissolved when "in our riper years we each pursued a different way." The friend became a wife and trod "The paths of usefulness,"

> As thou canst witness, thou dear Maid,
> One of the Darlings of her care;
> Thy *Mother* was that Friend . . . .

The poem returns to Jane's motherhood at the end, asking Jane to accept some guilt for the speaker's loss of those youthful dreams. Still addressing Julia, the daughter, she asks that if "this poor memorial strain"

> Should touch her Mother's heart with tender pain,
> Or call a tear into her loving eye,
> She will not check the tear or still the rising sigh.

By addressing Jane not directly but through her daughter, the speaker seems to address her friend's motherhood itself.

The association of the maternal smile with Jane's motherhood in this poem serves to dissociate the idea of the mother from the idea of nature, and it is this dissociation that allows the poet to write so fluently here, despite her disclaimer that she is not writing poetry. Earlier in the poem she defines poets as those "who sang in nature's praise" and tells us that she did not join them then because of her mother's gentle reproaches. The passage that opens the poem, a beautiful description of the rustic dream-cottage, is a song in nature's praise, but, far from its being linked to the image of the repressive mother, the idea of motherhood is here opposed to it. Jane's motherhood, the cause of her desertion of their shared dream, removed Dorothy from nature by depriving her of that particular "one dear Spot" embedded in the dell. Unlike the Cottage poems, this poem reveals the interior of the grove:

> A cottage in a verdant dell,
> A foaming stream, a crystal Well,
> A garden stored with fruit and flowers
> And sunny seats and shady bowers,
> A file of hives for humming bees
> Under a row of stately trees . . . .

Although the familiar enshrouding trees reappear, they have parted for a moment. The grove in the Cottage poems, the maternal smile of "Irregular Verses," and the guardian nature of the album poem and of "Holiday" are all related by the similarity of the feelings associated with each: they all menace as well as protect. Possibly the interior of the grove can be described in "Irregular Verses" because the blocking qualities of the grove fall away when the grove is no longer invested with maternal associations. That grove hardly symbolizes the mother, but it takes on the same emotional values.

Separating nature from its maternal characterization, turning Mother Nature back into nature, ought to alleviate one of the major difficulties experienced by a woman writing in the Romantic tradition. But although Dorothy may recognize the importance of making this separation, this recognition does not open the way to an untroubled or prolific poetics. The reason may be in the uneven balance between Dorothy's own

self-conception and her acceptance of the picture of herself she
receives from her brother, through the poetry that she daily
read and transcribed for him. In *The Prelude* Wordsworth
identifies her with nature's beneficence, sometimes specifi-
cally with nature's nurturant powers. "Nature's inmate," she
breathes a "charm / Of sweetness" that likens her to nature.
At a time when he was "endlessly perplex'd" and "wearied
out with contrarieties," "the beloved Sister" (1850) "pre-
serv'd me still / A Poet" by being identified with natural
forces. "The belovèd Woman . . . ,

> now speaking in a voice
> Of sudden admonition, like a brook
> That does but cross a lonely road, and now
> Seen, heard and felt, and caught at every turn,
> Companion never lost through many a league,
> Maintain'd for me a saving intercourse
> With my true self.
>
> (X, 909-916)

Dorothy's warning takes effect because Wordsworth hears it
in natural terms, and that transformation itself, more than the
content of her warning, is the first step to recovering his voca-
tion. He reacts to this "belovèd Woman" in the same way that
he reacts to all natural phenomena: hearing her causes him to
consider and return to himself. Her saving task has been to
"soften down / This over-sternness" in his soul engendered
by his love for "that beauty, which, as Milton sings, / Hath
terror in it" (XIII, 225-227). Like some nature spirit charged
with the care of his soul,

> thou didst plant its crevices with flowers,
> Hang it with shrubs that twinkle in the breeze,
> And teach the little birds to build their nests
> And warble in its chambers.
>
> (XIII, 233-236)

Wordsworth makes this identification between Dorothy
and nature primarily because Dorothy is such a receptive and
contented observer of nature. In Book VI Dorothy guides

him to the cure for a mind "haunted by itself" by sharing
with him her mode of grateful observation. On their excur-
sions to Brougham Castle during his vacation from Cam-
bridge they climb together to some precarious viewpoint and

> We look'd abroad, or on the Turret's head
> Lay listening to the wild flowers and the grass,
> As they gave out their whispers to the wind.
>   (VI, 230-232)

This is a vision of reciprocity within nature, not between the
self and nature. The flowers whisper to the wind, and the
human listeners are subordinate. Book XI (1850: Book XII),
like Book VI, presents Dorothy as an observer of nature, and
again as a corrective contrast to some overzealousness in the
poet, this time his tyrannous eye. Dorothy's "eye was not the
mistress of her heart" (1850, XII, 153), but instead

> She welcom'd what was given, and craved no more.
> Whatever scene was present to her eyes,
> That was the best.
>   (XI, 207-209)

Wordsworth thinks of Dorothy as being like nature be-
cause of occasions such as these when she looks at nature. Yet
for Dorothy there is a crucial distinction between identifica-
tion with nature, which she avoids, and observation, which
she carefully cultivates. The difference is the margin between
her not writing and her writing. For her to make such a con-
flation herself would be and is harmful to the flow of her writ-
ing, as when in the Cottage poems nature rises up between
her and her chosen object (the cottage) and abstracts her from
her project by causing her to identify with trees or storm.
Wordsworth, identifying her with natural forces in the same
way that he identifies fictive female figures with nature,
forgets the significance of her ability to stand off from them
and thereby misinterprets her. For Wordsworth and for Cole-
ridge, a too-great particularity of natural observation is det-
rimental to the harmonies to which poetry aspires. In order to

represent his alienation from nature in the Dejection Ode, Coleridge describes a landscape made up of discrete elements that do not harmonize. The "peculiar tint of yellow green" is artificially precise; the moon is "as fixed as if it grew / In its own cloudless, starless lake of blue"; the elements of the landscape are "them all," not "it." When Coleridge says of Dorothy, "her eye watchful in minutest observation of nature,"[25] he reveals that her way of seeing nature seems to him peculiar and obsessive, but Dorothy's descriptions view elements and harmonies simultaneously in order to testify that those elements composed themselves gradually before her eyes. For her, natural particulars always carry the potential of harmony, while for Coleridge and Wordsworth they compete against the mind's powers of synthesis. The internalizing imagination does not differentiate, as Dorothy does, between nature's gratuitous harmonies, performed without the intervention of the mind, and the burial or immersion of the self in nature, because in both cases nature in its otherness has priority over the self.

Nature's ministry of fear, that aspect of nature that taught Wordsworth visionary things, appears first in Book I of *The Prelude* when

> I heard among the solitary hills
> Low breathings coming after me, . . .
>
> (I, 329-330)

Wordsworth's closing tribute to Dorothy inverts that passage in order to identify her with nature's nurturant ministry of love:

> thy breath,
> Dear Sister, was a kind of gentler spring
> That went before my steps.
>
> (XIII, 244-246)

Whether she listens to flowers whispering in the wind, or is the planter of those flowers, these faculties are collectively opposed to visionary powers, and he leaves her as close to the heart of nature as Lucy.

CHAPTER III

Emily Brontë

To be told by her own brother that she is like nature, and implicitly or explicitly that she cannot have her own subjectivity, would seem to be the most compelling of reasons for a woman to feel dislocated from the poetic tradition in which these opinions originate. To receive these views personally as a sister and not just generically as a woman prevents Dorothy Wordsworth even from wishing to seek a way around them. And yet it appears that Dorothy's difficulties as a poet result not just from her unique personal situation, because although Emily Brontë proceeds much further toward the establishment of authentic poetic identity, her poems just as much as Dorothy's reveal that the sources of poetic power are not felt to be within the self. Brontë is troubled by the apparent otherness of her mind's powers, which she imagines as a series of masculine visitants who bring visionary experience to her. As the alien centers of imaginative power, they repeat, in a general way, Dorothy's implicit picture of her brother as a center of an imaginative power that is never hers. The major and obvious difference between these two configurations is that Brontë's masculine figures for poetic power are invented and contained within her poems, where William Wordsworth has his own irreducible existence, and that consequently they do share their power with the poet, if grudgingly, rather than keeping it perpetually apart.

Brontë's masculine visitants are comparable to a masculine poet's muse. The development of a masculine muse by a woman poet should not logically be surprising, but the phenomenon is new with Brontë (and recurs in Dickinson) and represents a first step toward the internalization of poetic power. There is no such thing, however, as a simple reversal of roles; unlike the usual situation in which a female muse's power exists to be overcome, the poet's ability to master her muse is in this case genuinely in question. Instead of invoking a visitant's aid and then proceeding with a poem on a chosen subject, Brontë often makes her entire poem an extended invocation. Many of her poems dwell on the masculine figures of alien power, elevating them from the status of agency to that of the major subject. This arrest itself suggests that she is not confident of having obtained the visitants' support, and the content of these poems is a continuous effort to wrest the visitants' power away from them and make it her own. It is not inherent in the concept of a masculine muse that he should take and keep more power than does the traditionally feminine muse, but in Brontë's poems he does.

Two comments about the poet's character by those who knew her suggest a biographical analogy for what the poems reveal. These comments share the assumption, hardly questionable in the nineteenth century, that power is synonymous with masculinity, in regard both to character and to accomplishment. Her French teacher in Brussels, M. Héger, said that "she should have been a man—a great navigator,"[1] and Charlotte Brontë writes that under a simple exterior "lay a secret power and fire that might have informed the brain and kindled the veins of a hero."[2] What is interesting here is not that Emily's strength of character should be considered manly, but that both these observers should compare this quality in her character to the character of a man of action, a hero or a navigator, rather than to that of a great author, even though Charlotte's words were written to accompany an edition of *Wuthering Heights*. This circumstance suggests that this sternness was not, or at least did not seem to be, fully integrated into Brontë's character, but stood apart. An inflexibility of will seemed to have her in its power, and to harm her more than it helped.

We can never know how far this lack of integration existed in Brontë's own character, but when Charlotte turns to discussing the novel itself, in the preface to her edition of *Wuthering Heights*, she continues in the same vein:

> Whether it is right or advisable to create beings like Heathcliff, I do not know: I scarcely think it is. But this I know; the writer who possesses the creative gift owns something of which he is not always master—something that at times strangely wills and works for itself. . . . Be the work grim or glorious, dread or divine, you have little choice left but quiescent adoption. (*WH* 12)

Possessed by a power not her own, the writer is "the nominal artist" and deserves neither praise nor blame. In the guise of defender, Charlotte does her sister considerable injustice, if she means that Emily was literally not in control of what she wrote. But as a conscious artist Emily does create a myth of imaginative possession. The account in Charlotte's preface is a literalization of figurative events in Emily's poems on the imagination, and although she betrays herself to be an insensitive reader of her sister's work, there is a certain truth in her misinterpretation.[3]

Brontë makes those visionary visitants an overt, even a major, subject of her poetry, but she also identifies another alien power of poetry that, perhaps because it is a more profound threat to her own identity, is less willingly acknowledged and therefore less apparent than the visionary power. This power belongs to nature, who inspires and endeavors to control the poet's speech in much the same manner as the visionary visitants. Nature is sometimes, though not always, characterized as feminine. For Dorothy to be identified by her brother with nature is to be silenced, because nature's language is not human; here, even though nature is a speaking object, the result is the same forfeiting of subjectivity that Dorothy experiences. As in Dorothy's "A Winter's Ramble in Grasmere Vale," Brontë portrays nature speaking in place of or in competition with the poet's own speech, and the poet must silence or turn away from nature in order to speak in her own right. Both Brontë's ambition and her success are greater in this regard than Dorothy's, but in her eagerness to defend against this alternate power of poetry, the poet overvalues and distorts the visionary experience offered by male figures without, however, decreasing her sense of its foreignness. Cutting herself off from one source of poetic identity, and not quite believing in the other, she finds nowhere a settled identity. The poet defends herself from the danger of becoming a feminine object by aligning her poetic self with the stage in feminine development in which the mother is rejected in favor of a turn toward masculine objects, but that turn cannot become an identity. Only in the novel, where she is free to displace the traditional feminine character of nature, can she return to what the reader senses is a more authentic belief.

What is of interest here is not so much the sexual identity of the mind presented in the poems, but the question of whether the poet can claim poetic identity at all, or whether the right to that identity is lodged in external powers, be they masculine or feminine. But the Brontës were also aware of the problem of sexual identity as it is represented textually. Charlotte shared a general cultural prejudice against "the poetry women generally write" (*WH* 4), and all three sisters must have defined themselves against this paradigm, consciously or not. In Charlotte's account of their choice of the sexually ambiguous pseudonyms, Currer, Ellis, and Acton, she says that they did not want to declare themselves women, because of a tendency among critics to condescend to "authoresses," "without at that time suspecting that our mode of writing and thinking was not what is called 'feminine' " (*WH* 4). Contemporary reviewers of *Wuthering Heights* spoke of Ellis Bell's "power" and "mastery." If Charlotte means that later on they did come to understand that their writing was not "what is called 'feminine,' " it is not clear whether she welcomed this distinction, thinking of "the poetry women generally write," or whether this distinction was an affront to her sense of identity and integrity as a woman. They did not want to abdicate their proper identity and assume "Christian names positively masculine," yet they could hardly wish, in the world in which they lived, to be grouped with authoresses.[4]

The pseudonyms were "veils," and perhaps insignificant in themselves, but it is impossible to imagine that the sisters could have questioned such a fundamental aspect of self-presentation without having felt, previously or at the time, a less trivial uncertainty about their sexual identity as writers. These considerations are as relevant to the poet's textual sense of identity as to her manner of presenting her works to the public, because the sense of literary identity is established through reading and through the poet's sense of her place in literary tradition. The choice to be named "Ellis," assuming that Emily participated in the decision, must represent the poet's wish not to have, as a writer, a determinate sexual identity. This wish may result partly from the desire not to be judged on the basis of gender, but sexual identification is problematic also because the two origins of poetry that she perceives as being available to her are sexually defined, and she can consider neither to be identifiable with the self. Feminine nature and forms of the masculine Word present her with a choice she does not wish to make. The arrangement of this choice is of course her own, but it may express her frustration at the sexual restriction of so many aspects of literary tradition and practice. Brontë's separation from the two sources of her power may be, then, the result not of any fragmentation of her own sense of identity, but of her uneasiness about their sexual orientation. She may not be able to, but also perhaps does not wish to, claim identification with either one.[5]

The history of the poet's negotiations for poetic identity is traced in a sequence of poems that forms the core of Brontë's canon. In 1844 Brontë made two books of transcriptions, for which she selected poems written at different periods in her life. She copied these poems into two notebooks, in a book-like printing and format that indicates that these were the poems that she considered to be her best. One notebook is a collection of poems about Gondal, the fictive land that in her adolescence she had invented and peopled, and whose sagas she continued to elaborate up to the year of her death. The other notebook, considered here, bears no title but consists largely of poems that are either explicitly or implicitly about imaginative experience. Of the poems that she published in the 1846 *Poems by Currer, Ellis, and Acton Bell*, five were chosen from the Gondal notebook and fifteen from the non-Gondal group. In making these transcriptions, Brontë retained many of the dates on which the poems were written, though arranging the poems in a new sequence that is roughly but not entirely chronological. The apparent care with which the poems were chosen and arranged indicates that, in the non-Gondal notebook, she is consciously developing a myth of the imagination; consequently this reading follows her arrangement of the poems rather than the chronological sequence. [6]

The pattern of borrowing an identity began very early, in the make-believe world of the Brontë children's "Young Men's Play," in which Emily represented the polar explorer, Sir Edward Parry. [7] In subsequent "plays" (the precursors of Gondal), in which the children invented nations and populations engendering lengthy prose tales and then poetry, the mobile adoption of fictive roles proliferates. In a child this borrowing is by itself unremarkable, and for an adult poet it is part of the procedure of any fictional writing to adopt various personae, but Brontë retains this pattern of supplanting identity even when it begins to produce sinister effects. It has been argued that in the conventional heroic posing of the Gondal poems (the first was written in 1836, when the poet was seventeen) she is concealing or suppressing her own identity, to the detriment of the poems, because she has difficulty representing her own genuine powers. [8] The figures she creates in the Gondal poems are often borrowed from gothic or Byronic sources, [9] and these borrowed personae are often themselves possessed by passions that they do not control, as for example in these lines from a poem of 1837:

The burning tears that would keep welling,
The groans that mocked at every tear
That burst from out their dreary dwelling

. . . .

Sometimes a curse, sometimes a prayer
Would quiver on my parchèd tongue.

(P 15)

In other early poems, the speaker is bound by "a tyrant spell,"
possessed in dreams by "the shadows of the dead," and in
many places overwhelmed by despair and by harrowing
memories.

The possession of these early poems is emotional rather
than creative, but when Brontë turns from the melodrama of
Gondal to poems about her own mind, she retains the lan-
guage of possession. The visionary visitant of later poems
takes many forms, but he is always masculine, and he is
threatening as well as inspiring, dangerous as well as be-
loved.[10] He is threatening more because, being external, he
can withdraw her poetic powers at will than because of any
dangerous content in the visions he brings. Her ambivalence
toward these figures produces an unstable relationship with
them. The poet early succeeds in exerting a measure of con-
trol over this figure, but this control succeeds not in har-
nessing the visitant's power but only counterproductively in
suppressing it, and later the visitant's power returns in a sinis-
ter form.

A poem of 1840 invokes a visitation from "thee," using the
language of romantic love augmented by devotional speech:

My worn heart throbs so wildly
'Twill break for thee.
. . . .
Will not mine angel comfort?
Mine idol hear?

(P 138, A 11)

The first three stanzas place the speaker at the mercy of this
figure, but the last appears to fulfill its own wishes: "O I shall

surely win thee, / Beloved, again!" "Mine angel" here is at
least fictively external to the poet, but subsequent poems trace
the internalization of this figure. The next poem, addressed to
"O Dream," records the passing of a Wordsworthian gleam
at the end of childhood. Though this figure has entity enough
to have an "angel brow," the darkening vision is the result of
dissociating the dream from external lights. Depriving this
figure of its illusory otherness decreases its powers:

> The sun-beam and the storm,
> The summer-eve divine,
> The silent night of solemn calm,
> The full moon's cloudless shine,
>
> Were once entwined with thee,
> But now with weary pain,
> Lost vision! 'tis enough for me—
> Thou canst not shine again.
>
> (P 86, A 12)

Whereas the discovery that this figure was not external but a
function of the self might be expected to increase the poet's
feeling of her own power, she experiences only loss. Turning
from the light vanishing "from off thine angel brow" to the
loss of "every joy that lit my brow," the next poem presents a
further stage in this internalization that merely contracts the
vision to a relic of his former power and makes the self a mor-
tuary without any compensatory gain in power.

> The barren mountain-side lies bare;
> And sunshine and awaking morn
> Paint no more golden visions there.
>
> Yet, ever in my grateful breast,
> Thy darling shade shall cherished be;
> For God alone doth know how blest
> My early years have been in thee!
>
> (P 135, A 13)

She internalizes this visionary faculty only as it diminishes be-
cause, like Dorothy Wordsworth, she cannot believe that any
poetic power could be at once internal and powerful.

The issue of visionary power is closed for four years and the next eight poems in the copybook take up different themes. The next poem on this subject, "My Comforter," (P 168, A 22), addresses a revived but very differently characterized figure. Having accepted the discovery of earlier poems that if visionary power is internal it must be weak, the poet now embraces rather than lamenting its triviality. Condescending to her comforter, she tells it that it has "not taught / A feeling strange or new; / Thou hast but roused a latent thought," and she guards from it the secret of the occasion for which she is being soothed: "What my soul bore my soul alone / Within itself may tell." The speaker's hollow gain is that she is in the position of power now in this relationship, and she reduces her "idol" to a "sweet thing" that calms but could not comprehend. The next two poems, though separated in composition by a year, are paired in the manuscript because they both involve a figure named "Fancy" who is, like this comforter, clearly a subordinate. The subject of the poem is the "Dark world" of actuality, and the speaker simply conjures a substitutive dream though the agency of this servile "Fancy . . . my Fairy love!" A fantasy of perfect and happy worlds in heaven is introduced by a fiat: "And this shall be my dream to-night— / I'll think . . ." (P 157, A 23). Acknowledged as a fantasy, this easy day-dream is hardly efficacious in any way. In assuming the powers of the figure she once pleadingly invoked and worshipped, she finds that its powers vanish. Its powers resided in its defiance and in her desire. Like Dorothy in "Holiday at Gwerndwffnant," "Irregular Verses," and the Cottage poems, she identifies her own poetry with fancy while readily admitting to its inferiority. As before, she does not conceive of a poetic power that would be both her own and powerful. The titling of the next poem in the notebook sequence, "To Imagination" (P 174, A 25), represents an effort to ennoble this faculty by association with the term that Coleridge reserves for the mind's highest powers. Indeed, it is here not quite so servile as before: it is a "benignant power" with a "kind voice," a "solacer of human cares," and "my true friend." But the poem still turns on a simplistic opposition between the hopeless "world without" that includes "Nature's sad reality" and "Truth," and the escapist "world within," comprising dreams and Fancy, which is the province of what she calls "Imagination." If not the fancy itself, it purveys a fanciful "phantom bliss" that the speaker mistrusts even while she welcomes it. What is significant here is that the poet recognizes that the moments of greatest power occur when this imagination voids the distinction between the "world within" and the "world without" to refer to a real but also desirable world elsewhere. She makes a continuity between fantasy and possibility:

> But thou art ever there to bring
> The hovering visions back and breathe
> New glories o'er the blighted spring
> And call a lovelier life from death,
> And whisper with a voice divine
> Of real worlds as bright as thine.

She increases the power of her imagination by associating it with "real worlds," but the cost of that gain in power is that voice returns to a source outside the self.

The poem transcribed next, written six weeks later, returns to a suspiciously harsh opposition between real worlds and reason, which must be renounced, and a "God of Visions," who, unlike her imagination, seems to require complete devotion. She calls it a "radiant angel," an honorific term that has dropped out of her vocabulary since the early poems. Shunning "the common paths that others run," she

> gave my spirit to adore
> Thee, ever present, phantom thing—
> My slave, my comrade, and my King!
> (P 176, A 26)

The next two verses explicate the last line. This passage is the main source for the myth of possession, as it is for comparisons between Brontë and Dickinson, who also addresses a power that is at once master and slave. Her accounts of "slave" and "comrade," though told with greater energy than before, are familiar, but when she turns to "my King" she is scarcely convincing:

> And yet, a king—though prudence well
> Have taught thy subject to rebel.
>
> And am I wrong to worship where
> Faith cannot doubt nor Hope despair
> Since my own soul can grant my prayer?

There is no apparent reason for inflating this figure into a king, since at the same time she so overtly makes it a part of herself and easily governable. Her insistence on intimacy must be concealing some unexplained alienation, of which the term "king" is the trace.

The account of the speaker's turn from reason to visions in this poem is framed by two opening stanzas and two closing lines that set the poem in a court of law. The poem's occasion is the speaker's invocation to her "radiant angel" to come to her defense against "Stern Reason" 's judgment. Reason "is mocking at my overthrow," as if the speaker had suffered or gone mad because of her preference. Her invocation is desperate:

> O thy sweet tongue must plead for me
> And tell why I have chosen thee!
>
> Stern Reason is to judgement come
> Arrayed in all her forms of gloom:
> Wilt thou my advocate be dumb?
> No, radiant angel, speak and say
> Why I did cast the world away.

The subsequent stanzas seem to do what the speaker is asking her God of Visions to do, in that they explain her choice, but that she closes with the same invocation with which she began indicates that this defense has been inadequate:

> Speak, God of Visions, plead for me
> And tell why I have chosen thee!

That implied inadequacy expresses powerlessness or subjugation far more vividly than does her guarded declaration that he is her king. If "my own soul can grant my prayer," the poem logically ought not to end with the implication that her God of Visions has not spoken and will not speak for her. The God is a tongue or a voice, and an advocate is one who speaks for someone else. That the speaker thus displaces her powers of speech indicates that language is alien to her. Her soul may be synonymous with her God of Visions, but without certainty of her power over language visions are of no use for poetry and she is alienated from her own poethood. That language is an alien power may account for the reduction of visionary power from "mine idol" to "sweet thing," coincident with its internalization. Mastering and containing the power undoes it, and yet to see it again as external threatens the poet's existence as a poet.

The next poem, "Enough of Thought, Philosopher," carries the implications of the danger of the externality of poetic power one step further by considering the possibility that there is not much difference between a sought-after "Spirit" (another imaginary visitant) and oblivious death. The Spirit represents a power to unify warring factions within human personality and to make their combined strength "far more fair / Than the divided sources were" (P 181, A 27). But the "lifeless rest" the speaker seeks when she abandons her futile search for this Spirit performs much the same function, if ingloriously:

> O let me die, that power and will
> Their cruel strife may close,
> And vanquished Good, victorious Ill
> Be lost in one repose.

This verse and the one preceding it were substituted for an original conclusion that characterizes death simply as "eternal

sleep" rather than as the closure of strife, so that the parallel
between death and the imaginative Spirit is not accidental, but
the product of purposeful revision. That death mimics the
Spirit here undermines imaginative efficacy. The speaker has
imagined this Spirit and has created a compelling visual image
of his powers of unification (the Spirit supervises the conflu-
ence of three rivers and kindles the "inky sea" where they
meet "with sudden blaze" so that "the glad deep sparkled
wide and bright— / White as the sun"). But only its mimicker
and antagonist, ironically, can fulfill the Spirit's promise.

"Enough of Thought, Philosopher," dated 3 February
1845, is the last of the poems in the non-Gondal notebook
to consider as overt subject matter the topic of imaginative
power. The poet does return to this subject, but as part of the
Gondal sequence, suggesting that although the poet no longer
wished to treat this difficult subject, and perhaps repressed it,
it must have been an unfinished issue of considerable impor-
tance to have found another way to surface out of place.
Rather than resolving the problem of her mastery over her
God of Visions, this poem allows her to express her fears
more freely because more indirectly. The poem in question is
the one that begins "Silent is the House—all are laid asleep,"
dated 9 October 1845. The passage on imagination is the first
three stanzas, which exist in an uneasy relation to the rest of
the poem, a narrative. Both Emily and Charlotte Brontë rec-
ognized this uneasiness, as the poem is printed only in ex-
cerpts in both the 1846 *Poems* and the group of poems pub-
lished by Charlotte in her 1850 edition of *Wuthering Heights.*
Emily selected parts of the narrative for the 1846 edition, and
Charlotte printed just the three stanzas about imagination,
with a two stanza conclusion of her own, under the title of
"The Visionary." The "I" in the first three stanzas of the orig-
inal poem is apparently the same as the "I" of the poems on
imagination in the non-Gondal notebook, while in the rest of
the poem the speaker is a dramatic character named Julian.

> Silent is the House—all are laid asleep;
> One, alone, looks out o'er the snow wreaths deep;

Watching every cloud, dreading every breeze
That whirls the 'wildering drifts and bends the groaning
   trees.

Cheerful is the hearth, soft the matted floor;
Not one shivering gust creeps through pane or door;
The little lamp burns straight, its rays shoot strong and far;
I trim it well to be the Wanderer's guiding-star.

Frown, my haughty sire; chide, my angry dame;
Set your slaves to spy, threaten me with shame:
But neither sire nor dame, nor prying serf shall know
What angel nightly tracks that waste of winter snow.

In the dungeon crypts idly did I stray,
Reckless of the lives wasting there away;
'Draw the ponderous bars; open, Warder stern!'
He dare not say me nay—the hinges harshly turn.

(P 190)

It is possible that the poet is identifying that Wanderer by
moving, without indicating any transition, into an imagina-
tive tale, as if the discovery of a topic for verse signaled the
Wanderer's arrival. The "I" idly straying in dungeon crypts
would be the mind searching for an adventure to recount, tak-
ing on the persona of Julian only in the next line.[11]

Once his friend, Rochelle is now Julian's "conquered foe,"
incarcerated in his dungeons. Julian visits the prison "reckless
of the lives wasting there away," and finds Rochelle beautiful
and sanctified by her hope for liberty through a quick death.
Falling instantly in love, he decides to free her, but not until
after some deliberations that confirm the implicit obnoxious-
ness of his idle stroll through his own dungeons. Having for-
gotten that he must have incarcerated her for a reason, he
worries that if he frees her she will not return his love,
whereas if he keeps her in prison she will remain subject to
him. Though he calls it "selfish love" and makes his decision
"short strife," that he must elaborate his decision at all is ap-
palling in a dramatic hero, given the romantic terms of the

tale. Having freed her, he takes her home and nurses her back
to health, self-righteously accruing a greater heroism by his
devotion to her and his sacrifice of the opportunity to go to
war, for which he is much scorned by his kin. Rochelle drops
out of the tale once she has been rescued, so that it is quite
startling when Julian thinks to refer to her at the end, even
though she is now merely the object of his self-serving sac-
rifice and the ground for his self-praise.

> Another hand than mine my rightful banner held
> And gathered my renown on Freedom's crimson field;
> Yet I had no desire the glorious prize to gain—
> It needed braver nerve to face the world's disdain.

> And by the patient strength that could that world defy,
> By suffering, with calm mind, contempt and calumny;
> By never-doubting love, unswerving constancy,
> Rochelle, I earned at last an equal love from thee!

This self-serving character who, unsought, frees Rochelle
from her dungeon invites comparison with the liberator she
does seek, who is described earlier in the poem. "A messenger
of Hope," she tells Julian scornfully, visits her at twilight, and
when he comes, "visions rise and change which kill me with
desire." She describes the advent of these visions as if they
were visions of poetic inspiration. First "a soundless calm de-
scends" in which she seems to forget her imprisonment,

> "—unuttered harmony
> That I could never dream till earth was lost to me.

> "Then dawns the Invisible, the Unseen its truth reveals;
> My outward sense is gone, my inward essence feels—
> Its wings are almost free, its home, its harbour found;
> Measuring the gulf it stoops and dares the final bound!"

Her "messenger of Hope" is a vision of death, but the vision
is described with Wordsworth's language for imaginative ex-
perience: ". . . we are laid asleep / In body, and become a liv-
ing soul." This allusion equates imaginative experience with

death. There is no room in the narrative for finding this equation faulty, since the life Julian offers is so unappealing and so distastefully achieved. Rochelle's vision includes a soaring bird as the traditional image of the soul's escape; Julian uses a bird as his metaphor for capturing her. He fears that she will fly away, in the passage on his decision between "ruth and selfish love:"

> Then like a tender child whose hand did just enfold,
> Safe in its eager grasp, a bird it wept to hold,
> When pierced with one wild glance from the
>   troubled hazel eye,
> It gushes into tears and lets its treasure fly, . . .

When she does not fly away upon release, it is because she is a "wounded dove." During her recovery, "Death gazed greedily / And only Hope remained a faithful friend to me." This possessive "to me" opposes Rochelle's claim to a different hope, who came "every night to me."

That Rochelle's vision of death is valued more highly than her human liberator, and that it appears to be so similar to imaginative experience, would seem to make that vision analogous to the Wanderer of the first three stanzas. Both the messenger of hope and the Wanderer are imaginary visitants. Rochelle's "My outward sense is gone, my inward essence feels" is quite like the poet's situation:

> Silent is the House—all are laid asleep;
> One, alone, looks out o'er the snow wreaths deep.

Rochelle's loss of self-consciousness is curiously paralleled by the use of "one" instead of "I" here, and by the trance of quietness in the poet's room. Furthermore, Julian, himself unimaginative, is associated with loss of voice. Rochelle seems delighted when the jailor's departure makes it possible for Julian to free her, but for this knowledge we are dependent on Julian's own untrustworthy reading of her expression, because she never speaks again after finishing her inspired description of the vision of death. Life with Julian is to be mute, but the vision of death inspires speech. Many commentators, reading Rochelle's vision as an extreme expression of mystical experience, identify that mystical experience as having been Brontë's own, and locate the passage as the culmination of a sequence of poems including those on imagination discussed above, thereby tacitly identifying mystical and imaginative experience.[12]

But the analogy between Rochelle's vision and the Wanderer cannot be made into an identity, because the poet is trying to avoid her suspicion that the Wanderer, as a muse-like bringer of poetry, is also a messenger of death. It cannot be that only the expectation of death is inspiring. Rochelle is entirely passive, and her desire fails, while the first three stanzas present an active self whose wish is efficacious: the Wanderer arrives. And what he brings is in itself efficacious. By relegating the fear of death, and passivity in relation to the control of voice, to the narrated story, the poet can exorcize these difficulties from the contemplation of her own imagination. Displacement fosters the belief that they are not her own. Still, the poet does not dispel her own intimation that imagination is the intuition and expectation of death. By setting the scene in winter the poet balances two possibilities. The snowy scene may exist to demonstrate the Wanderer's dependence on her: without the brightness and steadiness of her lamp's rays, the Wanderer would be lost in the snow, as Lockwood is lost in the snow at the beginning of *Wuthering Heights*. The poet makes that "wildering" and threatening landscape safe and intelligible, so that whatever the Wanderer brings—the story—depends on the poet's primary powers of clarification. But because he crosses a "waste of winter snow" the Wanderer may come from regions of death, like the messenger of hope. The room is warm and still because "not one shivering gust creeps through pane or door," suggesting a resistance to the visitor's entrance as well as a welcome.

The third stanza, though part of the prefatory material on the poet's own experience, disrupts the tone that the first two verses establish. Their apparent calm and confidence is broken by its defensive anger:

> Frown, my haughty sire; chide, my angry dame;
> Set your slaves to spy, threaten me with shame:
> But neither sire nor dame, nor prying serf shall know
> What angel nightly tracks that waste of winter snow.

The source of this sudden defensiveness is uncertain. Nothing in the first two stanzas seems to provoke it, yet suddenly the poet's world is populated by suspicious and ill-intentioned people. The line "Silent is the House—all are laid asleep" may refer to these people, whose silence would now be revealed to have been the result of suppression. The defense is against the inference that the Wanderer is a human lover, whether sire and dame are the house's inhabitants or the poem's readers. The poet may be disturbed at the unintentionally erotic implications of her myth. However, neither of these interpretations accounts for the abruptness of the tonal shift and for the energy of the poet's distress. There must be a quantity of pent-up anxiety that finds partial expression in these lines, as if redirected from its original goal. If the rest of the poem exhibits any potential source of anxiety, it is the association of the imagination with death, and it may be that the delusion of persecution in stanza three is a redirection of the poet's fears of her own imaginative experience. Those fears may have chosen this particular course with a certain design. Even though the poet's intention seems to be to discourage the view that the Wanderer is a human lover, it is she who first plants the suggestion in the reader's mind. It may be that she raises the erotic possibility as a screen to hide an even more threatening fatality. By invoking the presence of sire, dame, and serfs, no matter how nasty they are, she wakes the dead. "Laid asleep," they represented the proximity of death and imaginative experience; frowning and chiding, they sever that connection.

The Wanderer does not actually bring death in the same

way that Rochelle's messenger promises. It is because he may choose to give or withhold language that he is associated with death, because the withholding of language is death to the poetic vocation. The plea to "speak for me" in the poem addressed to the God of Visions (P 176, A 26) betrays the dangers of alien control of langauge. That plea reappears in the messenger's envoicing of Rochelle, in Julian's domineering way of speaking for her, and in the Wanderer's provision of a story to the hitherto silent poet. Feminine figures rely on masculine figures for their speech, and the poet herself defers first to the Wanderer and then to Julian as his chosen speaker. The poet has no rebuttal for Julian's deceptively cheerful interpretation of the final state of events. The poem never returns to her, as if she had set in motion a self-sufficient machine.

There are several earlier poems from the non-Gondal notebook that touch, as does "Silent is the House," on the matter of imaginative power without specifically addressing a personified dream or a God of Visions. Where the poet is not overtly myth-making, she can more easily find expression for anxieties and fears. As in "Silent is the House," the mind resists the sources of its own inspiration, and this resistance is in direct contrast to roughly contemporary poems about the imagination that simply plead for the return of a dream (A 11, 1840) or lament its departure (A 12, 1838; or A 13, 1840). In "Aye, there it is! It wakes to-night" (P 148, A 9), dated July 1841, the speaker describes the onset of a natural wind that acts as a supernatural influx into the mind of the poem's "thou," who is never named. The speaker mentions "thine altered cheek" and "thy kindled gaze" as evidence of "How wildly fancy plays." The "glorious wind / Has swept the world aside, / Has dashed its memory from thy mind," so that the experience described resembles Rochelle's "My outward sense is gone, my inward essence feels."

> And thou art now a spirit pouring
> Thy presence into all—

The essence of the Tempest's roaring
And of the Tempest's fall—

A universal influence
From Thine own influence free;
A principle of life, intense,
Lost to mortality.

One critic is prompted by tradition to read these verses as an address to the wind, because an influence or influx ought to be a wind, and because the lines resemble part of Shelley's "Ode to the West Wind."[13] But there is no indication that the speaker has turned from one interlocutor to another. The wind may initially have induced this outpouring of spirit, but the interlocutor's powers of influx are fully as great as the wind's. It is not that the interlocutor has assumed the wind's function, but that they have merged. Both wind and mind are spirit; both pour their presence into all; the mind has joined the wind in becoming a universal principle. Wind and woman are undifferentiated, and the vanishing of barriers between subject and object leads to an indifference to distinctions between life and death: "lost to mortality."

This exaltation is brought abruptly back to earth by the next and final stanza:

Thus truly when that breast is cold
Thy prisoned soul shall rise,
The dungeon mingle with the mould—
The captive with the skies.

There is apparently nothing in the poem to provoke this thought of death; on the contrary, the rest of the poem seems to be about an accelerating vitality. That this stanza might be an interpretation of the rest of the poem, as "thus truly" signals, is nonsense. There is no rational cause to call the soul that has previously been described as an ecstatic spirit a "prisoned soul." A "principle of life" that transcends distinctions between animate and inanimate can hardly be identified as a "captive" whose release must wait for death. Like the defensive third stanza of "Silent is the House," this stanza is dislocated from the rest by something that is not accounted for by the poem's ostensible plotting. The idea of death can only be a reaction to the foregoing ecstasies. The fusion of wind and mind in spirit is as threatening as it is exhilarating, because it necessitates the annihilation of individuality, perhaps even of individual life. "Lost to mortality" suggests "lost to life" as much as "lost to death." The narrative arrangement, with the speaker at once describing and addressing the poem's subject, indicates an aspect of that danger. In the poems on imagination there is normally a solitary inspired "I." Whether there are two distinct figures in this poem or two parts of one self, there has to be a watcher here because the one who is being described is incapable of speech. One of the signs of the wind's influx is "the words thou scarce dost speak." Her mode of expression becomes that of the wind; the "Tempest's roaring" is her roaring too. Ecstatic mergence with spirit or wind takes place at the price of language and perhaps of life.

That the speaker is not annihilated and the power of articulation is kept separate from the ecstatic spirit is the poet's signal that the "thou" 's experience, like Rochelle's vision of death, is not to be identified as a parable of the poetic imagination. "The Night-Wind," a poem of ten months earlier than "Aye, there it is," exhibits a similar association between death, loss of language, and mergence, but again outside the explicit discussion of the poetic imagination. The poem is about the night-wind's efforts to seduce the speaker, who is here a single consciousness. His seductions are all invitations to death, though not explicitly so, since the images of darkness and loss of self that he proffers are entirely lovely and beguiling.

> But still it whispered lowly,
> "How dark the woods will be!
>
> "The thick leaves in my murmur
> Are rustling like a dream,

And all their myriad voices
Instinct with spirit seem."

(P 140, A 7)

The night wind claims an inexorable power that belies his apparent gentleness:

The wanderer would not leave★ me;   ★or heed
Its kiss grew warmer still—
"O come," it sighed so sweetly,
"I'll win thee 'gainst thy will."

The speaker resists all these efforts because she understands what they mean. The poem ends, like "Aye, there it is," with a suddenly hard and explicit image of death:

"And when thy heart is laid at rest
Beneath the church-yard stone
I shall have time enough to mourn
And thou to be alone."

Barbara Hardy takes this "final darkness" to be "what the wind has always been uttering," and the explanation for its lures and for the speaker's resistance.[14]

However convincing, this reading does not account for the wind's projected lamentation of his beloved's death, as if his project required her vitality. It may not be her death that he wants, primarily; the state evoked is very like that in Wordsworth's Lucy poems, in which Lucy's death is incidental to her incorporation into nature. Part of the speaker's defense here is her insistence on maintaining a distinction between heaven and earth, human and natural. The wind wants to obliterate this distinction and in doing so to steal her linguistic powers, which derive from difference. Reading and perhaps seeing herself in the Lucy poems may have detracted from Dorothy's sense of identity as a poet, and the Lucy situation here threatens to have the same effect on this poem's speaker. The poem begins with an open window and a verbal opening toward nature, in that nature is described:

> A cloudless moon shone through
> Our open parlour window
> And rosetrees wet with dew.

When the wind, softly waving the speaker's hair, speaks of a continuity between heaven and earth, however, the speaker recoils from it.

> It told me Heaven was glorious,
> And sleeping Earth was fair.
>
> I needed not its breathing
> To bring such thoughts to me, . . .

Her recoil is against the wind's presumption in telling her her own thoughts, not against the thought itself; either way there is an undesired interpenetration of domains. The wind says that the voices are "instinct with spirit." She resists that interpenetration by countering with hierarchical thinking, speaking as if nature were low or childlike compared to the human mind. Addressing the wind, she says:

> "Thy wooing voice is kind,
> But do not think its music
> Has power to reach my mind.
>
> "Play with the scented flower,
> The young tree's supple bough,
> And leave my human feelings
> In their own course to flow."

It is not entirely certain that the interpenetration she defends herself against is death—or, if death is its final form, the immediate threat is the possible collapse of language. When the speaker recoils from the wind's telling her her own thoughts, part of her fear is that nature may preempt human speech. In the verse that follows, the wind's self-description is spoken from the point of view of the human listener, not the natural speaker:

"The thick leaves in my murmur
Are rustling like a dream,
And all their myriad voices
Instinct with spirit seem."

Only substituting "your" for "my," this is the kind of speech
that the human being should be making, full of metaphors
and an outsider's uncertainty about appearances. The wind
speaks for her. At least part of what disturbs her about the
wind's seductions must be the threat that human language
will cease. Her fears are justified by the wind's disregard of
her verbal protests. For the wind, word and kiss are one. In his
appeal to her nostalgia for childhood he almost images a re-
ciprocal love:

"Have I not loved thee long?
As long as thou hast loved the night
Whose silence wakes my song."

He reminds the speaker that she is a lover of the images of
death—silence and the night—as if answering her objections
to being herself silenced. In the image of death that the wind
proffers as his last persuasion, the dead one is "alone" and
therefore beyond communication, while the wind will go on
speaking: "I shall have time enough to mourn." Language
depends on keeping the human and other aspects of nature
separate; for the wind to speak in human terms violates intel-
ligibility. If the wind's seductions are to death, then it would
have to mourn its own deed, but "silence wakes my song,"
and the wind is intent on eradicating difference, which wakes
human song.

In "Shall Earth no more inspire thee" (P 147, A 6) the wind
has so successfully preempted human voice that he is the only
speaker; there is no human voice at all. He chastizes "thee" for
rejecting the earth's inspiration in favor of mental abstraction,
"regions dark to thee," and asks this "lonely dreamer" to
"come back and dwell with me." In the manner of the wind

in "The Night-Wind" the speaker blurs the distinction be-
tween heaven and earth:

> . . . none would ask a Heaven
> More like this Earth than thine.

The earth uses for himself the terms that the poet elsewhere
uses for imaginative power:

> I've seen thy spirit bending
> In fond idolatry.

The first line of the last verse, "Then let my winds caress
thee," recalls Wordsworth's address to Dorothy at the end of
"Tintern Abbey": ". . . let the misty mountain-winds be free /
To blow against thee." The speaker of "Tintern Abbey" is for
Brontë the type of the poet of the imagination, who domi-
nates the woman he addresses by his privileged discourse
with nature, by the maturity of his imagination, and also by
his masculinity. By having the earth speak with his words,
Brontë identifies the earth's powers with both imaginative
power and with sexual dominance.

The repeated identification of a masculine wind with the
preemption of language clearly refers to the tradition of the
Word as the spirit or breath of God, or wind blowing from
God. The poet's fear that she neither originates nor controls
her own speech, a fear that she presents as a fear of death,
arises from her being a woman writing in a masculine tradi-
tion. Coleridge's "The Eolian Harp" images the mind as both
passive and feminine, made to "tremble into thought" by the
passage of the "intellectual breeze" that is identified with (an
unorthodox) God. "That simplest Lute" is "by the desultory
breeze caress'd, / Like some coy maid half yielding to her
lover." For Coleridge himself, the alignment of the sexes in
this metaphor is not conducive to the highest imaginative
power. Instead of experiencing sublimity, "many idle flitting
phantasies, / Traverse my indolent and passive brain." And
the mind thus imaged gives way later in the poem to an ab-

surd orthodoxy. When Coleridge seeks an image of true imaginative power, the mind is no longer feminine or subject to the whims of the breeze, but the source of that breeze itself: "The primary IMAGINATION I hold to be . . . a repetition in the finite mind of the eternal act of creation in the infinite I AM." Whereas the image of the mind as feminine and passive is not definitive for Coleridge, it intrudes itself into Brontë's serious formulations about her identity as a poet, as when Dorothy Wordsworth consciously aligns her poetic voice with Coleridge's definition of fancy. Unable to identify with the masculine Word or breath of God, Brontë portrays herself as its passive object in "The Night-Wind" and in "Shall Earth no more inspire thee" (A 7 and A 6). Where in "Aye, there it is" (A 9) a female figure is united with an intellectual breeze, her assumption promotes thoughts of death, not of power.

Dorothy Wordsworth's lack of a central poetic self and her tendency to identify what faculties she possesses with an eccentric fancy are also negative responses to the Coleridgean formula, and like Dorothy's decentered self Brontë's myth of imaginative possession and her sense of obligatory deference to higher powers create great difficulties in her poems. Self-alienation in the poetry causes her to feel as much threatened as delighted by her gift. One cure for self-alienation is simply to give in to it and "sleep / Without identity," and in *Wuthering Heights* death's project is the reuniting, not of parts of the self, or of poet and poetic spirit, but of two individuals. Heathcliff is eager for death so that he and Cathy may "be lost in one repose." Loss of self, the dispersal of identity, leads to the merging and reunion of identities. This loss of identity may not be the same as Dorothy's self-dispersal, yet dispersal is the goal of so much in the novel that it seems reasonable to make a comparison. The dispersals in *Wuthering Heights* may represent a positive use of the very difficulty experienced both by Dorothy and by Brontë in her poetry. The form of the novel is fitted for dispersiveness as the Romantic lyric is not, and it may be that Brontë, experiencing Dorothy's difficulty, found in the novel the proper place for turning it to use. This transformation of a former difficulty may account, in part, for the novel's superiority to the poetry.

Many critics, writing on diverse aspects of the novel, have noted its drive both toward diffusion and toward reunion. Robert Kiely finds in it an underlying principle of dynamism that causes motion to be valued exclusively over stasis.[15] The novel defies its own potential categories, because it is constantly fusing polarities, whether of character, of landscape, or of morality (hell is heaven and heaven is hell). Leo Bersani's chapter on *Wuthering Heights* is about the dissolution and transference of identity, particularly in the exchange of identity between Cathy and Heathcliff.[16] Although Cathy insists "I *am* Heathcliff," and Heathcliff calls Cathy "my soul" and "my life," Bersani points out how different they are in character, a difference that transcends particular qualities because Heathcliff is the archetypal outsider in the story. Their fusion of identity is not a natural reunion, but a self-alienation and an identification with otherness that is both terrifying and appealing. Because death is the final form of dissolution, especially in Heathcliff's plan for the physical merging of his corpse with Cathy's, "death is the most appropriate metaphor for that radical transference of the self to another . . ." (pp. 211-212). The two houses, Wuthering Heights and Thrushcross Grange, are not the polarities they are usually taken to be, but have interchangeable characteristics. Even sexual distinctions cease to pertain: the second Linton is more conventionally feminine than any character in the novel, except his mother Isabella. The boundaries of identity are dissolved by the repetition of the generations and the recombination of family traits resultant from intermarriage. And the diffuse narrative structure dissolves this dissolution even further. There is no single controlling point of view that might preserve a remnant of stability.

There are novels by men that exhibit the same traits of diffuseness to be found in *Wuthering Heights*, though perhaps not to so great a degree. The novel is generically a more scat-

tered form than the lyric, and it would be impossible defini-
tively to trace this difference to sexual difference. Kiely points
out that Nelly's success as a narrator has to do with her lack of
egotism: "The fact is that neither Lockwood nor Heathcliff
could possibly tell the story without focusing almost exclu-
sively on himself. Nelly can do otherwise" (p. 237). This lack
of egotism may, however, originate in her being a domestic
rather than in her femininity; neither of the Cathys would do
much better as narrator than Lockwood and Heathcliff. But
insofar as the diffuseness of *Wuthering Heights* provides a suc-
cessful answer to difficulties in the poems that arise from the
poet's femininity, and insofar as it resembles the selflessness in
Dorothy's writing, it tentatively may be connected to the
novelist's femininity. The poet is never confident of her
power over language and over imagination because both are,
to her, alien and masculine, therefore dangerous to the self's
integrity. Whereas the poetic speaker must always fear her
own death, characters in the novel may die without im-
pinging on the continued life of the whole, and in fact their
deaths may contribute to continuity. There is no single self in
the novel to compare with the poems' troubled selves. The
only comparable figure is the surface of the entire text. If the
novel's text is like a psyche, this psyche is so diffuse as to in-
clude, and therefore not be threatened by, its own potential
destroyers.

In the poems the poet is obliged, unwillingly, to value pos-
session positively by characterizing it as transcendence. She
can overcome the threat of invasion or of possession only by
pretending that it is not threatening but welcome, deferring to
it either way. But the novel's inclusiveness allows her to avoid
having to overvalue external powers. There is an almost exact
correspondence between Cathy's words about Heathcliff and
the transcendent belief represented in "No coward soul is
mine" (P 191, A 31):

"If all else perished, and *he* remained, I should still con-
tinue to be; and, if all else remained, and he were annihi-

lated, the Universe would turn to a mighty stranger. I should not seem a part of it.'' (*WH* 74)

> Though Earth and moon were gone
> And suns and universes ceased to be
> And thou wert left alone
> Every Existence would exist in thee.

The similarity between these two passages is startling, but there are important differences as well. The prose passage consists of a pair of complementary statements whereas the verse is a single gesture, a stylistic difference that underscores a more basic difference. Cathy's speech is punctuated by an alternation of emphatic "I" and "he," but there is no "I" in the verse, only a "thou." Cathy's and Heathcliff's relation is reciprocal, but after an initial equality with the "God within my breast" the "I" in the poem defers to what she knows is a higher principle.[17]

> Life, that in me has rest
> As I Undying Life, have power in Thee . . . .

The symmetry of "in me . . . in Thee" suggests mutual dependence, but that life rests in her and she draws power from it is not an equal relation but a hierarchical devotion that operates only in one direction. All the sources of poetry seem to be external, and the poetic self invariably loses any competition with a divine figure external to the poem. The novel has better success, not by winning, but by avoiding the competition altogether.

When Charlotte Brontë mentions Heathcliff in the preface to her edition of *Wuthering Heights*, as quoted above, it is as an example of the horrors that a mind possessed by its creative gift may produce, and her theory of possession develops from her desire to excuse Heathcliff's presence in the novel. Heathcliff is himself daemonic, and although he hardly represents his author's creative powers, he is the main character and much of the action is presented from his point of view. He is in many ways similar to the figures of imaginative power in the poetry, in that he is powerful, at times visionary, and alien. This similarity may be Brontë's way of announcing that in the novel she has discarded her myth of visionary posses- sion, because there Heathcliff is only a character, dissociated from the creative process. He may retain the shape of the daemon of creativity, but his significance lies elsewhere. Heathcliff is himself possessed and driven to death by Cathy's ghost. In his human shape, the visitant is as much victim as victor, and his power is relative, not absolute.

THE NOVEL PRESENTS the overcoming of otherness as a rela- tionship between two characters whose powers are fairly equally matched; the poems present a continual struggle be- tween the poet and the sources of voice and vision. Creative power is held externally by various masculine figures of imag- inative visitation, and it never quite becomes the poet's own. At the same time, Brontë has an alternate myth of the origin of poetic voice that associates language not with a dream or vision but with nature. In the manner of the visionary poems, nature and the memory of nature are a source of voice either that the poet endeavors to adopt as her own or against which she defines her own voice. Just as her attitude toward the vi- sionary visitants is a mixture of desire and resistance, because their gift is precarious and untrustworthy, she treats nature's voice and powers with a mixed spirit of welcome and compe- tition. This origin of voice is no more native to her than is the alien visitation of a God of Visions.

Many of the earliest poems and verse fragments linger over descriptions of natural settings in a manner that suggests an uncomplicated love of nature. It is only when the poet begins to think of herself as a poet that she ceases to defer to nature. "To a Wreath of Snow" (P 39), written in 1837, gratefully welcomes nature as a speaker. Imprisoned, her heart "weighed with sinking gloom," A. G. Almeda (the heroine of the Gondal poems) wakes one morning to find blown into her cell this "silent sign of winter skies." She calls it a talisman, a "voiceless, soulless messenger," because it "sweetly spoke /

Of cloudy skies and mountains bare" and cheers her by re-
minding her of home.

A. G. Almeda is not a poet, and she welcomes this silent
sign unambivalently. The non-Gondal notebook (comprising
the poems on poethood) opens with a series of four poems,
written within a period of five weeks in 1838 (11 Nov.-18
Dec.), in which the poet both welcomes natural voices of this
kind and learns to extract her own voice from them. This ex-
traction is difficult because nature is a powerful speaker.

> Loud without the wind was roaring
>   Through the waned autumnal sky;
> Drenching wet, the cold rain pouring
>   Spoke of stormy winters nigh.

> All too like that dreary eve
> Sighed within repining grief;
> Sighed at first, but sighed not long—
> Sweet—How softly sweet it came!
> Wild words of an ancient song,
> Undefined, without a name.

>   (P 91, A 1)

This last utterance is timely because it shows the speaker that
she is not dependent on nature's speech for her own. Until the
arrival of the "Wild words of an ancient song," nature roars
and speaks while the speaker only sighs. Up to that point, her
utterance is limited to the expressive possibilities made avail-
able by nature. Her grief is passively "All too like that dreary
eve." The "ancient song" seems to originate externally, but it
is not a visionary visitation; rather, the song is the voice of the
speaker's own memory, and its imagined externality ex-
presses the poet's surprise at finding a voice of her own. Ac-
customed only to being addressed and spoken for, she does
not recognize her own voice.

Nature's speech can only imitate or react to natural events,
but poetic speech is able to create a landscape in nature's ab-
sence.

"It was spring, for the skylark was singing."
Those words, they awakened a spell—

. . . .

In the gloom of a cloudy November,
They uttered the music of May.

The bulk of the poem consists of three scenes from memory that appear to be exercises in the delight of using language to transcend present time and place. In none of these scenes, however, does the poet fail to include nature's voice beside her own exuberant descriptions. The first opens with an invocation to the wind, but scenic description begins only when the wind has in turn called to her "To walk by the hill-river's side." The second is a vision of a summer morning in childhood:

But blithely we rose as the dusk heaven
Was melting to amber and blue;
And swift were the wings to our feet given
While we traversed the meadows of dew, . . .

Though this verse almost moves out of the remembered and into the visionary, the poet ties the scene back to a dependence on a natural voice as the source of delight. The children race across the meadows

For the moors where the linnet was trilling
Its song on the old granite stone;
Where the lark—the wild skylark was filling
Every breast with delight like its own.

In the final scene emotion is expressed through an inadequacy in the speaker's language: "What language can utter the feeling / That rose when, in exile afar, . . ." Paired with the speaker's stated speechlessness and contributing to her distress is her recognition that natural objects are more articulate than she is herself. Her unnamed "feeling" is evoked by the sight of brown heather growing on "a lonely hill";

> It was scattered and stunted, and told me
> That soon even that would be gone;
> Its whispered, "The grim walls enfold me;
> I have bloomed in my last summer's sun."

These remnant flowers cast over the speaker a powerful but ambiguous and unspecified "spell," and the wish for liberty from that spell is expressed as a wish for tears, as if even the most rudimentary self-expression would of itself restore the speaker's power of articulation, both over herself and over nature.

> The spirit that bent 'neath its power,
> How it longed, how it burned to be free!
> If I could have wept in that hour
> Those tears had been heaven to me.

The wish for expression is not fulfilled, however, and the cryptic phrasing of this stanza suggests that the poem is ending as it began, with nature's speech taking precedence over poetic language.

But the closing stanza does something that nature cannot do and, although its meaning is unclear, it wins a power independent of nature. Part of nature's speech at the opening of the poem was a prophecy: "the cold rain pouring / Spoke of stormy winters nigh." The prophecy is synecdochal: rain speaks of more rain. Closing, the poem offers in competition with this natural prophecy a human prophecy that introduces an element from outside nature and outside the poem. Its disjunctiveness seems clumsy, but whereas nature can only speak of itself, this verse exists to show that human speech can refer to the absent and thereby multiply its scope and power.

> Well, well, the sad minutes are moving
> Though loaded with trouble and pain;
> And sometime the loved and the loving
> Shall meet on the mountains again.

The next two poems present a similar relation to nature, in which the poet's love for nature and for the memory of nature is strained by nature's undesirable preemption of human voice or thought. "A little while, a little while" (P 92, A 2) follows the pattern of "Loud without the wind was roaring," in which scenes from memory are framed by the wish to withdraw from an unpleasant present:

> Where wilt thou go, my harassed heart?
> Full many a land invites thee now;
> And places near and far apart
> Have rest for thee, my weary brow.

The first of these inviting places, though the product of a gothic imagination, is announced as a real memory: "There is a spot . . . ." She longs for "the hearth of home," but like the speaker of Dorothy Wordsworth's Cottage poems she is halted before entering by the natural objects and effects encountered just outside.

> The house is old, the trees are bare
> And moonless bends the misty dome
> But what on earth is half so dear,
> So longed for as the hearth of home?
>
> The mute bird sitting on the stone,
> The dank moss dripping from the wall,
> The garden-walk with weeds o'ergrown,
> I love them—how I love them all!

The speaker delights in her ability to transport herself, and the next scene is presented at first as an invention:

> Shall I go there? or shall I seek
> Another clime, another sky . . . ?

But this too is a memory, a reinvention of home in which conflict between nature and the human is simply avoided:

> A little and a lone green lane
> That opened on a common wide;
> A distant, dreamy, dim blue chain
> Of mountains circling every side;

> A heaven so clear, an earth so calm,
> So sweet, so soft, so hushed an air
> And, deepening still the dream-like charm,
> Wild moor-sheep feeding everywhere—
>
> That was the scene; I knew it well, . . .

The memory passes because the poet is recalled to work, caus-
ing her to complain that "truth has banished fancy's power,"
but the difference between the visionary promise of "another
clime" and "That was the scene; I knew it well" indicates that
truth to nature had already banished fancy's power.

In "How still, how happy!" (P 93, A 3), dated three days
later, nature is controlling present vision rather than memory,
but with the same strained effect. The speaker is conscien-
tiously trying to persuade herself that she loves the present
"December's smile / As much as July's golden beam," but she
cannot prevent her mind from wandering away from the
"wintry light o'er flowerless moors—"

> I could think in the withered grass
> Spring's budding wreaths we might discern;
> The violet's eye might shyly flash
> And young leaves shoot among the fern.

Nature forces a retraction of this rudimentary imaginative act:

> It is but thought—full many a night
> The snow shall clothe those hills afar.

The poet uses her retraction to split the next two verses be-
tween the here and the not here, the present scene and the
summer scene that language can evoke in its absence, but the
poem ends with a concession to nature both in vision and in
voice:

> Then let us sit and watch the while
> The blue ice curdling on the stream.

To sit long enough to watch ice form is to invite freezing and
to forgo human rhythms for nature's measureless pace.

The next poem, of a week later, takes place in the same situation, but the poet refuses to permit visible nature to dominate. The bulk of the poem consists of accounts of absent and beloved things, in defiance of winter's presence. In "Loud without the wind was roaring" (A 1) the inability to weep is a sign for the poet's difficulties of expression. Here in "The blue bell is the sweetest flower" (P 94, A 4), the speaker closes the poem's long and lovely descriptions of the vanished bluebell by saying "For these I weep," making mourning the source of verse, a source located in the self. At the close of the poem winter offers its own loveliness to contemplate, similar to the curdling ice of the previous poem, but the speaker turns away in favor of memory:

> If chilly then the light should fall
> Adown the dreary sky
> And gild the dank and darkened wall
> With transient brilliancy,
>
> How do I yearn, how do I pine
> For the time of flowers to come,
> And turn me from that fading shine
> To mourn the fields of home.

It is interesting to note that "O Dream, where art thou now?" (P 86, A 12), which is part of the sequence of poems outlining the visionary origin of poetry, was written at the same period as these other early poems that offer a natural theory of poetry—in fact slightly earlier (5 Nov. 1838). That Brontë, transcribing poems for her formal notebook, took it out of chronological sequence to place it with later poems about dreams and visions indicates that she was well aware of these two separate paths. It also indicates that the two theories are alternatives, operative at the same time, rather than a progression or sequence.

Several poems from about a year later exhibit a temporary resolution of the strain present in the first four poems of the non-Gondal notebook. Nature no longer endangers human

voice and thought because it is reduced simply to a figure for
whatever human subject is in the foreground. This reduction
resembles the pattern of the dream or visionary poems, traced
above, in which for a period the poet portrays herself as com-
pletely in control of her visitant. Both kinds of poetry origi-
nate in absence, but following an original lament they make
use of that absence to augment the poet's power. Loss of the
visionary gleam incites a visionary elegy. Loss of summer in
winter, or of nature at a time of confining labor, provokes the
poet to articulate her memories. Now those losses are trans-
formed into figuration, in which the natural object is itself ab-
sent and no longer a subject, though its name remains to be
used for human purposes. "The wind, I hear it sighing" (P
120, A 14), written in October 1839, is about the haunting re-
turn of once-pleasurable fancies, but it opens with a symbolic
landscape that serves to point the difference between then and
now: "Withered leaves as thick are lying / As spring-flowers
on the ground." The poem proper ends with a vacant op-
timism, but this setting suggests the more helpful possibility
of a Keatsian autumnal song. "Love and Friendship" (P 121,
A 15), the next poem chronologically and in the manuscript
order, points its minor moral by means of a simile from na-
ture, and the next after that makes nature's cyclical recoveries
an object lesson for the despairing. Nature in these poems
may initially be wiser than the human watcher, but its lessons
can always be explicated. As in *Wuthering Heights*, nature
employed as a figure loses all the dangerous potency it has
when considered as a subject in itself.[18]

As in the sequence of visionary poems, this subduing is not
permanent. In "O thy bright eyes" (A 26) the power that the
God of Visions retains over the otherwise powerful speaker is
the power of speech, creating a lack important enough to di-
minish the speaker's other powers. This recognition of pow-
erlessness opens the way to identifying the visionary with vi-
sions of death. The sequence of poems in which nature and
the memory of nature are the potential sources of poetic voice
follows a similar course. Though it is not nature's absence

that the poet mourns, nature's presence is threatening to poetic speech, and the early poems' energy is in the strained balance between invasion and invitation. In later poems, nature is associated with death just as much as the visionary visitants are. Nature is as alien a source for poetry as is the God of Visions, and the poet uses death to figure her alienation from its power. But whereas the visions of death can be made to seem transcendent, nature's death is final and bound to the earth. Where there is a choice, nature is treated as a greater threat than are those masculine figures of vision. Juxtaposing the two schemes for poetry, the poet diminishes nature by making the death associated with vision now suddenly transcendent and glorious. Other poems, such as the three poems about the wind (A 6, A 7, and A 9), have used death as a metaphor for the speaker's fear of and resistance to visionary experience, but by valuing the visionary exclusively, the poet finds a way to direct all negative feeling toward nature. The expectation of "everlasting day" becomes hyperbolic, and nature represents all the threatening aspects of death. Even life in nature is a life in death.

Other critics account for this phenomenon by describing it as a continuous part of Brontë's mystical or visionary experience. A painful conscious existence leads to, and is perhaps even necessary for, transcendent experience or transcendence after death.[19] This reading assumes that there is nothing unusual or questionable in this hyperbolic valorization of these religious hopes, because it is assumed that that is where her interest exclusively lies. But it may be that her hyperbolic view of heaven is not spontaneous, but conditioned by her view of nature, and she frequently qualifies her belief in transcendence after death even while she is stating it.

The first text that exhibits this radical split between natural and transcendent death is the essay "The Butterfly," written as an exercise in French during the period of Emily and Charlotte's stay in Brussels in 1842.[20] Because it is prose it has been cited as a doctrinal statement of Brontë's attitude toward nature,[21] but the essay form is no less inherently fictive than

poetry. Two of the other "devoirs" have overtly fictive
speakers, and all are highly dramatic. Because it was written
as a school exercise and therefore with a knowledge of its au-
dience, "The Butterfly" ought logically to be further from
personal belief than the poetry, not closer. The first part of the
brief essay is a ghastly account of the "insanity" of all crea-
tion. "Life exists on a principle of destruction; every creature
must be the relentless instrument of death to the others, or
himself cease to live." The speaker finds as a case in point a
flower being devoured from within by a caterpillar, and,
crushing it melodramatically under foot, sees the universe as
"a vast machine constructed only to bring forth evil." At that
moment she sees a butterfly and is reminded of transcendent
possibilities:

> Here is a symbol of the world to come—just as the ugly
> caterpillar is the beginning of the splendid butterfly, this
> globe is the embryo of a new heaven and of a new earth
> whose meagerest beauty infinitely surpasses mortal
> imagination.

The essay concludes with the orthodox metaphor of the di-
vine harvest that will follow mortal suffering and that will
lead to the "eternal realm of happiness and glory." This strin-
gent portrayal of nature is the reverse of the poems of 1838-
1839. There, the speaker may betray some resistance to na-
ture's apparent powers of speech, but nature remembered is
beloved. Even in the poems about the wind, of 1840-1841,
natural beauty is chosen as the figure for visionary experience
because it is genuinely seductive, even when fatal. Here nature
is unambiguously hated and even its use as a figure does not
decrease its evil potency.

But valorized though the "new heaven" is, it deprives the
essayist of her own speech. In the negative part of the essay
she is quoting her own exclamations as she walks through a
wood; the energy of her pessimism is her own. But when the
butterfly appears, "I was silent, but an inner voice said to me
. . ." and the rest of the essay is given over to received ortho-

dox views. Earlier, the speaker evokes this influx of orthodoxy by repeating the prophecy of Genesis: crushing under foot the caterpillar, which she calls a reptile, she bruises the head of the serpent. The speaker also asks her reader to doubt the genuineness of the whole discussion by telling us at the beginning that she is in the darkest of moods:

> In one of those moods which sometimes lay hold on us, when the world of imagination suffers the blight of winter; when the light of life seems to go out and existence becomes a barren desert in which we wander exposed to all the tempests which blow, without hope of rest or shelter—in one of those dark moods, I was walking . . . .

The implication here is that normally "the world of imagination" and "the light of life" preserve her from such gloomy views. The orthodoxy that enters at the end is only a borrowed light, taken up in despair and presumably to be made superfluous by the return of imaginative strength.

A later poem that, like "The Butterfly," might appear to represent Brontë's hatred of nature and her supposed mystical hopes, is also set in a time when the world of the imagination is dark. We find the speaker of "A Day Dream" (P 170, A 24) "sullen" and "in a fit of peevish woe." The natural scene is a lovely day of early summer, but the speaker is thinking of winter, and her gloominess about nature equals that of "The Butterfly."

> "The birds that now so blithely sing,
> Through deserts frozen dry,
> Poor spectres of the perished Spring
> In famished troops will fly.
>
> "And why should we be glad at all?
> The leaf is hardly green,
> Before a token of the fall
> Is on its surface seen."

The day dream that follows is a vision of transcendence, couched in pagan or fanciful terms, but as orthodox in spirit as the "eternal realm of happiness and glory" of "The Butter-fly."

> "Let Grief distract the sufferer's breast,
> And Night obscure his way;
> They hasten him to endless rest,
> And everlasting day.
>
> "To Thee the world is like a tomb,
> A desert's naked shore;
> To us, in unimagined bloom,
> It brightens more and more.
>
> "And could we lift the veil and give
> One brief glimpse to thine eye
> Thou would'st rejoice for those that live,
> Because they live to die."

Mortal death may lead to eternal day, but at the cost of trivializing the earth.

If this poem's "fit of peevish woe" may be identified with the essay's mood "when the world of imagination suffers the blight of winter," the cumulative effect of the two works is to suggest that this evocation of orthodoxy is due to a failure of the imagination. By a series of references, "A Day Dream" sets itself against Coleridge's naturalized imagination in "The Rime of the Ancient Mariner," as if this were even more a rejection than a failure of the imagination. The poem opens with nature's loveliness pictured as a marriage between May and "her young lover, June," an image that permits the speaker to enter into the context of "The Rime."

> And I, of all the wedding guests,
> Was only sullen there.

Spoken by the single outsider at a wedding, Coleridge's poem is in its own way a "spousal verse" for the marriage between the mind and nature, but the sullen speaker here refuses to lend her voice to the celebration. The Mariner looses the albatross' spell "unawares" by blessing the slimy sea snakes through finding them beautiful, but Brontë's speaker gratuitously curses a beautiful setting, when she prefers to think of winter as the proper character of nature, and "these bright things" as "a vision vain, / An unreal mockery." The Mariner's imaginative love is rewarded by the arrival of the "troop of spirits blest" who revive him and inspirit the dead sailors to begin the journey home. The spirits are "sweet sounds," and they are followed later in the poem by a troop of silent seraphs who are "all light." The speaker cursing natural cycle in Brontë's poem hears the dreamt song about everlasting day from similar spirits, comprising light and sound:

> A thousand thousand glancing fires
> Seemed kindling in the air;
> A thousand thousand silvery lyres
> Resounded far and near:
>
> Methought the very breath I breathed
> Was full of sparks divine,
> And all my heather-couch was wreathed
> By that celestial shine.
>
> And while the wide Earth echoing rang
> To their strange minstrelsy,
> The little glittering spirits sang, . . .

But though the Mariner's "sweet sounds" seem to sing of imaginative reunions between the human spirit and nature, Brontë's "glittering spirits" sing of the fortunate separation death makes between spirit and nature.

In this poem and in "The Butterfly" the value placed on excluding nature from transcendence, and the necessity for demeaning nature (or worse) in order to attain transcendence, are made to appear highly suspect. Yet not only has this been taken as Brontë's mystic doctrine,[22] but also Brontë herself seems to wish to believe what she propounds. These doctrines ring false because they are poetically suicidal. In turning over her discourse to orthodoxy, she silences herself; and in rejecting the Mariner's blessing of the snakes she rejects the poetic

strategy most available to her. The more hyperbolic her vi-
sion of transcendence, the less convincing it is, even without
the doubts she builds into the structure of these texts. Are we
really to put our faith in "little glittering spirits," and to be-
lieve that Brontë does too? The most persuasive lines in the
poem, the ones that seem to describe heartfelt experience
rather than the outlines of a fable, are not in the vision itself
but in the passage about its onset:

> Methought the very breath I breathed
> Was full of sparks divine,
> And all my heather-couch was wreathed
> By that celestial shine.

The vision is still contextualized in nature here. To breathe in
"sparks divine" is to make transcendence tangible and vivid.
The "celestial shine" here decorates the heather, rather than
the heather serving the shine. Most important, the speaker is
still present. The lines enact an interplay of nature, vision, and
self. The speaker's wonder in the line "Methought the very
breath I breathed" is as palpable as the glowing heather. The
vision is located in a place, and it is personal. To this point the
reader is asked to care about what effect the vision has, even
more than what its content will be. But the vision itself, be-
ginning two stanzas later, is unmediated by the speaker, who
presents it as if at dictation and without any framing com-
mentary beyond the wish that it were true. Although it is of
course the product of the speaker's own fancy, she presents it
as much as possible as a received truth, in much the same way
that the essay's speaker defers to an "inner voice" that speaks
the language of orthodoxy. Neither text returns to the
speaker's self nor to the natural context, because the orthodox
vision is not really part of the poem. There is no way to have
it make sense in the foregoing natural world, and the self in
the poem does not integrate it as part of her own. By not re-
turning to the speaker, the poem avoids testing the vision
against her "fit of peevish woe," and by overriding these
built-in doubts, the vision of transcendence claims the last

word, and therefore, apparently but fraudulently, the poem's entire investment of belief.

Although the poet convinces neither herself nor her reader of her belief in transcendence after death, she clings to the effort to do so because to abandon it would be to concede that nature's death is final. The tenacity of her effort to deny this finality suggests that she knows quite well that beyond the bulwark of a fiction of transcendence there is no transcendence in nature or in natural life. Although in many poems she returns to the orthodox fiction that suffering on earth leads to a transcendent afterlife, she considers only once the possibility that this sequence does not really work. "I see around me tombstones grey" (P 149, A 19) is unique in its vehemence and in its subject matter, and even in its versification, and this uniqueness suggests that the poem stands for many unwritten poems, because it has the energy of suppressed feeling.

The poem entertains the same categories of a dark and fatal earth and an eternally happy heaven that form the structure of "A Day Dream" and "The Butterfly," but the path from one to the other is blocked. To the extremely bitter speaker life on earth is a death-in-life, but death promises no respite, because the earth prevents her passage to the "sweet land of light." The poem's tone is difficult to read because the speaker is half convinced that she prefers to remain with the earth, even though she knows that that preference is enforced and imprisoning. Her loyalty to her jailor causes her to speak mockingly of heaven as being reserved for those who have not, unlike her, suffered and sinned on earth; its inhabitants are happy because their innocence has never been tested.

> Let me remember half the woe
> I've seen and heard and felt below,
> And Heaven itself, so pure and blest,
> Could never give my spirit rest.
> Sweet land of light! thy children fair
> Know nought akin to our despair;
> Nor have they felt, nor can they tell

What tenants haunt each mortal cell,
What gloomy guests we hold within—
Torments and madness, tears and sin!

The speaker pretends ironically that she has control over her deprivation, and consigns these innocents to their heaven as if it were a curse:

Well, may they live in extasy
Their long eternity of joy;
At least we would not bring them down
With us to weep, with us to groan.

Earth jealously guards her "cup of sufferings drear," not to share it with heaven, "And only mourns that *we* must die" and perhaps desert her for heaven's attractions. The rest of the poem is an account of how "we" take pity on the bereft earth and choose to remain with her when we die. The earth's bereavement is a mock misery:

Ah mother, what shall comfort thee
In all this boundless misery?
To cheer our eager eyes a while
We see thee smile; how fondly smile!
But who reads not through that tender glow
Thy deep, unutterable woe?

Earth's beauties cause us to think that she is a feeling creature too, but the only unutterable woe is human woe. The choice to remain in the earth is a mock choice:

Indeed, no dazzling land above
Can cheat thee of thy children's love.
We all, in life's departing shine,
Our last dear longings blend with thine;
And struggle still and strive to trace
With clouded gaze, thy darling face.
We would not leave our native home
For *any* world beyond the Tomb.
No—rather on thy kindly breast
Let us be laid in lasting rest; . . .

Yet in spite of the bitterness of the entire poem so far, it ends on a note that cannot be ironic:

> Or waken but to share with thee
> A mutual immortality.

This must be genuine loyalty, uttered in spite of the speaker's certainty that there can be no mutual immortality. The couplet seems intended to deny the preceding bitterness, even though the poem cannot be unsaid.

Thinking of the earth as "mother" is what stops the speaker from condemning and dismissing her, as she does in other poems where the earth or nature is neutral. As for Dorothy Wordsworth, the received maternal characterization of nature on the one hand generates a distrust for nature on the part of the feminine poet; on the other, it prevents her from fully acting on that distrust. Nature can be condemned more easily where it is not explicitly named as maternal, but that maternal characterization may be a repressed presence in all the poems that devalue nature, even those where nature appears neutral. If earth is mother, then "Heaven itself, so pure and blest" is cast into the orthodox position as the heaven of God the Father, and in fact heaven in this poem is closer to the heaven of Sunday-school instruction than in any other poems. The denunciation of nature in favor of "everlasting day," here and elsewhere, represents what Freud describes as the feminine turn from mother to father. No matter how highly that turn is valued, those poems must include doubts and qualifications because, as in Dorothy's *A Narrative Concerning George and Sarah Green*, to make a complete rejection of the maternal figure endangers feminine identity fully as much as does maternal dominance. The heartfelt lines at the end of the poem may be a recognition that the poet's identity is bound up with that of the maternal figure.

A text of a year later, concerning a human mother rather than Mother Nature, repeats the complexity of feeling brought by Brontë to any consideration of the maternal figure. The French "devoirs" include a letter to a fictional mother from her fictional daughter, who, away at school, complains pathetically of the mother's neglect, the mother having neither visited nor written for what seems to the girl to be a long time. The letter's mixture of yearning and suppressed anger repeats, if less vehemently, the attitude expressed in the final lines of "I see around me tombstones grey," and it also recalls Dorothy Wordsworth's ambivalence about blaming the mother in *A Narrative Concerning George and Sarah Green*. The girl reproaches her mother with her absence and then apologizes for the reproach by finding other causes for her sadness, and then apologizes for having written about herself at all:

> I am afraid that you think less often of your daughter when she is away; lately very small things make me sad, and especially when I think of this I can't help crying. They tell me that my health is weak, and they make me stay in my room and leave my studies and my friends; maybe this is the reason I'm so sad, because it's so tiresome to be shut up all day in an isolated room. . . .
>
> I long to come home again and see the house and the people I love so much. If only you could come here, I think your presence by itself would cure me. So come, dear mother; and forgive this letter for speaking only of me; I myself will talk to you of plenty of other things.[23]

If the girl is in quarantine, nineteenth-century experience and literary convention make it likely that she is dying; suppressing her reproaches against the mother, the girl instead identifies with her, with fatal results: the mother's abandonment will issue in the child's death. M. Héger's comment at the end of the letter is a reminder of a further absence: "Aucune marque de souvenir p[ou]r papa—c'est une faute." Himself a figure of paternal authority, Héger is the appropriate defender of deference to the father. If the letter itself is a gloss on the poems' ambivalence about maternal figures, this addendum points to the fragility of the poems' overvaluation of the orthodox alternative. It may be fatal to choose the mother, but apparently there is no other choice.

The bitter refusal of heaven in favor of earth in "I see around me tombstones grey" is familiar from *Wuthering Heights*, except that in the novel this gesture is utterly sincere. The major characters valorize nature in an unequivocal manner entirely different from its valuation in the poetry, and the poetry's hyperbolic investment in transcendence after death is absent from the novel. The reasons for this change may be in the radical difference between the form and traditions of poetry and of prose fiction, which make possible the novel's removal from nature of all the complex feelings associated with the maternal figure.

Cathy is telling Nelly Dean that she once dreamt that she was in heaven:

> "Heaven did not seem to be my home; and I broke my heart with weeping to come back to earth; and the angels were so angry that they flung me out, into the middle of the heath on the top of Wuthering Heights; where I woke sobbing for joy." (*WH* 72)

The dream is an allegory of Cathy's dilemma: she associates Linton with heaven and Heathcliff, implicitly, with "the heath on the top of Wuthering Heights," even though Heathcliff's nature has been degraded by Hindley's treatment. This passage prepares for the equation that Cathy makes, in her delirium, between nature and the death she desires. Having in her delirium imagined herself back at Wuthering Heights with Heathcliff and as a child, she wakes to find herself, as Mrs. Linton, "an exile, and outcast, thenceforth, from what had been my world" (*WH* 107). This thought of the heaven where she earlier predicted she would be an exile makes her think of the earth, her proper home.

> "I'm sure I should be myself were I once among the heather on those hills. Open the window again wide, fasten it open! Quick, why don't you move?"
>
> "Because I won't give you your death of cold," I answered.

"You won't give me a chance of life, you mean," she said sullenly.   (*WH* 107-108)

Cathy opens the window herself, "and bent out, careless of the frosty air that cut about her shoulders as keen as a knife." We cannot know at this point whether Cathy intends a suicidal illness or whether she simply wants to recover nature and her childhood. She does not overtly wish to die, but neither does she differentiate between death and returning to nature. Death is always a physical place, never transcendent. Linton's lamentations

"can't keep me from my narrow home out yonder, my resting place where I'm bound before spring is over! There it is, not among the Lintons, mind, under the chapel-roof; but in the open air with a head-stone . . . ."
                                    (*WH* 109)

A moment later she tells Linton "my soul will be on that hilltop before you lay hands on me again." It should be her body that will be on the hilltop, not her soul, but the only transport she seeks is into nature. Like the speaker of "The Night-Wind" Cathy is in a situation similar to Lucy's, but because Cathy is a character, not a poetic voice, the Lucy situation is not threatening to the act of writing or of speaking here as it is to Dorothy Wordsworth or to the speaker of "The Night-Wind," and incorporation into nature need no longer be negatively valued.

The novel correspondingly abandons the valorization of a transcendent death that poems like "A Day Dream" propound so effortfully. On the day before Cathy's actual death, months after her formulation of death as a return to nature, Cathy and Nelly conspire to have us think that her death is, to the contrary, to be transcendent. There is "unearthly beauty" in her changed appearance. Her eyes

no longer gave the impression of looking at the objects around her; they appeared always to gaze beyond, and far beyond—you would have said out of this world.
                                    (*WH* 131)

Cathy, frustrated with her efforts to take Heathcliff with her, says,

> "I'm wearying to escape into that glorious world, and to be always there; not seeing it dimly through tears, and yearning for it through the walls of an aching heart; but really with it, and in it. . . . I shall be incomparably beyond and above you all." *(WH* 134)

Though in the earlier scene it was nature to which she wished to escape, now "that glorious world" is clearly some transcendent heaven, even if not the heaven of orthodoxy. But she makes this speech only after Heathcliff has balked at the reunion she seeks, as if to spite him. Nelly's pious interpretation of Cathy's death the reader takes with the usual room for doubt, since it has more to do with Nelly's state of mind than with Cathy:

> No angel in heaven could be more beautiful than she appeared; and I partook of the infinite calm in which she lay. My mind was never in a holier frame than while I gazed on that untroubled image of Divine rest. I instinctively echoed the words she had uttered, a few hours before. "Incomparably beyond, and above us all! Whether still on earth or now in heaven, her spirit is at home with God!" *(WH* 137)

Nelly's orthodoxies if anything incline the reader to doubt that Cathy is "incomparably beyond," and in any case the reader is left to prefer Heathcliff's certainty that she is neither in heaven nor entirely extinguished in the earth.

In the earlier passages, from Cathy's delirium, the purpose of returning to childhood and to nature is to return to Heathcliff, the "earth" alternative in her earlier cosmic comparison between the two suitors. Nature is associated with Heathcliff, and is entirely free of the maternal associations that trouble the poetry. This may be because the novel affords the author a way to step outside poetic traditions. Free to create her own symbolic landscape, she can more easily discard the feminized nature she inherits from the Romantic tradition. Furthermore

it is Cathy, not the poetic self, who sees nature in this new
way. Although the poems' speaker is not to be identified with
Emily Brontë, a fictive character is much further from the
self. Heathcliff's vision of nature is feminized, in a way, but
that is because he sees Cathy there (and everywhere), not a
mythic maternal presence.

> "What does not recall her? I cannot look down to this
> floor, but her features are shaped on the flags! In every
> cloud, in every tree—filling the air at night, and caught
> by glimpses in every object by day, I am surrounded
> with her image!"   (*WH* 255)

Like Cathy during the first part of her illness, Heathcliff is
eager to be out of doors, just before his death, to commune
with her spirit.

Both of them believe in a very physical union or reunion
with one another after death, a merging of identity through
the dissolution of physical entity. Cathy associates this re-
union in death with regression to childhood. Thinking she
sees the lights at Wuthering Heights, she says,

> "Joseph sits up late, doesn't he? He's waiting till I come
> home that he may lock the gate. Well, he'll wait a while
> yet. It's a rough journey, and a sad heart to travel it; and
> we must pass by Gimmerton Kirk, to go that journey!
> We've braved its ghosts often together, and dared each
> other to stand among the graves and ask them to come.
> But Heathcliff, if I dare you now, will you venture? If
> you do, I'll keep you. I'll not lie there by myself; they
> may bury me twelve feet deep, and throw the church
> down over me, but I won't rest till you are with me. I
> never will!"   (*WH* 108)

This memory of ghost-baiting turns real death in the present
into a return to that childhood game, and by making death a
game Cathy metaphorically accomplishes the return to child-
hood that she seeks. That she haunts him after her death ex-
tends the game to Heathcliff's eagerness for death, years later.

That death should fulfill both the desire for reunion and the desire for regression is exactly what Freud shows in *Beyond the Pleasure Principle*, and Leo Bersani finds in *Wuthering Heights* the characteristics of the Freudian death instinct.[24] Bersani's primary interest is in the relation between the death instinct and the notion of self-alienation as proposed in the second section of *Beyond the Pleasure Principle*, but his argument leads back from "being different from ourselves" to the strange nature of the relationship between Heathcliff and Cathy, which appears to represent other aspects of the death instinct as well. The death instinct is a desire for "the restoration of an earlier state of things" (p. 37), and at the end of his discussion Freud shows how the sexual instincts also share this regressive character, by referring to Plato's primordial unity of the sexes in the *Symposium*. Regression thus provides a ground for connecting and perhaps identifying the sexual instincts and the death instinct.

The proper aim of what is manifested as the death instinct is not death, but a restoration of the past. The path backward is blocked by the resistances that maintain the repressions, so that the instinct is redirected toward the future (p. 42). This blockage of the path suggests that the desired and unattainable "earlier state" might be the same as the object of the oedipal desires. Freud is able to make that connection between the death instinct and the sexual instincts because he is considering the matter from the masculine point of view, in which that primordial sexual unity is appropriately modeled on the child's memory of the happiness of earliest infancy. The child's sense of unity with his mother, long since lost, is the goal of these regressive wishes, and the return to "mother earth" is a substitute for the impossible return to the mother herself. This coincides roughly with the darker side of Wordsworth's love for nature.

For a woman, the death instinct should not, by Freud's own account elsewhere, follow the same configuration, because a "restoration of an earlier state of things," if it were a reunion with the mother, would mean something quite different to her than it would to a man. The difficulty with Freud's theory, for a woman author and her female characters, is that the feminine desire to be reunited with the mother is considerably less fervent than it is for males. The significance of Cathy's death instinct is that, at the same time that it is a sexual instinct, it is not the same as a desire for a return to first things. The reunion that Cathy and Heathcliff seek is not primordial, but a reunion with each other as consciously known and loved individuals, however the reader may qualify that love. Both Cathy and Heathcliff are reborn on the occasion of their becoming friends as children, and their identification with each other forms a new origin that replaces parental origins. Their regressive wishes go back only to that second origin, and no further. It is this invented origin that permits the novel to value Cathy's desire for death so highly. Were nature associated with the maternal figure and were Cathy's death wish as Freud describes it, it would have all the ambivalence of the attitude toward death in "I see around me tombstones grey" and elsewhere in the poetry. Dorothy Wordsworth, too, creates a second origin for herself in attributing to her brother parental qualities. This free origin is created in letters; when she turns to poetry and to other self-conscious writing, she is snared by maternal origins. The novel permits Brontë to depart from the poetic traditions that enforce maternal origins, and allows her to remake nature in the form of a chosen beloved.

During her delirium Cathy sees Nelly as a witch who inhabits and commands nature.

> "I see in you, Nelly," she continued, dreamily, "an aged woman—you have grey hair, and bent shoulders. This bed is the fairy cave under Penistone Crag, and you are gathering elf-bolts to hurt our heifers; pretending, while I am near, that they are only locks of wool."
>
> (*WH* 105)

Later, when she half understands that Nelly has been keeping the knowledge of her illness from Linton, she exclaims,

"Nelly is my hidden enemy. You witch! So you do seek elf-bolts to hurt us!" (*WH* 110). In a novel in which biological mothers die off rapidly and in obscurity, Nelly is the only durable maternal figure. She points out that the second Cathy and Hareton are "in a measure, my children" (*WH* 254), but she also helped raise the older generation of which she was a part. Nelly as a "withered hag" in the landscape represents Cathy's fearful image of motherhood, both her neglected maternal origins and the maternal presence buried in nature. The withered hag is also Cathy herself, however, and that recognition renders the image maddening. Directly after the speech about the aged woman Cathy looks in a mirror across the room and recognizes neither herself in it, nor that it is a mirror. Literally self-alienated, her own image "haunts" and terrifies her. Nelly's persuasion that the face is really Cathy's own is even more terrifying than an unknown demon: " 'My-self!' she gasped, 'and the clock is striking twelve! It's true, then; that's dreadful!' " (*WH* 106). What it is that is dreadful, we are not explicitly told. During her delirium, Cathy habitually imagines that she is back at Wuthering Heights as a child, and it is her adult self that frightens her and from which she is alienated. The ghostly face in the mirror might be the image of her own impending motherhood.

This reading may be extravagant, but one of the late poems requires a similar reading. "Stars" (P 184, A 28) is usually classed among those poems in which imaginative or mystical vision is figured as possession by a masculine figure.[25] The night and stars in this poem appear to constitute a figure similar to Rochelle's messenger of hope, or to the God of Visions of "O thy bright eyes," or to the various personifications of dream and vision that the poet apostrophizes elsewhere:

> All through the night, your glorious eyes
> Were gazing down in mine,
> And with a full heart's thankful sighs
> I blessed that watch divine!

The speaker "revelled in my changeful dreams" while

> Thought followed thought—star followed star
> Through boundless regions on,
> While one sweet influence, near and far,
> Thrilled through and proved us one.

The situation is somewhat different from that of the other poems of masculine possession, because in addition to the stars, there is another possessive figure, the sun, who is associated with violent masculinity: "Blood-red he rose, and arrow-straight / His fierce beams struck my brow." The poem can be read as an allegory of the competition, in the speaker's mind, between two modes of poetry and life.[26] To sketch briefly the poem's plot, the speaker is lamenting the night's departure and the intrusion of the dazzling sun. Through closed eyes she sees him blaze "And bathe in gold the misty dale," eradicating the last hiding places of sublimity. The speaker's only action in the poem is a futile gesture of choice:

> I turned me to the pillow then
> To call back Night, and see
> Your worlds of solemn light, again
> Throb with my heart and me!

Although the day's demands are inexorable, the poem ends with the speaker's impassioned plea to the stars to return and hide her from the arriving day.

The difficulty with assimilating the night and stars to other masculine figures of imaginative possession is that nowhere is it indicated that they are masculine. Addressing the stars, the speaker has no recourse to a pronoun, and those attributes of the stars that might indicate gender are feminine and maternal as often as they are masculine.

> I was at peace, and drank your beams
> As they were life to me.

These lines could refer as well to a recovery of infant relations with the mother, as to heterosexual romance, and the metaphor of nursing affects the surrounding metaphors. "Your glorious eyes" keep watch over the speaker, and at the poem's close it is protection she seeks. The contrast in the poem is not between two masculine figures so much as it is between a rich, almost pre-lapsarian undifferentiated sexuality and violently overt sexual opposition:

> Blood-red he rose, and arrow-straight
> His fierce beams struck my brow:
> The soul of Nature sprang elate,
> But mine sank sad and low!

The sun's presence is painful because of his fierce beams and scorching fire, but even more because of the response he evokes in nature. Nature is not explicitly feminine here but, compared to the speaker's refusal to respond, it is the proper mate for this phallic sun. The best and most original lines in the poem are inspired not by the speaker's beloved stars, but by a hallucinatory and horrific nature:

> It would not do—the pillow glowed
> And glowed both roof and floor,
> And birds sang loudly in the wood,
> And fresh winds shook the door.
>
> The curtains waved, the wakened flies
> Were murmuring round my room,
> Imprisoned there, till I should rise
> And give them leave to roam.

Nature as a feminine figure so readily and so efficaciously empowered by a masculine one is more threatening than the sun himself.

This image of nature should not of itself threaten the speaker's self-image, but nature gives the speaker an unfavorable image of herself as jailor, through wakening those flies that are "Imprisoned there, till I should rise / And give them leave to roam." Usually nature is the jailor. In "I see around me tombstones grey" maternal nature is a hypocritical jailor who uses love to prevent the speaker from passing natural limits. The prison is the commonest image for the mortal condition, as when in "Silent is the House" the soul is imprisoned in the body or in natural life. Nature can also be a liberator, but to be identified with nature in her character of jailor is to see oneself not as a poet but as the antagonist of poetry. Nature as jailor definitively resists propriation by human act or language, by turning propriation back on humanity. It is that final otherness that the human poet cannot and should not try to grasp, like the natural violence that Dorothy Wordsworth depicts in her *Journal of a Tour on the Continent*. To be identified with beneficent nature, as Dorothy is by Wordsworth in "Tintern Abbey" and *The Prelude*, is sufficiently problematic to put a stop to her writing, since this identification entails a dissolution of self in deference to nature's self. To be identified with threatening nature, as Brontë is on the verge of becoming here, would bring about an even greater dissolution of self. When Dorothy is identified with nature, she is still within the borders of humanity. To become identified with this aspect of nature that is entirely resistant to humanization would be to cut off all human ties. Cathy and Heathcliff desire to make just such a transference of self to other but they do so only by dying, a possibility appropriate only for characters within a framing fiction.

That the novel succeeds in areas where the poetry breaks down is due, in part, to the novel's abandoning the traditional identification of nature as feminine or maternal, thus avoiding some of the risks encountered in writing poetry. The novel makes use of a strategy similar to that which Dorothy uses briefly in "Irregular Verses" ("To Julia Marshall—A Fragment") but does not sustain. In that poem, she frees nature of its problematic maternal configuration by introducing a human mother whom she has intelligible reasons to blame. This disassociation allows the poet to cease depicting nature as the ominous shroud surrounding human habitation in related poems (see above, pp. 99-100). In *Wuthering Heights*, Brontë does not entirely forget nature's ominous maternal configuration, but she presents it as a function of madness. As the witch of Penistone crags, Nelly is only a vestigial and distorted image of Mother Nature. Like repressed material that surfaces in a dream, the image vanishes after a brief appearance, clearly a figment of Cathy's fevered brain and not adopted by the rest of the novel.

Excluding from the novel the poetic tradition of maternal nature permits the novel to abandon the poems' investment in transcendence after death that defaces the authenticity of many of the poems. The poems' unconvincing belief in transcendence is made necessary because the image of maternal nature makes natural death horrific. In the novel, free from maternal characterization, the earth need hold no particular terrors. It ceases to threaten the author's powers because nothing about it is predetermined, and she is free to characterize it as she chooses. It holds no thematic terrors for Cathy and Heathcliff because they are free to identify it with each other and with a restoration of their childhood. Instead of an investment of belief in transcendence after death, images of continuance in the novel are all invested in heterosexual love, regardless of how the reader judges the specifics of Cathy and Heathcliff's relationship. Freed from the poems' distorted and distorting fixation on the extremes of hyperbolic transcendence and tellurian darkness, the novel locates in Cathy and Heathcliff a compromise that is both conducive to writing and humanly convincing.

CHAPTER IV

Emily Dickinson

Dickinson thought of herself not just as a poet but as a woman poet. The first and most obvious evidence for this statement is that she searched for models among the famous women writers of her day, admiring George Eliot, the Brontës, and Elizabeth Barrett Browning in particular. This interest was more personal or biographical than it was literary, but this indicates no disparagement, since her poetry was scarcely influenced by literary men, either.[1] In her letters she mourns the deaths of these great women as vehemently as she admires their work. She inquired insistently after the prospects for a biography of George Eliot in an exchange of letters with the Boston publisher Thomas Niles in April 1882. In March 1883 Niles sent her Mathilda Blind's *Life of George Eliot*, and in 1885 she received the first volume of Cross's *Life* from her literary correspondent Thomas Wentworth Higginson. After reading Blind's biography she commented, "A Doom of Fruit without the Bloom, like the Niger Fig," which echoes an earlier comment, made shortly after Eliot's death, indicating a range of biographical affinities between the two women:

> Now, *my* George Eliot. The gift of belief which her greatness denied her, I trust she receives in the childhood of the kingdom of heaven. As childhood is earth's confiding time, perhaps having no childhood, she lost her way to the early trust, and no later came.[2]

She possessed portraits of Mrs. Browning and was even sent a picture of her grave, testifying to her friend's knowledge of

her interest. She found A. Mary F. Robinson's biography of
Emily Brontë "more electric far than anything since 'Jane
Eyre' " (*L*, III, 775). Again alluding not to Brontë's own
work but to what was written about her—Charlotte Brontë's
1850 Biographical Notice—Dickinson refers to Brontë as a
person more than as a writer in the following comparison
with her friend Mrs. Holland: she was

> humbled with wonder at your self-forgetting, . . . Re-
> minded again of gigantic Emily Brontë, of whom her
> Charlotte said "Full of ruth for others, on herself she had
> no mercy."   (*L*, III, 721)

In these comments she extends her sympathies to these
women as suffering human beings, not as women, but she
also considers them as women, and is aware of special difficul-
ties that were perhaps similar to hers.

> That Mrs. Browning fainted, we need not read *Aurora
> Leigh* to know, when she lived with her English aunt;
> and George Sand "must make no noise in her grand-
> mother's bedroom." Poor children! Women, now,
> queens, now!   (*L*, II, 376)

She also uses womanhood specifically as a literary classifica-
tion. In 1871 she wrote to Higginson, "Mrs Hunt's Poems are
stronger than any written by Women since Mrs—Browning,
with the exception of Mrs Lewes" (*L*, II, 491). She must be
making a special point in referring to George Eliot as Mrs.
Lewes and in using a dash to emphasize Elizabeth Barrett's
marriage, but it is unclear whether this is a private reference to
her metaphor of wife and bride for poetic power, or whether
she is thinking of the difference marriage might make to a
woman writer. In 1870 she held a curious exchange with Hig-
ginson about another married woman poet.

> You told me of Mrs Lowell's Poems.
>   Would you tell me where I could find them or are they
> not for sight?   (*L*, II, 480)

Maria White Lowell's poems were published in 1855, but Higginson had apparently been referring to her poems in a metaphoric sense, because in her next letter Dickinson says

> You told me Mrs Lowell was Mr Lowell's "inspira-
> tion" What is inspiration?
>   (*L*, II, 481)

Dickinson is incensed that, when she has a chance to read a woman's poetry, or, just as good, to learn of another woman poet as private as herself, Higginson, a self-proclaimed champion of women's rights, asks her to consider the poetess in her more acceptably feminine role as her husband's muse.

That Dickinson can compare reading Emily Brontë's life with reading *Jane Eyre* indicates that she groups real and fictive biographies under the category of exemplary lives. When she turns from the lives to the works of these women writers, it is usually without reference to gender. Her comments on Eliot and Emily Brontë suggest affinities between their work and aspects of her own work that seem to have nothing to do with femininity.[3] She characterizes Eliot as "she who Experienced Eternity in Time" (*L*, III, 689).

> "What do I think of *Middlemarch*?" What do I think of glory – except that in a few instances this "mortal has already put on immortality."
> George Eliot is one. The mysteries of human nature surpass the "mysteries of redemption," for the infinite we only suppose, while we see the finite.
>   (*L*, II, 506)

Dickinson is perhaps expressing her surprise and delight that a novel can do what she expects of poetry; in any case it is Eliot's encompassing mind that she is considering, and not "Mrs Lewes." Several very late letters quote one "marvelous" stanza from Brontë's "No coward soul is mine," each time subsuming it to the expression of her own sentiment (*L*, III, 802-803, 844, 848). One of these quotations includes an illuminating misinterpretation. Writing in 1883 of the "sorrow of so many years" brought by the deaths of so many beloved friends and relatives, she says "As Emily Bronte to her Maker, I write to my Lost 'Every Existence would exist in thee –' " (*L*, III, 802-803). Dickinson must have known that Brontë was referring not to "her Maker" but to a more personally defined deity, a conception much closer to Dickinson's own than Dickinson seems willing to acknowledge. She treats Brontë the poet as a rival and distances her, while at the same moment welcoming an affinity on the personal level.

Just as Dickinson compartmentalized her own interest in women writers, studies of her have tended to consider her femininity at the level of biography and to leave her femininity out of critical readings of her poems. Even though she seems to have been more openly conscious than Dorothy Wordsworth or Emily Brontë about the difficulties of being a woman and a poet, any treatment of her specifically as a woman poet runs the risk of being either confining or tangential, because she has too large and brilliant a body of poetry to be adequately interpreted from any single perspective.[4] However, this chapter will argue that Dickinson derives her unique power from her particular way of understanding her femininity, and that her work is as complex and profuse as it is, at least in part, because she is able to put behind her problems of identity that make Dorothy and Brontë linger over the same themes and issues in poem after poem. For example, in the letter discussed above in which she quotes from Brontë, she telescopes Brontë's long and arduous struggle to center an external poetic power within herself, and although this telescoping may be unfair, it suggests what Dickinson views as a crucial difference between Brontë's concept of language and her own: for Brontë linguistic power is a single entity, which may or may not be possessed, but Dickinson goes on in the rest of the letter to sketch obliquely her concept of language's doubleness. The most recent and stunning of those deaths, that of her eight-year-old nephew Gilbert, has broken language into its components. Naming is difficult and self-conscious:

Sweet Sister.
Was that what I used to call you?

.   .   .   .

The Physician says I have "Nervous prostration."
Possibly I have – I do not know the Names of Sickness.

Her disease is unnameable because it is a disease of referents
lost through the recent deaths. Gilbert's last words—" 'Open
the Door, open the Door, they are waiting for me' "—have
set her thinking about what is for her an ultimately missing
referent, where just previously she has supplied one for
Brontë. "*Who* were waiting for him, all we possess we would
give to know. . . . All this and more, though *is* there more?
More than Love and Death? Then tell me it's name!" She
splits language to find genuine mysteries, and she finds in lan-
guage's doubleness, paradoxically, a way around the hierar-
chizing dualism that impedes Dorothy Wordsworth and
Brontë.

IN A LETTER to her friend Abiah Root written when she was
nineteen, Dickinson tells an extravagant and amusing story
about a cold, and then, in a gesture that distinguishes artist
from anecdotist, she exposes her fictive strategy:

> Now my dear friend, let me tell you that these last
> thoughts are fictions – vain imaginations to lead astray
> foolish young women. They are flowers of speech, they
> both *make*, and *tell* deliberate falsehoods, avoid them as
> the snake, and turn aside as from the *Bottle* snake, and I
> dont *think* you will be harmed.
>
> (*L*, I, 88; 29 Jan. 1850)

Although this letter dates from well before Dickinson's first
serious poetry, such self-consciousness establishes this and re-
lated passages as the proper place to begin an investigation of
her sense of identity as a writer and as a woman. The writer
here is logically, though never overtly, associated with the
snake, since she is the inventor of the "vain imaginations,"

and in a postscript she refers to her story about the cold as "mistakes" and "sin." Her interlocutor, so innocent that she must be told that the story is a fiction, plays Eve to Dickinson's Satan. At the end of the passage the writer renounces her guise as a fiction-maker and turns abruptly to what she announces to be her sincerer feelings. Searching for a better topic she says, "Oh dear I dont know *what* it is! Love for the absent dont *sound* like it, but try it, and see how it goes." She signs the letter "Your very sincere, and *wicked* friend," as if to demarcate, retrospectively, two separable styles of address and of self.

These are sins in jest, of course, but the reader is provoked to take this language seriously because of the context in which it occurs. In a letter to her friend and former teacher Jane Humphrey, written only six days earlier, she uses the same language to describe her own life as genuinely wicked. Charitable works would provide an opportunity "for turning my back to this very sinful, and wicked world. Somehow or other I incline to other things – and Satan covers them up with flowers, and I reach out to pick them" (*L*, I, 82; 23 Jan. 1850). The letter to Abiah simply transfers the metaphor of flowers and falsehood to a less serious tenor. The origin of this fatal view of herself is her failure to become converted to the evangelical Christianity that most of her friends were then embracing. She herself views it as a failure: in the sad discussions of religion of this period and earlier she never expresses a doubt that Christianity has a patent on goodness and that in not accepting Christ it is she who is in the wrong.[5] In 1846 she had, from her report, experienced a temporary conversion, and in describing its aftermath she uses the unequivocal language of true and false: "I had rambled too far to return & ever since my heart has been growing harder & more distant from the truth" (*L*, I, 31; 28 March 1846). If truth is a place, then her dislocation from it repeats the Fall:

> I think of the perfect happiness I experienced while I felt I
> was an heir of heaven as of a delightful dream, out of

which the Evil one bid me wake & again return to the
world & its pleasures. Would that I had not listened to his
winning words! . . . I determined to devote my whole life
to [God's] service & desired that all might taste of the
stream of living water from which I cooled my thirst.
But the world allured me & in an unguarded moment I
listened to her syren voice.   (*L*, I, 30)

Her transfer of religious metaphor to fiction-making later
on is not fortuitous. Religious and literary concerns converge
at the idea of truth. In the passage above, both orthodoxy and
her fall are portrayed as fictive: one was a delightful dream,
the other the product of winning words and a siren voice. Her
insistence in these religious passages that there is such a thing
as the truth may be a defense against her growing knowledge
that there is no absolute truth or literal meaning. The Bible is
said to be a true text, yet her own experience shows her how
easily figurative language can deceive, and the Bible is figura-
tive. That the satanic storyteller in the letter about the cold is
a guise does not necessarily make the contrasting sincerity
genuine. If she can speak in one invented style, all forms of
address may be fictive. When she writes to her more religious
friends, her apparently genuine self-depreciation may be as
fictive as the most extravagant of her announced fantasies.
She is writing to please her readers, and she may also be con-
vinced of her own sincerity, writing to please herself as well.
But she depicts such a worldly sinner and such a radical fall
that it is hard to believe that she did not see, or even intend,
the melodrama. The modern reader prefers to think that she
saw the religious fervour of her day as a delusion, and in ret-
rospect it is easy to doubt that she would ever have considered
entrusting her mental faculties to the keeping of her saviour.
But a parodic element is coextensive with whatever sincere re-
ligious sorrow she expresses; and to mean two opposing
things at the same time would very likely debase the writer's
faith in the possibility of a literal truth, whether secular or
Christian.

A few months prior to the letter in which she invokes the language of the Fall, she jokingly identifies herself with Eve on the grounds that there is no account of her death in the Bible, and the Bible must be taken at its word. "I have lately come to the conclusion that I am Eve, alias Mrs. Adam. You know there is no account of her death in the Bible, and why am I not Eve?" (*L*, I, 24; 12 Jan. 1846). This is the kind of remark that is entirely parodic and entirely serious at once. If the Bible is the source of the truth, then she is indeed Eve, because she has picked Satan's flowers and fallen from an Eden of perfect belief. In the letter about the cold she transforms herself from tempted into tempter. There, Abiah is an innocent Eve, and Dickinson as the writer of fictions is implicitly identified as the tempter. In the letter to Jane Humphrey of the same week, excerpted above, in which the writer pictures herself as led astray by Satan, she also identifies herself as the tempter: "you are out of the way of temptation – and out of the way of the tempter – I did'nt mean to make you wicked – but I was – and am – and shall be – and I was with you so much that I could'nt help contaminate" (*L*, I, 83). Again there is a note of parody, even though the tone of the whole letter is sincerely pained: "I was - and am - and shall be" makes her wickedness as immutable as God's divinity. It disturbs her to find that the fictions she delights in are indistinguishable from the words of the "Evil one," in that she is the speaker of both, and they are equidistant from the truth. Implicitly her own fanciful words led her astray: she is self-tempted. The difference between Eve and Satan is enormous, but that she moves between the two as metaphors for herself reminds the reader that Eve became Satan's accomplice and is a tempter herself—both tempted and tempter.

Later in the same letter she speaks of her angry impatience to see Jane and again condemns herself. "Is it wicked to talk so Jane – what *can* I say that isn't? Out of a wicked heart cometh wicked words." Though hating the intervening time may be reprehensible, her friendship, the source of that animosity, is not. The wickedness may refer instead to the vivid metaphor with which she describes her impatience, just previously: "Eight weeks with their bony fingers still poking me away – how I *hate* them – and would love to do them harm! Is it wicked to talk so . . ." (*L*, I, 83). The danger of fictions, here or in the story about the cold, is that they tempt her to say things that she does not literally mean, but which will be read literally by others. Such talk is "wicked" only if those vividly personified weeks are really animate, but a vocabulary of hate leaves corrupting traces in the minds of writer and reader. Furthermore, the use of metaphor may itself be wicked, since orthodoxy might call fiction a falsehood.[6]

It must have made a considerable difference to one's sense of self to have been a girl instead of a boy growing up in a context in which Biblical history was the dominant metaphorical framework in which human activity was viewed. Even if Dickinson's Puritan heritage did not plentifully reinforce the cultural prejudice that, if we are all sinners, women are a little more sinful than men, to read Genesis (and Milton) and see oneself in Eve rather than in Adam would lead to an entirely different sense of self in relation to language. Emerson's attack on orthodoxy, if that might have furnished the young Dickinson with support for her own independent views, only strengthens the identification of poetic language with a masculine tradition. By insisting on the proximity between poetic speech and the divine Word in "The Poet," Emerson makes poetry as masculine a province as does Coleridge with his inheritance of the "infinite I AM," despite other differences in their theories of poetry. Emerson invokes the tradition that Adam was the first and best speaker when he says that the poet is "the Namer or Language-maker," who gives to every thing "its own name and not another's . . . . The poets made all the words."[7] Dorothy Wordsworth may have been discouraged from writing poetry in part by the appropriation of poetic language by those who can consider themselves the inheritors of a masculine divinity. However unlike the God of orthodoxy Emerson's powers of divinity may be, he retains the masculinity of the verbal tradition.

Eve's words are secondary and stray from the truth. Because she learns Adam's language rather than inventing it with him (Adam having named the living creatures before Eve's creation), she can learn another as well, and she learns Satan's. Satan teaches her to doubt the literal truth of the language that God and Adam share, and to interpret and demystify God's prohibition about the tree of the knowledge of good and evil. Wrong though she is to take the fruit, she proves God's words to be not literally true, because it is not, in fact, the case that "in the day that thou eatest thereof thou shalt surely die." Satan's words are no less accurate than God's: her eyes are opened, as he promises, and she learns good and evil. It is Eve's discovery that both God and Satan are fictive speakers, and that no discourse is literally true. Adam becomes the traditional symbol for literal language in which words are synonymous with meaning, but Eve is the first to question that synonymity, the first critic, the mother of irony. It is in this sense that she is similar to Satan, and in making tempter and tempted synonymous Dickinson is recognizing this aspect of her inheritance from Eve. When she talks about wickedness, then, in the context of fiction or of religion, what she fears is not the conventional notion of sin, but rather the figurativeness of language that allows even the most sincere speech to be a fiction among other fictions.

When male Romantic writers identify themselves with Satan it is in order to annex the energy of his revolt against a bland orthodoxy. In *Paradise Lost*, by the time Satan is instructing Eve in the ways of deceptive speech nothing admirable remains, but it is this aspect of Satan's history that Dickinson invokes, an entirely different paradigm from that provided by his earlier career.

An enormous change takes place in Dickinson's tone concerning tempters between the two letters of January 1850 and a letter of April of the same year. Writing again to Jane Humphrey, she extols, as she has before, the "marvellous change" that belief brings to those around her. But when she turns to her own doings, she suggests for the first time that she may be as justified as the orthodox believers. "I have dared to do strange things – bold things, and have asked no advice from any – I have heeded beautiful tempters, yet do not think I am wrong" (*L*, I, 95; 3 Apr. 1850). Whatever her belief is, she views it as a center of truth rather than as a deviation. Or rather she uses the metaphor of religious belief without any worry that she is infecting orthodoxy by pairing it with "tempters." "I hope belief is not wicked, and assurance, and perfect trust – . . . I hope human nature has truth in it – Oh I pray it may not deceive – confide – cherish, have a great faith in . . . ."

Between January and April, Dickinson wrote her first (extant) poem—a valentine addressed to a friend, dated March 4—and a prose valentine published in the Amherst College paper, *The Indicator*, in February.[8] The prose valentine's exuberant effect comes from its deliberate word consciousness. It revels in language, using many words where one would suffice, as if the lethal fictiveness of language had become a matter of delight. "Sir, I desire an interview . . . . And not to *see* merely, but a chat, sir, or a tete-a-tete, a confab, a mingling of opposite minds is what I propose to have" (*L*, I, 92). Those "beautiful tempters" might be words themselves, like Whitman's "dumb, beautiful ministers," so that her use of the word "tempter" might itself be the first evidence of her own "marvellous change:" one word with two happily opposite meanings. The extensiveness of her language, which both multiplies language and elevates the speaker into "Judith the heroine of the Apocrypha, and you the orator of Ephesus," is figurative speech.

> That's what they call a metaphor in our country. Don't be afraid of it, sir, it won't bite. If it was my *Carlo* now! The Dog is the noblest work of Art, sir. I may safely say the noblest – his mistress's rights he doth defend – although it bring him to his end – although to death it doth him send!

This kind of fanciful language is exactly that which she told Abiah jokingly to "avoid . . . as the snake;" the directive not to fear its bite might be better directed at herself than at the "sir." The passage in effect frees her, by parodying it, from the connection she had created between falsehood in language and real "wickedness." The vehicle of this parody is the contrast between harmless language and the bite of a real dog, but the last sentence in the passage renders the dog fictive, too. Because the dog dissolves into a nursery rhyme, there is no difference, at the level of the letter, between a metaphoric bite and a "real" one. This glimpse of the nonreferentiality of language has a momentary liberating effect, regardless of whether or not she would subscribe to the theories of deconstructive criticism. The biblical names she adopts remind the reader that her identification with Eve, earlier, both in play and in earnest, depended on a literal reading of the Bible. If orthodoxy depends on literal reading, then this is a declaration of freedom from orthodoxy, and from her notion that she must define herself as an exile from orthodoxy, either as the fallen Eve, as Satan, or as both.

The virtue of this provisional freedom from referentiality is that it enables her to use metaphoric language without anxiety. In the letter about the cold, fictions were dangerous only figuratively. Fictions, momentarily personified, tell falsehoods but are not synonymous with them, and she advises Abiah to avoid fictions "as the snake." In the April letter she uses metaphoric language to describe her special "truth," that belief that has resulted from heeding "beautiful tempters," showing how far she has advanced from her belief that metaphor and truth were incompatible:

> What do you weave from all these threads, for I know you hav'nt been idle the while I've been speaking to you, bring it nearer the window, and I will see, it's all wrong unless it has one gold thread in it, a long, big shining fibre which hides the others – and which will fade away into Heaven while you hold it, and from there come back to me   (*L*, I, 95)

Never before has she found an explicit metaphor to be adequate for the expression of heartfelt concerns. She emphasizes its status as metaphor by privileging the signifier, asking her reader to believe that the golden fibre is a tangible and visible object as well as a verbal figure. At the same time, the image she chooses is a neat transformation of her earlier metaphor for metaphor. The "long, big shining fibre" must be art's redeemed version of the snake, serpentine but crafted and beautiful, issuing from and returning to the artist rather than invading her integrity.[9]

The snakes in the letter about the cold belong to a sequence of images of the Fall, and take their significance from this association with wickedness and with questioning literal truth. An equally traditional interpretation would be to read them as phallic images, related to but distinct from Satanic imagery. As a personal expression, the passage may or may not be about sexual fears, but what is important is that the text engages the idea of masculinity as a literary term.[10] That Dickinson combines these two sets of significations is already an interpretive gesture. For wickedness and temptation to be characterized as masculine presents an alternative to or defense against the identification of Eve with Satan that also lurks in the passage. Instead of reading her own words as vain falsehoods, as when she says, "Out of a wicked heart cometh wicked words," identifying falsehood with masculinity would allow her to see it as alien and therefore not a reflection on herself. Her flights of fancy would be proper extravagances: moments when she borrows a language not her own. (This would hardly be a helpful paradigm for her poetic vocation, and is not long retained.)

At the same time that she identifies lies as masculine, she also sees religious orthodoxy as masculine. In the early letters about religion she limits herself to a choice between her saviour and "the world," but each alternative is equally alien to her own identity, if she characterizes them both as masculine. For the girls in her adolescent circle, "loving Christ" clearly had romantic overtones. Religion was the one permissible romance, and provided a sanctioned outlet for feelings otherwise suppressed. She loses female friends to Christ as she

later loses them to husbands. Wishing she could console Jane
Humphrey for the loss of her father she says, "She has the
'Great Spirit' tho', and perhaps, she does'nt need me" (*L*, I,
100). A long passage about marriage in a letter to Sue Gilbert,
the future wife of Dickinson's brother Austin, begins by
using marriage as a metaphor for religion and turns impercep-
tibly to its major subject by transforming the vehicle into a
new tenor. Walking with Sue's sister Mattie, we "wished for
you, and Heaven. You did not come, Darling, but a bit of
Heaven did, or so it *seemed* to us, as we walked side by side
and wondered if that great blessedness which may be our's
sometime, is granted now, to some" (*L*, I, 209; early June
1852). This blessedness, so far, seems to refer to a religious
state of grace, but the passage continues, without a break:

> Those unions, my dear Susie, by which two lives are one,
> this sweet and strange adoption wherein we can but look,
> and are not yet admitted, how it can fill the heart, and
> make it gang wildly beating, how it will take *us* one day,
> and make us all it's own, and we shall not run away from
> it, but lie still and be happy!

By the end of the sentence it is clear that the subject is mar-
riage, but it is impossible to say where the transition occurs.
"It" renders all mysteries equivalent. The next paragraph is
explicitly about marriage, but it uses language drawn from
orthodoxy. The terms of secular romance and marriage in-
clude a sacrifice of autonomy, as does, by analogy, "loving
Christ:"

> I was almost inclined to yeild to the claims of He who is
> greater than I. . . . I hope the golden opportunity is not
> far hence when my heart will willingly yield itself to
> Christ, . . .

> I know that I ought now to give myself away to God &
> spend the springtime of life in his service . . . .
>
> (*L*, I, 28, 31)

This sacrifice of autonomy goes far to explain Dickinson's resistance both to marriage and to orthodox religion.

Dickinson's way of characterizing many external things as masculine—truth and falsehood, the world and its renunciation—illustrates a mind defining its own interior operations as feminine. It is also typical of a rhetorical pattern, prevalent throughout her work and not just as this early period, of rendering equivalencies from polarities. Her freedom from literal meaning originates in her sense of femininity, from her identification with Eve, and it permits her a special use of irony to draw disparate meanings from a single term. This pattern is not the same as a satanic equivalency of good and evil, even though Eve and the Tempter are closely related. If it verges on the satanic, it is only because Dickinson pursues language's own logic to that point. It is a question more of tonal than of moral values, and the manipulation of tone readily permits such divergent readings. One case in point is the way in which an apparently transparent poem invites two mutually exclusive readings. Published anonymously in 1878, Dickinson's "Success is counted sweetest" (P 67) was taken to be the work of Emerson.[11] Slipped in to the volume of poetry Emerson published in 1876, or read in the context of the later essays, it might well be taken as a straightforward account of a pessimistic view of the doctrine of compensation. Read as early Dickinson, the poem is surely a bitter parody both of orthodox thinking and of the principle of compensation that the Emersonian reading would endorse.

> Not one of all the purple Host
> Who took the Flag today
> Can tell the definition
> So clear of Victory
>
> As he defeated – dying –
> On whose forbidden ear
> The distant strains of triumph
> Burst agonized and clear!

By compensation Emerson means a tendency in nature for all oppositions to balance out: losses are compensated for here on earth, not in heaven. In this context, the soldier is compensated for his dying by a gain in understanding. But Dickinson may be undermining the poem's ostensible moral as she utters it: "forbidden ear" suggests not just that the soldier is dying as he hears the "distant strains of triumph" but rather that he cannot hear them at all and that with his death he has purchased nothing whatsoever. The poem suggests that where Emerson would find a balance of price and purchase, Dickinson finds an equivalence of valuelessness. That the attribution of this poem could even today be mistaken is a measure of one of the challenges of reading Dickinson: it is often very difficult to know when she is being ironic and when we are to take her at her word, and often she seems to have contrived this difficulty. To speak of opposing readings of the same poem is in itself risky with Dickinson, because the poems seldom permit such comforting distinctions. But the difference between these two readings is characteristic of Dickinson's way of treating oppositeness. The poem makes its critique of an idea about oppositions, compensation, by entertaining two irreconcilable readings. It is also characteristic of a major disagreement between Dickinson and Emerson: Emerson begins with polarities and works toward reconciling them, but Dickinson works toward undermining the whole concept of oppositeness.

The language Dickinson uses to describe her idea of heaven is often the same as the language she uses to satirize the heaven of orthodoxy, so that there is only a difference of tone between heaven and one version of hell.

> "Heaven" – is what I cannot reach!
> The Apple on the Tree –
> Provided it do hopeless – hang –
> That – "Heaven" is – to Me!
>
> (P 239)

However, "the unknown is the largest need of the intellect."
The vanishing and the elusive are genuine objects of faith and
desire, as in "A Light exists in Spring" (P 812). This rare light
"passes and we stay,"

> A quality of loss
> Affecting our Content
> As Trade had suddenly encroached
> Upon a Sacrament.

If we suddenly recall that communion is only a transaction,
belief vanishes; the vanishing light is an image of faith. But
the same light is found in the nasty orthodoxy of the last
stanza of poem 239: "Her teazing Purples – Afternoons – / The
credulous – decoy –." The second stanza includes "The in-
terdicted Land –" among examples of teasing heavens. This is
one of several references to Jehovah's cruelty in letting Moses
see but not enter Canaan. It is not Canaan itself as an image of
desirability that she satirizes, but God's method of consecra-
tion, inflating the value of Canaan for others by depriving
Moses, making unattainability a pure and empty status sym-
bol.

"Success is counted sweetest" is one of many poems, early
and late, that take up the theme of the relativity of knowledge,
of emotion, or of achievement. These poems have largely
been taken as straightforward statements of her belief, as is
also true of a similar group of poems by Brontë (see above,
p. 141).[12] Joy is apparently unknown without the experience
of pain, and only what is inaccessible is attractive.

> Water, is taught by thirst.
> Land – by the Oceans passed.
> Transport – by throe –
> Peace by it's battles told –
> Love, by Memorial Mold –
> Birds, by the Snow.

(P 135)

She rarely punctuates with periods, and her use of them here is the first signal of irony, as their authority and finality suggest dogmatism. The problem in the poem is that the innocent speaker seems not to know the qualitative differences among the six pairs. The first and last refer to simple and remediable absences: thirst teaches the value of water, winter teaches us to miss the birds. But to group with these innocuous forms of relativism "Transport – by throe –" is overtly bitter. Though the speaker seems to miss its power, the bland context makes the line stand out for the reader: it is not just different, but nonsensical, too.

Our appreciation of the bitterness of the line depends on our seeing its contrast to the other lines' variations on the same structure. The speaker who believes in the instructional value of relativity can do so only through deafness to the poem's tonal contrast, but we can criticize the poem's ethic of relativity only by relying on such a principle in reading the poem's language.

Two poems overtly consider the idea of oppositeness by name. [13] "The Zeroes – taught us – Phosphorus" is, like poem 135, organized on an instructional principle, but the instruction is faulty. Not only are mild and bitter mixed indiscriminately, as if for camouflage, but some of the pairs of oppositions are simply not opposite. The speaker's critical faculties may be oppressed by orthodoxy.

> The Zeroes – taught us – Phosphorus –
> We learned to like the Fire
> By playing Glaciers – when a Boy –
> And Tinder – guessed – by power
> Of Opposite – to balance Odd –
> If White – a Red – must be!
> Paralysis – our Primer – dumb –
> Unto Vitality!
>
> (P 689)

The exclamation marks raise a facade of false assertiveness, in the manner of the periods in poem 135. "When a Boy" denotes a time prior to cultural or linguistic differentiation, just as, in a different context ("A narrow Fellow in the Grass," P 986), the same expression denotes innocence of sexual difference. Zeroes and phosphorus, like red and white, are as opposite to him as are glacier and fire. We learn that there is no innate sense of relativity, because it must be acquired, and it can be acquired faultily. Because the poem mixes faulty and true oppositions, the final one, for which the others are a preparation, is undecidable. We may learn to value vitality by experiencing paralysis, but as in "Success is counted sweetest" that is a final frustration, not an education, and it invites an ironic reading. Or if paralysis refers to the constrictions of life on earth and vitality to a freer life after death, the logic is that of an oppressive orthodoxy that endorses suffering by reversing the meanings of life and death. Either way, the poem invites both ironic and non-ironic readings, and having established that the simple reversal of meaning is central to orthodox rhetoric, the poet allows orthodoxy's own principles to undermine themselves.

" 'Tis Opposites – entice" considers the satanic deception, corollary to this orthodox belief in deferred rewards, that whatever the believer lacks must be the good. Opposites may entice but it is because they are constructed to do so; the valuation conferred by lack is a distortion.

> 'Tis Opposites – entice –
> Deformed Men – ponder Grace –
> Bright fires – the Blanketless –
> The Lost – Day's face –
>
> The Blind – esteem it be
> Enough Estate – to see –
> The Captive – strangles new –
> For deeming – Beggars – play –
>
> (P 355)

The final form of these overvaluations is projection:

> To lack – enamor Thee –
> Tho' the Divinity –

> Be only
> Me –

Assuming that "Thee" has all that "Me" lacks is not far from saying that what this divine interlocutor has is what the self has too but cannot recognize. Divinity is only as powerful as the mind of its imaginer.

Most of the poems that consider the idea of opposites or of relativity admit of ironic readings, but Dickinson's use of irony is itself involved in what she criticizes. Saying one thing in order to mean its opposite is the rhetorical analogue of what she criticizes. Her ironies are so fine that it is quite hard to say if she is in earnest or ironic, and several poems do in fact celebrate what she elsewhere mocks, or, like poem 355, combine sincerity with irony. She mocks the very structure of language by writing ironically about irony. Read without irony, these poems would celebrate antithesis as the fundamental of knowledge or desire, as when transport is known by pain. Taken ironically they decry that definition of knowledge. But to take them ironically the reader must use a principle of antithesis; to decry antithesis the reader must concede antithesis. Or, in the first case, to read these as celebrations of antithesis requires that the reader become—or be, innocently—deaf to antithesis.

Poem 1036 is one of many poems about deferment whose ostensible theme is that unattainability confers value, and proximity or achievement is disappointing.[14]

> Satisfaction – is the Agent
> Of Satiety –
> Want – a quiet Comissary
> For Infinity.

This stanza plays on the idea that one polarity demands or requires the other, not on the instructional model of poems 67, 135, and 689, but in terms of an economy of feeling. Satisfaction and satiety, used here as opposites, come from the same root, *satis* or enough. That an affective opposition ought to be or once was an identity is a self-critique of the cultural shaping of language, and threatens the poem with collapse by undermining the validity of its apparently valorized oppositions, such as want and infinity. Presenting want and infinity as a pair of opposites renders infinity a plenitude, but etymologically infinity is as negative a concept as want. The second verse complements the thought of the first by apparently opposing possession and joy:

> To possess, is past the instant
> We achieve the Joy –

All the oppositions in this poem are slightly askew. The achievement of joy may precede possession, but nothing except traditional expectation precludes joy from continuing into possession. Achieve and possess are close enough to reproximate "possess" and "the instant we achieve the Joy."

> Immortality contented
> Were Anomaly.

"Immortality contented" is presented as if it ought to be an oxymoron, since it parallels the pairing of want and infinity in the first verse, as if immortality were a process of constant desire. Anomaly usually implies deviance, more than simply difference, with negative connotations that enforce the inappropriateness of "immortality contented," but since it derives from "without law" it may have positive value here as well. To be without or outside the law, if it is the law of orthodoxy, would be freedom. The poem has used a commercial or legal metaphor throughout, in "Agent," "Comissary," and possibly "possess." If that is the kind of law that "Immortality contented" violates, then it is to the discredit of those already dubious transactions, not of the immortality. The poem would then double back and mean that satisfaction is not the agent of satiety, or that the two terms are simply returned to their original identity, cancelling the poem.

In order to show that "Immortality contented" is not an oxymoron or a self-opposition, it was necessary to show that anomaly is, in that it suggests two opposing sets of meanings.

On one level the poem states that satisfaction and satiety are opposites, affectively, at the same time reminding us that they are the same, by reminding us of their common root. But these readings make sense only when opposed to first or non-ironic readings: they deny an impossibility rather than making a positive statement. Like her self-contradictory use of irony described above, this poem opposes opposition only by way of a rhetorical strategy based on oppositions.

Despite the transparency between self and world that Emerson prophecies, and the infinitude of his individual man, his philosophic universe depends on dualism as much as any in tradition. Though he parodies the orthodox preacher of deferred rewards in "Compensation," the dualism that that essay extols includes a dichotomy between matter and spirit among others, and from Dickinson's point of view there cannot have been much difference between parodier and parodied. The essay *Nature* is dualistic throughout. His account of the origin of language assumes a basic dualism: "Every word which is used to express a moral or intellectual fact, if traced to its root, is found to be borrowed from some material appearance" (*W*, I, 18). The purpose of his essay is to prove the congruence of spirit and nature, but manifestly there would have been no need for such a proof if the reverse were the accepted case, and his proof of the transparency between natural facts and spiritual facts begins with their separation.

> All the facts in natural history taken by themselves, have no value, but are barren like a single sex. But marry it to human history, and it is full of life.   (*W*, I, 19)

His manner of arguing demands that he postulate an original division. His first example of the uses of nature is the orthodox analogy between the germination of seeds and the rising of the spirit after the body's death. This analogy and that between the seasons and the sequence of human life, which Emerson lists next, figure largely in Dickinson's poems, but their validity is constantly questioned. Her reason for using them is probably not that Emerson does, but for the same reason: they are clichés, the most accessible examples of orthodox metaphor. She does not take that "marriage" to be inevitable, perhaps because Emerson assumes subservience on the part of the bride. Oppositions in orthodoxy are kept apart by deprivation. Blake's chimney sweeper in the *Songs of Experience* tells of "God & his Priest & King / Who make up a heaven of our misery." Figurative language depends on, or brings about, the absence of the tenor.

The account of the origin of language presented by Freud in "The Antithetical Meaning of Primal Words" (1910, *SE*, XI, 155-161) is very different from Emerson's in *Nature* but also centers on a dualism, that of relativity. Freud's account sounds very much like the relativity that Dickinson parodies as orthodox. I cite Freud here, ever though Dickinson could not have known the work, because it helps demonstrate that certain assumptions are held in common by a wide range of phallogocentric philosophies. Freud's essay is a review of a work by the philologist Karl Abel (1884) and the theory of language is not so much Freud's own as his interpretation of Abel's interpolation of the philosopher Bain. Because of "the essential relativity of all knowledge" (p. 159) language ought theoretically to have originated (according to Bain), and did originate, according to Abel's discoveries about the ancient Egyptian language, in antithesis. No concept is imaginable without being measured against its opposite: we know darkness only because we know light; we understand far only in comparison with near. In this primitive language, the word for far and the word for near are conjoined, and take one or the other of the two meanings according to the speaker's gesture. But although conjoined, the word must already be read or heard as two, because it is a compound. As in *Nature*, which assumes the existence of division in order to insist on its closure, the speakers of this primitive language must have recognized difference at the same time that they denied it (or they were emerging from not recognizing to recognition). Although *Nature's* dualism is different, Emerson's "Compensation" matches Abel's theory in designating those qualitative oppositions as a primal dualism.

> Polarity, or action and reaction, we meet in every part of nature; in darkness and light; in heat and cold; in the ebb and flow of waters; in male and female; . . . An inevitable dualism bisects nature, so that each thing is a half, and suggests another thing to make it whole.
>
> (CW, II, 96-97)

This passage sweeps the dualism of spirit and matter of *Nature* into an encompassing, universal structural principle.

Freud's interest in Abel's work stems from his perception that it supports one aspect of his theory of dreams. In *The Interpretation of Dreams* he notes that reversals occur frequently in representations in dreams because something can be said in reverse that would be censored in its proper shape (*SE*, IV, 326-329). The idea of the antithetical meanings of primal words provides a paradigm and possibly a source for the reversals formulated by dreams, by showing how close in the primitive levels of the brain oppositions lie. The analogy in Dickinson's rhetoric is to the moments when she brings back together words that have come to have opposite meanings, as when satiety and satisfaction are made compatible through the irony of poem 1036. But what about the complementary case in Dickinson, when one word is taken apart and shown to have two opposing meanings? There is a corresponding phenomenon in Freud's essay, which he does not explain, although he implies, by offering no other account, that Bain's theory of the relativity of all knowledge explains both the compound words mentioned above and this other sort. In addition to compounds that rely on relativity for meaning, there are in the same language unitary words that have two opposing meanings simultaneously. For these, a different sort of conceptualization seems necessary. Rather than containing two opposing meanings, they are prior to differentiation into opposites. We must translate Latin *altus* by deep *and* high, but the Romans must have known the word as a unitary concept.

It is a strain on the imagination to conceive of a language that differentiates only between ranges of qualities, for example between the spectrum of color and the range of temperature, but this is what Abel tells us was the habit of the primitive mind. This is a language (or a part of a language) without value judgments, which already appear in the compounds analyzed later in the essay. Relativity simply does not account for this phenomenon. There is a slight but crucial difference between saying that a primitive language system entertains mutually exclusive oppositions (in the same word) and saying that it does not know that they are opposite, or what opposition means.

None of this enters into Freud's considerations; rather, he considers that there is conceptually no difference between the two phenomena, except to say that the compound words are "a further stage in this unintelligible behaviour of the Egyptian language" (p. 157). This conflation is surprising in the light of Freud's own views. His essay opens with a reference to the problematic discovery that dreams often represent two opposites as one thing. Anna Freud offers this unity of opposites as one of the defining characteristics of the id:

> In the id the so-called "primary process" prevails; there is no synthesis of ideas, affects are liable to displacement, opposites are not mutually exclusive and may even coincide and condensation occurs as a matter of course.[15]

It is the ego that makes value judgments. Anna Freud notes that children are able to counteract experienced pain by means of fantasy without asking that the fantasy be experientially true. Prior to the development of a powerful ego, the young child is capable of feeling two contradictory states of mind to be equally valid, and two reports about experience that adults perceive as opposite to be equally true, without experiencing a sense of conflict or contradiction. In "The Zeroes – taught us – Phosphorus –" the boy must acquire his knowledge of contradiction. It is the synthesizing ego, by all accounts, that objects to contradictions. Because of the hierarchical nature of relations between id and ego, and because they develop sequentially, Anna Freud suggests that the id is prior to differentiation, unfallen rather than simply resistant to progress. The id, if it spoke, might invent a unitary term that meant both of two opposites, unperceived as opposites; the ego would be the one to insist that this is not one term but a composite, and would separate it into two. Abel's unintended implication that there was once a time when the mind did not discriminate between what we perceive as opposites may not be verifiable, but his suggestion makes a suitable myth of the id; and his account of the compound words sounds like an account of the ego.

Dreams do not exclude the use of consciousness's language, and they may function in ways analogous to the functioning of language, but they originate in the unconscious, which for Anna Freud is synonymous with the id. It is therefore curious that Freud blurs the distinction between the two ways of experiencing opposites which offers so excellent an analogy for his own structures. The reversals that occur in dreams are closest to the idea of the unitary word that contains two meanings, but the explanation he favors is the one that accounts only for the compound words. This lapse on his part is consistent with the pervasive dualism of his thinking, but it also shows how difficult it is to escape dualism.[16] Dickinson's language is a departure from dualistic thinking, and from the phallogocentrism in which it originates, but it is difficult to comprehend the extent and value of this departure, so firmly are her readers' imaginations shaped by dualism.

The price often paid for this departure is loss of communicability, as she indicates in a poem that enacts this departure as a journey.

> I saw no Way – The Heavens were stitched –
> I felt the Columns close –
> The Earth reversed her Hemispheres –
> I touched the Universe –

And back it slid – and I alone –
A Speck upon a Ball –
Went out upon Circumference –
Beyond the Dip of Bell –

(P 378)

The hemispheres here are the concentric spheres of the earth
and the heavens, and they are halves in the sense that neither is
complete without the other, but by calling them hemispheres
the poet limits them to the oppositeness of east and west or
north and south. Then by referring to them as "it" she puts
oppositeness behind her. This departure from a dualistic uni-
verse takes her "Beyond the Dip of Bell," or beyond signifi-
cation, especially beyond a system of signs with ties to con-
ventional religion, if the bell here is a church bell. The poet
knows that by forgoing the tradition of language that relies
on oppositions or relativity for meaning, as she often does,
she may forgo the possibility of communicating what she dis-
covers. To the extent that her poems are readable, she is still
relying on the conventions of unreversed hemispheres.

HIERARCHY OR relativity in language is fundamentally the
same as propriation in language, because both fulfill the need
for the center to posit an eccentricity, or for the primary to
posit a secondary. Emerson's definition of language balances
human spirit against nature's matter, in a neat symmetry of
relativity. This use of nature as the ground for human mean-
ing is also propriative, in the manner of Derrida's account of
the operation of language, because it subjects nature to human
usage and denies its separate identity. Dickinson's objections
to hierarchy in language extend, as might be expected, to lan-
guage's appropriation of nature, and to overthrow this subjec-
tion of nature she makes use of strategies similar to those that
she employs in her disruption of language's hierarchical struc-
ture. Dickinson's sense of the foreignness of nature is com-
monly recognized, but nature's distance is due as much to her
sense of the fictiveness of language as to qualities inherent in

nature. Nature's defiance of human comprehension should not be credited entirely to nature's power, or to Dickinson's supposed timidity; nature is "graspless" at least in part because of a conscious and voluntary resistance to possessiveness on Dickinson's part. Nature's resistance to human language could be a model for Dickinson's own project to overthrow ordinary terminology, yet to call it a model of any kind is to violate the first principle of that non-appropriative project.

"What mystery pervades a well!" is often cited as the extreme case of Dickinson's wariness about human efforts to possess nature.[17] The poem's rhetorical mode is paradox, which stretches the oxymoronic style of poems like "Success is counted sweetest" to a limit where it approaches meaninglessness. Whether or not the contradiction is resolvable, paradox articulates the possibility of pure contradiction, which also typifies relations between the human and nature. The water in the well is "A neighbor from another world," the first of a series of paradoxical epithets about the mistaken belief that nature participates in the human community of understanding. Here are the final stanzas:

> But nature is a stranger yet;
> The ones that cite her most
> Have never passed her haunted house,
> Nor simplified her ghost.
>
> To pity those that know her not
> Is helped by the regret
> That those who know her, know her less
> The nearer her they get.
>
> (P 1400)

Those who know her know that she is inaccessible to language, so that even to make such a statement is to make nonsense of terms like knowledge. Her apparent presence seems to invite knowledge but her absence makes knowledge impossible; furthermore, presence and absence are imposed terms. The terms "her ghost" and "her haunted house" demonstrate the difficulty that even the sardonic speaker has in writing any account of nature. They implicate her in the same error made by "The ones that cite her most," because to separate matter from spirit is to impose on her an artificial system. The ones who cite her most are the more at fault, however, because they have reduced nature to her matter component.

"The ones that cite her most" perform an act of naming that implies appropriation of the named. Citing is naming with the specially active sense of bringing forward for purposes of argument, so that what is cited is made secondary to the argument. The ones who cite her most believe that they can use her as, for example, a metaphor for human activity. But nature escapes and leaves language a husk. Those citers, if they can be cited, must be Emerson and the Transcendentalists. Insisting that nature and spirit are indissolubly linked, their rhetoric depends on a separation. Emerson cites nature in *Nature* as the matter that human history elevates when the two are wed. He also cites nature according to the whim of his argument. At the outset he distinguishes between two uses of nature, nature as the "NOT ME" and the nature of "the river, the leaf." As his argument continues, nature becomes the reverenced repository of spirit, or the barren matter which the mind must enliven. "Nature is thoroughly mediate. It is made to serve" (*W*, I, 25). Dickinson is warning against such an appropriative project because it risks an ignorance of fatality. Those who get near to nature know her less by comprehending her resistance to our inquiries, but they also know her less because to get near to nature is to die, and to know everything less.

"What mystery pervades a well!" is often grouped with other poems apparently concerned with nature's inaccessibility, particularly to the poet's art, in order to arrive at a general statement about Dickinson's distance from nature. " 'Nature' is what we see —" exposes the futility of efforts to master nature by finding linguistic equivalencies for it:

"Nature" is what we see –
The Hill – the Afternoon –
Squirrel – Eclipse – the Bumble bee –
Nay – Nature is Heaven –
Nature is what we hear –
The Bobolink – the Sea –
Thunder – the Cricket –
Nay – Nature is Harmony –

                                        (P 668)

The listing of natural elements is insufficient and provokes a "Nay" each time, but the abstract terms that seem intended to correct that insufficiency—"Nature is Heaven," "Nature is Harmony"—not only remain distant from nature but they also produce a stuttering effect that threatens to bring the poem to a halt. Putting "Nature" in quotation marks in the first line is Dickinson's way of separating herself from the poem's definitions of nature, and it may also be a specific reference to the essay *Nature*. The poem's rapid shifting from one definition of nature to the next suggests that Dickinson is again mocking Emerson's belief that nature "is made to serve" the ends of whatever argument he happens to be pursuing. If the poem is in this way a response to the essay *Nature*, the poet is suggesting that Emerson's appropriative definitions are damaging not so much to nature (that was Dorothy Wordsworth's fear) as to Emerson himself: he is wasting his efforts. The poem's conclusion cautions the reader against trying to "say" nature:

Nature is what we know –
Yet have no art to say –
So impotent Our Wisdom is
To her Simplicity

Even "her Simplicity" is an imposed and abstract term, even though what it stands for is nature's resistance to human language.

Dickinson elaborates elsewhere on the way that nature surpasses human language:

> The Veins of other Flowers
> The Scarlet Flowers are
> Till Nature leisure has for Terms
> As "Branch," and "Jugular."
>
> We pass, and she abides.
> We conjugate Her Skill
> While She creates and federates
> Without a syllable.

(P 811)

A conjugation is an uncreative exercise in repetition that is set against nature's highly efficient substitute for language, the soundless federation of the scarlet flowers with the apparently bloodless ones. Typical of Dickinson's rhetorical mobility, a poem from the same packet precisely reverses this poem's metaphor for nature's separateness. Where poem 811 has "We pass, and she abides," poem 812, referring to the fleeting "Light" that "exists in Spring," says, "It passes and we stay – ." This juxtaposition, of opposite expressions that have the same import for human relations to nature, expresses nature's inaccessibility as effectively as could any single expression. It seems to make no difference what language is used, because, although the two lines would seem to cover all possibilities, they play against each other rather than touching nature.

As Charles Anderson points out, language relates happily to nature only where it forgoes the effort to imitate nature literally.[18] It is worth considering here that Dickinson welcomes a limitation in language that Dorothy Wordsworth also celebrates, but for very different purposes. Dorothy's wish not to try to appropriate nature by means of language contributes to her resistance to poetic identity, because to her that is the characteristic operation of poetic language. Dickinson's art is not impeded in any way by her recognition that nature is not to be possessed, because she understands and makes use of a general dislocation between words and their referents that includes, but is not limited to, language's relation to nature. Because she knows that all language is figurative, she feels no special distress at the discovery that actual nature is not the same as the words used to name it. Emerson, even though he shares some of Dickinson's knowledge of the vertiginous freedom of language, is disconcerted by nature's elusiveness, because his views of language include its powerful propriation of nature.

The test of Dickinson's equanimity about language's supposed failure to possess nature is that for every poem about nature's evasion of language there is a poem in which poetry matches or surpasses nature, or in which such comparative terms may be discarded in favor of an indication of pure difference. Something small (a poem) can be larger than something big (the summer, a sunset), when the terms of relativity are abandoned. "When I count at all – ," the poets merely head a numbered list of priorities, but "looking back," reversing the order of the counting, poets "Comprehend the Whole" (P 569). In a mock competition with the day the poet makes two sunsets "and several Stars – / While He – was making One – ." The day's was "ampler," but "Mine – is the more convenient / To Carry in the Hand –" (P 308). In a similar stalemate, poem 811 appears to value nature's visual language over human language, but to conjugate is to conjoin as well as to repeat, and in fact it is only through the poem's juxtaposition that the scarlet flowers have any relation to the others. Nature's language is at once superior to and dependent on a human viewpoint. The first two verses of "The Brain – is wider than the Sky – ," in which the brain contains the sky and absorbs the sea, demonstrate that scale is irrelevant to power, by lifting the small over the large (P 632). But the poem presses past this point. The third stanza violates the expectation raised by the first two, of a pattern of such displacements, by abandoning the language of scale altogether, even as a metaphor. Competition for status as the largest in the first two stanzas gives way to a recognition of difference that is neither spatial nor temporal. The brain and God differ here "As syllable from Sound – ." They may be coextensive, or even occupy the same place. Syllable is articulate and sound is unintelligible, but articulation may equally be a diminishing of pure and primal sound. It is impossible to find here an order of valuation, and the poem teaches us not to wish to impose one.

Both Dorothy Wordsworth and Emily Brontë have difficulty writing about nature because they inherit a tradition in which nature is Mother Nature, and, in the mythic family dynamic, the mother is the object of their jealousy rather than of their devotion. Dickinson's sense of the fictiveness of language finally frees her from this problematic tradition. But at the same time that she is learning to become a daughter of Eve, she is also a daughter of Mother Nature, and it is evidence of the tenacity of this tradition that Dickinson's liberation from it is a process that extends past the time of her understanding of the powers of irony. Mother Nature holds her to the terms of literal competition or identification. Dickinson is, however, helped in this regard by the fact that her American predecessors are not so prolifically enamored of nature as are their British counterparts. Nature is not so unavoidable a subject of verse for an American poet.

Dickinson very early becomes involved in a minor competition with maternal nature when the love of a beloved male figure is in question, though it is a competition that stirs her to write, not to stop writing. The second poem in the Harvard edition, actually the prose conclusion to a letter written to her brother Austin in 1851, is read by some critics as a veiled sexual invitation, and certainly it is a love poem with a female speaker. Out of context, as verse, the alternative nature that the speaker offers is a metaphor for her love, in the tradition of the Song of Solomon, where the woman is a garden:

> There is another sky,
> Ever serene and fair,
>
> .   .   .   .

> Here is a brighter garden,
> Where not a frost has been;
> In its unfading flowers
> I hear the bright bee hum;
> Prithee, my brother,
> Into *my* garden come!
>
> (P 2)

While the "another sky" and "brighter garden" retain their
status as metaphors when restored to their context in the let-
ter, that they follow a passage about actual nature puts them
in a slightly different light:

> The earth looks like some poor old lady who by dint of
> pains has bloomed e'en till *now*, yet in a forgetful mo-
> ment a few silver hairs from out her cap come stealing,
> and she tucks them back so hastily and thinks nobody
> *sees*. . . . Dont think that the sky will frown so the day
> when you come home! She will smile and look happy,
> and be full of sunshine *then* – and even *should* she frown
> upon her child returning, there is *another* sky ever serene
> and fair, . . .   (*L*, I, 149)

The "brighter garden" is called into being in response to an
inadequacy in real nature, so that as well as functioning as a
metaphor for the writer's love, those lovely images compete
with real nature on the literal level. That nature is charac-
terized as a woman in this passage emphasizes the femininity
of the speaker, making the sequence a competition between
two women for the love of the man.

Because the rhyming lines seem to grow spontaneously out
of prose, they appear (whether or not Dickinson contrived the
effect) to represent the untutored origins of poetry, as if
poetry originated in imitation of nature. This moment of
origination stands at the beginning of a project for poetry
quite different from that which her objections to hierarchical
language produce. Many of the poems from her first year of
writing seriously (1858, seven years later) enact this implicit
competition with nature by assuming nature's voice. Domes-

ticating small natural objects by personifying them, she then joins them as if to test the hypothesis that poetry might substitute for nature. Other poems were sent with flowers as greetings, making an equation between flowers and speech and between nature and the speaker.

> She slept beneath a tree –
> Remembered but by me.
> I touched her Cradle mute –
> She recognized the foot –
> Put on her carmine suit
>   And see!
>
> (P 25)

If nature wakes the tulips with a touch and without voice ("I touched her Cradle mute –"), then she is hardly a model for the aspiring poet, but the poet here seems to desire nothing further than simple presence ("And see!"), deferring to nature. Elsewhere the poet constructs a rose out of language, but her speaker's purpose, as before, is only to approximate nature's activity, and no more:

> A sepal, petal, and a thorn
> Upon a common summer's morn –
> A flask of Dew – A Bee or two –
> A Breeze – a caper in the trees –
> And I'm a Rose!
>
> (P 19)

The impulse to compete with or correct nature seems to have disappeared in favor of an apprenticeship in innocence.

This apprenticeship is essentially stultifying, and Dickinson knows it. Another letter from the 1851 correspondence with Austin anticipates and characterizes the feminine voice of the 1858 poems so accurately that she cannot have been unaware of their trite effect. Austin has apparently admonished her for a grandiose style in previous letters and has recommended a simpler one. Her letters at this time are full of the flights of borrowed fancy that she identifies as masculine. Perhaps he objected to her satiric tone in her letter of June 15, or her hyperbole of June 22, the two letters just previous to this response. In either case, his admonition causes her to be defensive about pirating an alien style.

> I feel quite like retiring, in presence of one so grand, and casting my small lot among small birds, and fishes – you say you dont comprehend me, you want a simpler style. *Gratitude* indeed for all my fine philosophy! I strove to be exalted thinking I might reach *you* and while I pant and struggle and climb the nearest cloud, you walk out very leisurely in your slippers from Empyrean, and without the *slightest* notice request me to get down! As *simple* as you please, the *simplest* sort of simple – I'll be a little ninny – a little pussy catty, a little Red Riding Hood, I'll wear a Bee in my bonnet, and a Rose bud in my hair, and what remains to do you shall be told hereafter.
>
> (*L*, I, 117; 29 June 1851)

The humor here almost makes us forget that this letter represents the usual relations between men and women. The godlike admonisher and the little ninny are all too recognizable, and Dickinson portrays them repeatedly in the letters and poems about Master and the daisy, satirized there as they are here. She outwits her critic but she also sketches what will become, strangely, a serious program of poetry writing. The nature poems of 1858 may represent an effort to show that wearing a rosebud does not necessarily make the wearer a little ninny, but benighted as her attempt may have been, it is necessary to put into context her lack of success. Identifying the empyrean style as alien, she chose to begin writing by first investigating the possibilities of a style that was definably feminine and ought to have felt native.

Fortunately, among these early poems are some that perform the salutary task of proving to their writer the impossibility of an innocent or entirely natural speaker. She deduces figuration out of the context of her loyalty to this natural style, and so makes the use of figuration more genuinely her own.

The morns are meeker than they were –
The nuts are getting brown –
The berry's cheek is plumper –
The Rose is out of town.

The Maple wears a gayer scarf –
The field a scarlet gown –
Lest I sh'd be old fashioned
I'll put a trinket on.

                                                        (P 12)

The innocent "I" thinks that she is deficient in ornament rela-
tive to nature, but the poem shows us that her deficiency is in
her critical faculties, in that she misinterprets the meaning of
nature's bright coloring. Like Blake's *Songs of Innocence*, this
poem is ironic without having an ironic speaker. Reading na-
ture with the assumption that it participates in the community
of human meaning, the speaker takes brilliant color to signify
decoration, not death. This misreading may be innocent, but
it is dangerous. Rather than humanizing nature, the speaker
risks her life in naturalizing herself: for her to put on a trinket
is, in the context of nature's language of gayer scarf and scar-
let gown, to prepare for death. The speaker requires the con-
cept of metaphor in order not to make this error, even though
metaphor would confirm the separation between nature and a
no longer innocent speaker.

    This natural speaker finds that there is no equivalent for na-
ture's voice, and that nature cannot be spoken of without the
defense of figuration. Mother Nature disappears as a major
subject after these very early poems, and when she does ap-
pear it is her silence and her defiance of poetic language that
are emphasized. As for Dorothy, nature's real power is no
help to those among her daughters who aspire to be poets, be-
cause it is a power against articulation. "Nature – the Gentlest
Mother is" is a counterpart to Dorothy's "Irregular Verses"
("To Julia Marshall—A Fragment") in presenting a maternal
figure who conceals oppression beneath kindness:[19]

> Her Admonition mild –
>
> In Forest – and the Hill –
> By Traveller – be heard –
> Restraining Rampant Squirrel –
> Or too impetuous Bird –
>
> (P 790)

In what way can a bird be "too impetuous"? What is the need for these restraints? Nature inspires worship, a traditional notion, but the description of her worshipers emphasizes their inferiority. Her voice

> Incite the timid prayer
> Of the minutest Cricket –
> The most unworthy Flower –

Granted that crickets are small, it makes no sense to say that a flower is unworthy. Earlier in the poem, Mother Nature is called gentle because she is "Impatient of no Child – / The feeblest – or the waywardest." The poem makes Nature superior to and separate from natural objects, an odd notion that reappears in another poem naming nature as mother:

> If Nature smiles – the Mother must
> I'm sure, at many a whim
> Of Her eccentric Family –
> Is She so much to blame?
>
> (P 1085)

Where nature is Mother Nature she is outside nature, making herself implicitly the center from which nature (with a small n) is eccentric.

In "Nature – the Gentlest Mother is," Mother Nature is primarily represented as a voice, speaking "Her Admonition mild" and vocally inciting prayer; a day's beauty is "How fair Her Conversation – / A Summer Afternoon –." Though this voice is metaphoric, it is perhaps a sign that the poet's own voice has been preempted. The last two stanzas are about the silence Mother Nature condescends to confer on nature:

> When all the Children sleep –
> She turns as long away
> As will suffice to light Her lamps –
> Then bending from the Sky –
>
> With infinite Affection –
> And infiniter Care –
> Her Golden finger on Her lip –
> Wills Silence – Everywhere –

This might have been a charming allegory of the coming of night, except that Mother Nature "Wills Silence" only after her children are asleep. This silence must be more than sleep, then. "Infiniter Care" is also overabundant. "Infiniter" makes no sense in natural terms and, like "Silence – Everywhere – ," goes beyond the harmonious imagery of night and sleep that Nature is promulgating. "Infiniter" is also parodic, undermining the hypnotic effect of "Her Golden finger on Her lip –." The "Silence – Everywhere –" must be death masquerading, as in the Lucy situation, as an entirely harmonious part of natural process.

In these two poems (P 790 and P 1085) Mother Nature is separate from nature. This separation is in distinct contrast to Mother Nature in both the Wordsworths and in Brontë, where she is by definition a presence immanent in nature. Knowing that nature is not to be possessed by means of any human construct, Dickinson is not taking Mother Nature to be a personification of nature, but a figure imported from tradition and extrinsic to nature. To Dorothy and to Brontë, Mother Nature appears to be part of nature's reality, because they do not separate literary tradition from actuality. Dickinson, with her greater sense of the potential detachment of words from their referents, is able to see with greater clarity the difference between Mother Nature and actual, unnameable nature. The concept of Mother Nature is only a fiction among other fictions. This is the most effective answer to the women poets' struggles with that maternal figure. Dickinson abandons the struggle after her earliest attempts at verse, and simply removes the grounds for the struggle altogether. Nature, "graspless," is alien, but its foreignness ceases to pose a threat to the existence of poethood. With nature no longer maternal, the woman poet need not feel a daughter's conflicting wishes to subdue and at the same time to identify.

THIS RECOGNITION OF the fictionality of nature's traditional sexual identification is part of Dickinson's larger discovery about language's fictiveness. Her resistance to appropriating nature is one model for improving the status of the woman writer in relation to the tradition; another lies in her challenge to the assumption that opposition is necessary for language to have meaning. Her undoing of rhetorical dualism becomes a model for a revised pattern of relations between the sexes, in her recognition that the opposition of the sexes is as figurative as any other kind of opposition, not a literal necessity. The traditional determinisms that have maintained this opposition need no longer operate, just as the tradition of Mother Nature, once it is recognized as a tradition and therefore figurative, not actual, ceases to be confining. A tradition of masculine dominance may be at the root of dualistic language, and her feminine identity, particularly her sense of inheritance from Eve, may be the origin of her readiness to object to that structure of language. She disrupts traditional relations between the sexes by means of the kind of undoing of hierarchical language that she employs in poems about the idea of opposition itself. Dickinson brings to those poems in which the poet's identity is explicitly feminine her knowledge that her best power lies in the manipulation of language to reverse its ordinary meanings. She uses that linguistic power first to reverse the ordinary direction of power between a feminine self and a masculine other, and then, as in the poems where she undoes antithetical language, uses it to discard the idea of dominance altogether.

There is a group of poems in which she pictures herself as a tiny being, typically a daisy and typically in relation to some figure of masculine power. As in the many poems in which she criticizes dualism or polarity, she entertains, in order to challenge it, the convention that women remain childlike or regress in romantic relations. In all these poems the positions are reversed by a slight disjunction.[20] In the manner of the poems that mock human competition with nature, the daisy may be tiny, but she is also larger than Master. If the poet's purpose were simply to prove her power, she would hardly portray herself as a daisy in the first place. Her point is that power is not relative, and cannot be described in the terms of relativity.

> In lands I never saw – they say
> Immortal Alps look down –
>
> (P 124)

"They say" always signals the false authority of convention, which she defies. In this case the "they say" refers to both expressions, preceding and following. She doubts "their" view that she never saw these lands; but she also reports that they say that immortal Alps look down. In the world of "they say," hierarchies of up and down obtain, but she has never seen such a place, which is to say that she never herself entertains such hierarchical thoughts. The ambiguous positioning of "they say" makes equally plausible two readings that contradict each other, in that she insists both that she might have seen and that she has not, and this confusion is paradigmatic of the procedure of the poem. An apparent opposition is resolved by lifting the convention: the poet can see perfectly clearly if her vision is not occluded by "them."

The power of these condescending Alps is next reduced by the contrivance of a figure that miniaturizes them:

> Whose Bonnets touch the firmament –
> Whose Sandals touch the town –
>
> Meek at whose everlasting feet
> A Myriad Daisy play –

"Daisy" was printed as "daisies" in the 1891 edition of Dickinson's poems, accurately destroying the very precise effect of these lines. A myriad daisy turns multiplicity into a fantastic unity. Where bonnets and sandals rationalize Alps, by rendering their size accessible, the myriad exalts the daisy, because "Myriad Daisy" defies not only sense but logic and reason too.

> Which, Sir, are you and which am I
> Upon an August day?

These lines have been cited as an example of the poet's confusion, intentional or not, about sex roles.[21] But if she were genuinely confused, she would hardly make so bald a statement. Instead, she voices the form of such a confusion in order to show its inapplicability: by now the reader ought to see that the question is not a question. Most sirs would still opt for Alps, but the choice has been minimized; there is no longer a clear opposition of high and low. The poem is about the invidiousness of ascribing conventional characteristics to the sexes.

This poem offers an interpretive key to related poems. Poem 106 presents the daisy again at someone's feet, shy here instead of meek, using the sun's grandeur to enlarge her own.[22]

> The Daisy follows soft the Sun –
> And when his golden walk is done –
> Sits shily at his feet –
> He – waking – finds the flower there –
> Wherefore – Marauder – art thou here?
> Because, Sir, love is sweet!
>
> We are the flower – Thou the Sun!
> Forgive us, if as days decline –
> We nearer steal to Thee!

The daisy is better at most things than is the admired sun. She knows him, but he is ignorant of her. Her gentility is superior to his, as is her command of articulation. When, surprised, he calls her "Marauder," she not only has a loving answer, but also manages to transform his rudeness into the language of her own adoration: "We nearer steal to Thee!" As in poem 124, the daisy multiplies her size and number till she becomes an omnipresent "we" who attends the sun's every motion, east and west. Her name means "day's eye," making her etymologically a mock sun. Having equalized their powers, the poet now renders the daisy and the sun even more similar by giving them the same view of each other. Her apparent reliance on his power parodies the dependence of the weak on the strong, because it is his absence that she desires, not his presence.

> Enamored of the parting West –
> The peace – the flight – the Amethyst –
> Night's possibility!

The daisy is in the end no less self-centered than the sun, who resented her presence at the opening, because "We nearer steal to Thee" in order to look beyond. Self-representation makes the other disappear, and the daisy has the last word in the poem because she has made the sun vanish. The poem parodies the faulty relations between the sexes that obtain when the conventional attributes are assigned, such as the equation of weakness with femininity and of power with masculinity. This exclusiveness isolates the sexes. The daisy can acquire power in this system only by mocking the sun, thereby depriving him of some of his power.

The daisy does not just desire the sun's absence, however. The last three lines (quoted above) project a kind of presence as well as absence: amethyst as well as parting, flight and peace. "Night's possibility" suggests transcendence, a third term outside the narrow competition between the daisy and the sun, but, like the moment of leaving the dualistic universe defined by hemispheres and going "out upon Circumference – / Beyond the Dip of Bell –" (P 378), if it represents a possibility beyond the isolation of sexual characteristics, it is also beyond communicable terminology. Incommunicability is the risk of any strategy that denies or surpasses oppositions, whether rhetorical or thematic, where conventional terminology depends on relativity.

Many of the Daisy poems simply enact reversals of size and power as related to gender. Poem 85 elevates the daisy to Christlike status. Jesus' brave statement is

> "They have not chosen me," he said,
> "But I have chosen them!"

The daisy's response is that although Jesus hasn't chosen her, she has chosen him, so that she is the inheritor of his position:

> Sovreign! Know a Daisy
> Thy dishonor shared!

In the Master letters the writer uses Daisy as a proper name for herself. The first of these letters, from about the same period as the Daisy poems, opens with a reversal similar to that of the poems: "I am ill, but grieving more that you are ill, I make my stronger hand work long eno' to tell you" (*L*, II, 333; about 1858). Competition is not far from the surface of this apparently self-abasing text. She slights his faulty powers of understanding: "You ask me what my flowers said – then they were disobedient – I gave them messages." Stooping to explain, she says that her message was no less than apocalyptic, and should not have been difficult to read. "They said what the lips in the West, say, when the sun goes down, and so says the Dawn." Though she defends the possibility of intelligibility, the role reversal here does not simply cause unintelligibility, it is founded on it.[23]

The daisy that addresses the sun as sir and the humble voice that speaks to her Master have, among other sources, a literary source in the manipulation of power in the relationship between Jane Eyre and Mr. Rochester in Charlotte Brontë's novel, which Dickinson greatly admired. Jane refers to Rochester as her master, at first in the literal sense that he is her employer and later generically, as her private deity. She always addresses him as sir, as a form of deference behind which she conceals her growing sense of equality with him. It permits her to exercise what powers she chooses without ever deserving a reproach, from herself or from the critical world, for forwardness or immodesty. He is her superior in every way—as her employer, in age and experience, and by virtue of being a man—so that her language is initially unremarkable. At the end of the novel when Jane, now independent both financially and morally, returns to find Rochester blind and helpless, the balance of power has become reversed. She torments him briefly with jealousy, ritually, in order to cancel the symmetrical power he once held over her. She profits from his crippling: "I love you better now, when I can really be useful to you, than I did in your state of proud independence, when you disdained every part but that of the giver and protector."[24] But the special quality of his dependence is that she retains the form of the usual relation of power. Walking, she leads him by letting him place his arm around her shoulders, as if it were he who protected her: "being so much lower of stature than he, I served both for his prop and guide" (p. 278). She retains the same form of address throughout, though in these last pages her "sir" becomes almost a parody of servility:

> "Am I hideous, Jane?"
> "Very, sir: you always were, you know."
> (p. 265)

The daisy's mock humility is similar in tone to Jane's. It is not disrespectful, but at the same time that it pretends to a continuity of relationship it measures the change in it, and it emblemizes the way in which power is augmented by disarming the governed. Jane Eyre's "sir" permits both of them to be powerful, as does the daisy's. When, in poem 124, she asks "Which, Sir, are you and which am I / Upon an August day?" she is not confused about sex roles but rather she is demonstrating their dispensability.

This alteration of ordinary relations between male and female figures may extend beyond the patently fictive voice of the daisy to a relationship that involves the poet's identity as a poet. Like Emily Brontë, Dickinson invokes an array of masculine figures of power in reference to the poetic process. Brontë's visitants—her dream, her God of Visions, her Wanderer, and others—invite comparison with a similar group in Dickinson. Many of Dickinson's poems on poetry are also about, or enact, relationships between the speaker and a range of powerful masculine figures. The speaker's attitude shifts, from poem to poem, between love, anguish, desire, fear, and humility, and the figure addressed may be God, an apparently human lover, death, awe, Master, or some other being or abstraction, but they are all masculine and they are all addressed as other, while the speaker characterizes herself as queen or wife or some other female figure. These poems sometimes follow the Daisy poems' pattern of inverting our expectations about gender roles, but sometimes they do not. For both poets these masculine figures function as something like a muse. Both poets both love and fear these figures, and both indicate a sense of alienation from their poetic powers, though Dickinson far less than Brontë.

Two critics have directly and extensively considered the gender or genders of Dickinson's mind, and though their arguments differ greatly, both find those figures to be a masculine component of Dickinson's mind. Albert J. Gelpi, addressing the issue of Dickinson's femininity along Jungian lines in *The Tenth Muse*, describes the masculine figures listed above as versions of the animus and discusses the poems in terms of their negotiations between feminine self and a masculine part of the self that is nonetheless other. He is clearly right in associating these figures and in emphasizing their status as figures rather than as actual persons (every reader of Dickinson should be grateful for his putting to rest the search for the biographical identity of Master). But the Jungian system leads Gelpi to a reductive formula—feminine self plus masculine mind equals complete poet—and to a static critical program of demonstrating Dickinson's ceaseless effort to "adapt the masculine characteristics of mind and will to the achievement of an integral identity as a woman" (p. 267). Dickinson assimilates those internalized figures to varying degrees, but by identifying intellect, will, and imagination as perpetually masculine, Gelpi (with Jung) insures that these powers must be uneasily appropriated and are never inherent. As with Emerson's marriage of natural history to human history, the objection to this system, both for Dickinson criticism and for human experience, is that while proposing to restore humanity to its primordial integrity, it only further divides and creates hierarchies.[25]

Joanne Feit Diehl (in the works already cited) identifies an analogous range of masculine figures as the poet's internalization of her poetic precursors, arguing persuasively from Freudian and Bloomian theory for a structure of mind that is similar to, though more complex than, the one Gelpi describes with reference to Jung. Because these masculine figures double as precursor and as muse, the poet's antithetical struggle to defend herself against her precursors, which she shares with male poets, causes her at the same time to defend against the beloved sources of her own inspiration, which for male poets are feminine and therefore distinguishable from the paternal precursors. This identification of precursor and muse accounts for Dickinson's ambivalence about the poetic art that she experiences as a dangerous, destructive power. Although Joanne Feit Diehl does not discuss Brontë, there is a remarkable similarity between this reading of Dickinson and Brontë's identification of the sources of poetry both with masculine figures of power and with death. This similarity could make one of the strongest cases for the existence of a common and recurrent experience of feminine poethood. However, while this alienation is Brontë's major experience of poetry, for Dickinson it is only one aspect, perhaps a stage, of her endeavor to establish her own poetic voice outside the tradition of masculine discourse. Brontë is genuinely "stalled" by the danger and power of the masculine figures she invokes, but to say this about Dickinson is to overrate the importance of the masculine in a poetics that endeavors to liberate itself from restrictive terms like those of gender.

Both of these ways of reading are persuasive, but both privilege poems that delineate internal struggles between masculine and feminine in such a way as to retain the hierar-

chical terms of self and other or subject and object. It may be
that Dickinson's greatest originality is in her breaking out of
the terms of gender altogether, in other poems in which the
mind appears to be divided into identical halves and in which
identical terms replace the expected terms of opposition or
complementarity. Gelpi cites in support of his argument
about Dickinson's difficulties in controlling her masculine
mind several poems, including the following one, that sketch
a balance, or sometimes a stalemate, between parts of the
mind that are explicitly unlabelled, and that are, in fact, not
separable parts at all.

> Me from Myself – to banish –
> Had I Art –
>
> . . . .
>
> And since We're mutual Monarch
> How this be
> Except by Abdication –
> Me – of Me?
>
> 　　　　　　　　　　(P 642)

Written out of her recognition that to use gender terms is un-
avoidably to use the hierarchical terms of self and other, these
termless poems indicate Dickinson's objections to the con-
ventional language of sexual opposition (as exemplified in
Brontë's poetry) and her effort to do without it.

This balance within the mind is not a confrontation be-
tween qualitatively different parts of the mind, nor a mirror-
ing of one part by another, but a balance of two parts that are
neither different nor the same. This self-doubling is a form of
irony carried from rhetoric to the level of poetic identity. Just
as a word may be asked to bear antithetical meanings, thereby
denying the reader's expectation of a stable or consistent read-
ing, the self may split into antithetical parts; but this irony of
the self is even less easily read than the rhetorical ironies of
other poems. Rhetoric demonstrates the self's divisions by a
doubling in language, as in "Abdication – / Me – of Me?" or

in lines like "Ourself behind ourself" or "Itself – it's Sovreign
– of itself." These repetitions seem to reach the limit of mean-
ing, because meaning depends on difference. As in the poems
in which the poet exploits the antithetical meanings of words,
that she avoids labeling her various powers of mind, either
sexually or hierarchically, creates a risk of obscurity. These
parts of the self may be provisionally labeled with gender or
other terms, but that these terms are variable suggests that
these characterizations are not proper differences:

> The Soul unto itself
> Is an imperial friend –
> Or the most agonizing Spy –
> An Enemy – could send –
>
> (P 683)

The terms "friend" and "Spy" represent the poet's efforts to
render comprehensible this division between the soul and it-
self. The poet falls back on the oppositional structure of lan-
guage, as a self-defense, even though she has elsewhere
proved to herself that that structure is obsolete. The language
of hierarchy is used in these poems only in order to be un-
done. The poem closes,

> Itself – it's Sovreign – of itself
> The Soul should stand in Awe –

The soul should stand in awe, but it cannot. Could the soul
transform its self-duplicated friend or enemy into sovereign
or into monarch, the doubling would cease to be so prob-
lematic. Hierarchy would restore a temporary and inauthentic
calm. (It is instructive to compare this structureless structure
to the hierarchy that preserves Whitman's divisions of the self
from becoming a splintering.)

   Most of these poems intensify the concept of rhetorical op-
position through a metaphor of combat or defense within the
self. The poem that begins "Me from Myself – to banish – "
represents a fortress within the self that cannot resist when
"Myself – assault Me – ;" and in the poem "One need not be a

Chamber – to be Haunted – " (P 670), "Ourself behind our-self" is "a superior spectre" whose dangerousness exceeds that of "External Ghost" or "Assassin." This violence is due not to the problem of masculine power, because these poems use no terms of gender, but to the sense of risk implicit in the act of self-division. Language's capacity for splitting into an-tithetical or free meanings is a powerful weapon when turned against itself and against sexual hierarchy, and when applied to identity it is equally dangerous. Eve's discovery of irony is liberating, but it is, after all, fatal. Yet at the same time that the poet is demonstrating this strategy's dangers she is using it to enlarge language's possibilities. Her repetitions cause differ-ence to emerge from sameness: when she says "Itself – it's Sovreign – of itself," the two words are distinct without being separately characterized. She makes us understand how richly duplicitous any word can be.

Dickinson's sense of herself as two selves, rather than as a unitary self in relation to others or as the other in relation to a self perceived elsewhere, is probably the most radical and conceptually challenging answer possible to the dualism of self and other that empowers the masculine tradition and that troubles its female inheritors. The same structural principle pervades and underlies the poetic strategies sketched in this chapter: it makes her ironies undecidable, it stalemates poten-tial power struggles as they arise, and it splits words into etymological and connotative meanings while refusing to hierarchize them. Brontë's efforts to master her master never quite succeed because of her assumption that there is a unitary power of speech and that it can reside only in one place. The external and powerful keepers of language make imaginative experience either unavailable or fearful as death. Because Dickinson places linguistic power in the context of her under-standing of the fictiveness of language, she denies the single-ness of that control, democratizing the structure of poetry. At the same time she revises for positive use what was a major difficulty for Dorothy Wordsworth. Dorothy allows her lack of a central sense of self to arrest her writing poetry, because her inherited definition of poetry necessitates a central speaking self. Dickinson's self-division allows her to avoid direct competition with the masculine unitary self, while at the same time also allowing her a power of her own. Dickinson's self-division approaches a stoppage like Dorothy's, but she uses it to press more meaning out of a word, and in the end to extend language rather than to collapse it.

IT MUST NOT be forgotten that Dickinson's recognition of language's fictiveness, which has the effects charted above, came originally from her sense of femininity and of its place within the tradition that she then undoes. Once she has used her femininity as a force for disruption, she liberates herself from that too, because sexual determinism of any kind must be antithetical to her concerns.

The proof of her freedom is that where she sees an image of power she is free to consider adopting it as her own, late in her life, even though it represents the masculine tradition from which she was originally alienated. "A Word made Flesh is seldom" aligns the poet's linguistic powers with the incarnation of the Word that represents a masculine God's specifically masculine powers of creation. The poem has been cited for its resemblance to other poems about the power and efficacy of language, but this way of reading, though it describes the religious content of the poem, does not indicate its significance in relation to her sense of identity.[26] Dickinson is not simply making use of a clever metaphor for language's power; she is entertaining a long tradition of the inheritance of divine language by human language. Conflating the sequential transformation of word into flesh and of flesh into bread and wine, incarnation and Eucharist, the poet claims a protestant privilege of individual communion:

> A Word made Flesh is seldom
> And tremblingly partook
> Nor then perhaps reported
> But have I not mistook

Each one of us has tasted
With ecstasies of stealth
The very food debated
To our specific strength –

(P 1651)

As the poem continues, the poet's operations are revealed as being like these manifestations of the Word. The Spirit dwells in the poet's words as much as in the divine Word: "Made Flesh and dwelt among us" is "Like this consent of Language / This loved Philology."

Neither the poem nor a prose fragment that it resembles (*L*, III, 912) can be securely dated, but the poem is likely to have been written late in the poet's life because of its similarity to a passage from a late letter.

> All grows strangely emphatic, and I think if I should see you again, I sh'd begin every sentence with "I say unto you – " The Bible dealt with the Centre, not with the Circumference –
>
> (*L*, III, 849–850; late autumn, 1884)

The "Word made Flesh" of the undated poem is the speaker of "I say unto you." The Bible makes pronouncements and requires that its language be taken as the literal truth. The incarnation is the type of literal language, and that is what is meant by language as a center, as opposed to Dickinson's usual rhetorical indirection, which she often identifies as "circumference." To model her poetry after God's or Christ's speech would be to change to an entirely new paradigm, and to concede her fictive gains.

But have I not mistook? This alternate source of power would not be incorporated into poetic identity without qualification. "A Word that breathes distinctly"

. . . may expire if He –
"Made Flesh and dwelt among us
Could condescension be

Like this consent of Language
This loved Philology

A living word in a poem may lose its inspiriting power if the incarnation, as a provisional model for poetry, is a condescension. Consent is an agreement among equals, and that is how Dickinson's language normally operates. The phrase "This loved Philology" enacts that "consent of Language" by pairing two etymologically equivalent words. The difference between consent and condescension is small in sound and appearance, but the poet splits a sound to find a vast difference in meaning: where consent implies equality, condescension is a reversion to hierarchical ways. That love of the Logos is loved only as long as it is a consent. It would be too easy for the rhetoric of the center of "I say unto you – " to become a hierarchy of condescension. She would adopt a masculine prototype for the self's power, but only if it could be free from determinism. Rather than a revision of her own model for poetry, she proposes a revision in the entire structure of patriarchal religion, to the effect that the incarnation might become more like her poetry, instead of poetry aspiring to resemble the incarnation.

A Feminine Tradition

Association with nature and exclusion from speaking subjectivity amount to two different ways of placing the woman in dualistic culture on the side of the other and the object. Although the configurations of Mother Nature and Romantic egotism create problems specific to the nineteenth century, and although society and literature have undergone enormous changes since then, our language is still what it was and it continues to create for the woman poet many of the same impediments encountered by nineteenth-century women, if in different forms. Returning these specifically nineteenth-century problems to their context in a general and continuing tradition of the objectification of women, I should like to suggest in this chapter that poetry by women is still and is likely to remain conditioned by its response to various manifestations of masculine authority, and that women poets today might learn from the nineteenth century's range of failed and successful strategies for writing within the same tradition. The women poets then and now must distinguish the advantageous from the detrimental in their inheritance from Eve. Eve as she is read by masculine culture is interchangeable with Mother Nature: the object of men's conversation, beautiful but amoral, the "mother of all living" (Genesis 3:20), and best kept under control and silent. Eve as Dickinson reads her and as she might be read by others is the first human speaker to learn a non-literal language, and therefore the most suitable prototype for poetic subjectivity. Dorothy Wordsworth is a docile daughter of nature, hoping that her docility will make up for the fall; Brontë is like a guilty Eve, repeating over and over a violation of male authority for which she believes the punishment is death; Dickinson celebrates Eve's duplicity, her invention of the art of concealment. To become poets, women must shift from agreeing to see themselves as daughters of nature and as parts of the world of objects to seeing themselves as daughters of an Eve reclaimed for their poetry.

With the aim of countering the traditional illusions about femininity, the prevailing feminist opinion is that poetry by women must report on the poet's experience as a woman, and that it must be true.[1] Although it is appropriate that readers learn to expand their notions of what constitutes acceptable poetic subject matter—motherhood is as universal and as potentially imaginative an experience as, say, romantic love—this emphasis on truth implies a mistaken, or at least naïve, belief about language's capacity not just for precise mimesis but for literal duplication of experience. In chapter I, I cited the use of Muriel Rukeyser's phrase "No more masks!" to call for a feminist poetry that would resolve women's difficult position within a dualistic culture simply by declaring an end to dualism; another anthology's title, *The World Split Open*, refers to the consequence of "one woman's" telling "the truth about her life" in Rukeyser's "Kathë Kollwitz."[2] Whether or not these borrowings represent Rukeyser fairly, they assume that telling the truth without any sort of mask is both possible and desirable. Patriarchal culture may have particularly misused language in its perceptions of women, as feminist arguments maintain, but language is inherently fictive and creates masks whether or not the speaker or writer wishes it. The hope that language can gradually be released from a heritage of untruths about women may not be entirely deluded, but when those lies reinforce and are reinforced by the inherently fictive structure of language, it is chasing phantoms to expect that language will suddenly work for the expression of women's truth. This aim is fundamentally antithetical to the aims of poetry, and it dooms itself by denying itself the power that poetry genuinely offers.

Dickinson's discovery that to depart from dualistic lan-
guage is to risk becoming either silent or incomprehensible
was prompted by conditions that still prevail. Since her day
writers and readers have become even more aware of the way
dualism pervades language, in part through semiology, which
has made a science of the necessary discrepancy between a
word and its referent. Though Dickinson made a private and
relatively early revolution in challenging herself and her fu-
ture readers to imagine alternatives to dualistic thinking, no
self-conscious writer today can believe in the goal of a unitary
language such as Dickinson's contemporaries could still have
imagined. The call for a women's language that, on the model
of a single-sex society, would be free of masculine fictions
about women is just such an anachronistic dream. A close
reading of Dickinson demonstrates that the best course is to
embrace and exploit language's inherent fictiveness, rather
than to fight against it. Almost nothing would remain after
the excision from language of undesirable fictions and the
hierarchical structures that support them. Luce Irigaray ar-
rives by way of psychoanalysis at a position quite close to
Dickinson's poetic sense of language's limits, a hundred years
later, when she says that there may well be a woman's lan-
guage, but that it sounds like babbling; free from dualism, it
does not make any of even the rudimentary distinctions upon
which ordinary comprehensibility rests.[3] Because the very
notion of a sign is based on dualism, the words of this lan-
guage bear indeterminate and non-repeating relations to their
referents, and its syntax, lacking the ordinary relationship be-
tween subject and object, excludes logic and any possibility of
linear reading. Impracticable as it may be, this projected
non-dualistic language is at least more genuinely revolu-
tionary and poetically suggestive than the goal of a feminist
literal language in which words and their referents would be
exactly determinate—a language, furthermore, whose origi-
nal is Adam's speech.

The naïve wish for a literal language and the belief in poet-
ry's capacity for the duplication of experience foster a concep-

tion of the feminine self in poetry that is, paradoxically, even more egotistical than some of the masculine paradigms from which it intends to free itself. In the poetics of "female experience," the poet's own female "I" must be unabashedly present in the poem, in order for the poem to be true. The poet must not hide behind a mask of convention or let her modesty exclude her from the poem altogether. This emphasis on self sounds at first like the answer to Dorothy's evasions of self, or to Brontë's uncertainty about the external sources of her power, as if these impediments to poetry had been removed by twentieth-century women's increasing self-confidence. But when Rich says ". . . I am Adrienne alone" or when Alta names herself in a poem ("my name is Alta. / I am a woman."), that particular, personal "I" differs greatly from the sense of self that underlies much of Romantic poetry.[4] Wordsworth, egotist though he is, does not name himself Wordsworth; "creative soul" and "Poet" are names that enlarge the self, where explicit naming would diminish it. Claiming one's own subjectivity seems, from the example of the nineteenth-century poets, a necessary precondition of writing poetry, but the unmasked and reductive "I" is only a further function of that belief in the literal, that it can be expressed and have literal effects. The new "I" has nothing to do with creative power; its purpose is to make poetry approximate as closely as possible a personal, spoken communication.[5] It will not do simply to perform a poor imitation of the masculine "I" for the sake of asserting equality, because true equality is inconceivable within the conceptual framework of dualism. Dickinson's poems in which the self is composed of two identical, self-regarding parts point to a sense of self that undermines dualism far more effectively than the self-centered, single "I" of feminist poetry.[6]

To place an exclusive valuation on the literal, expecially to identify the self as literal, is simply to ratify women's age-old and disadvantageous position as the other and the object. Contemporary poetry by women that takes up this self-defeating strategy risks encounters with death that are destructive both poetically and actually. The current belief in a literal "I" present in poetry is responsible for the popular superstition that Sylvia Plath's death was the purposeful completion of her poetry's project, the assumption being that if the speaker is precisely the same as the biographical Plath, the poetry's self-destructive violence is directed toward Plath herself, not toward an imagined speaker. This reading of Plath is unfair to the woman and, by calling it merely unmediated self-expression, obscures her poetry's real power. In poem after poem depicting or wishing for physical violence, the imagery of violence is part of a symmetrical figurative system, and death is figured as a way of achieving rebirth or some other transcendence.[7] Plath's project may not thus be very different from that of Dickinson, who speaks quite often from beyond the grave, reimagining and repossessing death as her own in order to dispel the terrors of literal death. However, within that figurative system the poet embraces a self-destructive program that must soon have been poetically terminal, even if it did not bring about the actual death.

Several of Plath's late poems come to terms with a father figure (who may include the poetic fathers she acknowledges in *The Colossus*), whose crime, no different from that identified by nineteenth-century women, is of attempting to transform the feminine self into objects. "Lady Lazarus" borrows the most appalling of Nazi imagery to accuse a generalized figure of male power of the ultimate reification. Not only is the dead victim of "Herr Doktor" and "Herr Enemy" an object in being dead, but she is also reduced to the actual physical objects from which the Nazis profited by destroying human bodies: "a Nazi lampshade,"

> A cake of soap,
> A wedding ring,
> A gold filling.[8]

The poem combines the tradition of woman as medium of exchange with that of woman as object to produce a desperately concise picture of literalization.

> I am your opus,
> I am your valuable,
> The pure gold baby

> That melts to a shriek.

Though the poet is here objecting to literalization, not embracing it, the poetic myth of suicide through which the oppression may be lifted amounts to the same thing: the speaker must submit to this literalization in order to transcend it.

> Out of the ash
> I rise with my red hair
> And I eat men like air.

Their death costs her death, and powerful though the poem is, this is an extraordinarily high price for retribution. And as always, it is the process of objectification that makes up the poem, not the final, scarcely articulable transcendence.

"Daddy" uses Nazi imagery to make the same accusation about objectification brought against men as oppressors in "Lady Lazarus" and makes the corollary accusation against the father (and the husband modelled after him) that objectification has silenced her:

> I never could talk to you.
> The tongue stuck in my jaw.

> It stuck in a barb wire snare.
> Ich, ich, ich, ich,
> I could hardly speak.

In this context defiance and retribution take the form of her speaking, but again this counterattack is counterproductive. Punning on the expression "being through" to mean both establishing a telephone connection and being finished, she at once makes and conclusively severs communication:

> So daddy, I'm finally through.
> The black telephone's off at the root,
> The voices just can't worm through.

The poem concludes, "Daddy, daddy, you bastard, I'm through." Suppressing the power of the one who silenced her, she simultaneously returns herself to the silence that the poem came into being to protest.

If being "through" is the ambiguous, counterproductive solution in this poem, "Edge" makes the final pun on the ambiguity of the word "perfection" to mean both the highest ideal of art and death. The traditional association of art with static perfection serves to separate life as much as possible from art, but Plath revises this tradition to associate art's perfection at once with immortality and with an actual perfecting or finishing of life:

> The woman is perfected.
> Her dead
>
> Body wears the smile of accomplishment,
> The illusion of a Greek necessity
>
> Flows in the scrolls of her toga.

A woman's dead body literalizes the beautiful, frozen forms on the grecian urn of Keats' "Cold Pastoral." The final perfection toward which the myth works requires that the figure of the woman become an object, in the double sense of her being dead and also an object for aesthetic contemplation. The way of escaping the father's imposed definitions is again synonymous with a celebration of woman as object.

Both as Wordsworth portrays it and as Dorothy Wordsworth, Brontë, and Dickinson echo and respond to it, the feminine figure who becomes an object by merging with nature, dying as a result, represents the masculine appropriation of femininity. The woman in Plath's poems dies in an effort to avoid this appropriation, whereas Lucy and Margaret and their successors yield to it—yet in both situations it is the appeal of the literal that is destructive. In the Lucy situation literal nature swallows the woman; for the women in Plath's poems the danger is that by provisionally accepting the old equation of woman and object in order to destroy it, they destroy themselves in the process. The result is the same.

That "Edge" makes the equation between woman and object in terms of an aesthetic object raises the question of the relation between Plath's real life and her art. Anne Sexton's memorial, "Sylvia's Death," makes the death a byproduct of the poems, endorsing the belief that Plath is literally identical with her speaker:

> what is your death
> but an old belonging,
>
> a mole that fell out
> of one of your poems?[9]

Although Plath's own death was not simply a repetition of the deaths enacted in her poems—had she literally believed in her suicidal myth, she would never have written a word—it is possible that she did give way to that literal belief about poetry in a different way. She shared with other women poets the overwhelming conflict, created by social and literary custom, between the vocations of woman and of poet, and demanded in spite of that conflict that the life of the mind be as actual as the life of the woman and mother, or that the life of the mother be as perfect as the static life of art. Whether or not she came to believe that her poems model a way for conducting her life, that her poems find only one way around the masculine objectification of women—death—suggests that from her life she could adduce no better way.

A mask, however despised by those who call for an end to them in women's poetry, provides for any poet a necessary separation between the self and the poem, just as the knowledge of language's fictiveness, the origin of masks, can mediate between a woman poet and the cultural dictate that women are objects. To embrace a belief in the literal means to embrace death, not death transformed but actual death. Rich's poem "Diving into the Wreck" became for many readers in the early 1970's a manifesto of feminist poetry, because of its androgynous collectivity and because of its polemic about discarding our old myths about the sexes in order to see "the wreck and not the story of the wreck / the thing itself and not the myth."[10] And yet even here, the diver depends on the mask that permits her to see these things under water and that in fact stands between her and death: "my mask is powerful / it pumps my blood with power." The poem thus qualifies its own wish for total revelation, knowing that such qualification is not an evasion but a necessity if the poet is to go on writing. The poem, further, makes its point about discarding myths in the highly figurative framework of a miniature allegory, demonstrating as part of its polemic that the mask that figuration provides is not incompatible with feminist rhetoric. A belief in figuration is life-giving.

The dangerous acceptance of literalization appears also in poems bearing on the idea of the mother, making a related point of contact between the poets considered in this study and their recent inheritors. None of the nineteenth-century poets were themselves mothers, but all the modern poets mentioned here were or are mothers. The nineteenth-century poets could consider motherhood from the removed viewpoints of tradition and of their remembered daughterhoods; even so, the subject was troubling. Whatever difficulties they experienced in relation to the concept of motherhood are multiplied for the women for whom it is not a concept but a consuming reality. Motherhood is literal creativity. It must be difficult for a woman to choose as her vocation poetry or figurative creativity, perhaps to the detriment of the maternal vocation with which she is expected to be contented, because the values associated with motherhood and with poetry are so very different. It may be that developing a poetics of literal truth, however impossible an aim, is the most logical response to this situation, the only poetics that might be expected to compete with motherhood on motherhood's untranslatable terms. When Rich turns her attention to motherhood, she writes in non-fiction prose rather than in verse, explaining, analyzing, and arguing rather than inventing. The term "non-fiction" helps to account for the switch: the subject of motherhood calls forth a desire to avoid fictions and to approximate the truth. Motherhood resists incorporation into the traditional values of poetry.

The entrance of psychoanalytic insights into common language has made it possible for a woman's identity with her mother to be openly accepted and for her struggles with this relationship to become appropriate topics for poetry. Relative to the covert mentions of the mother in works by Dorothy and Brontë, the mother's inhibiting influence is all on the surface in Sexton's poetry, perhaps fulfilling Irigaray's aim to have women reclaim their maternal origins. Yet because motherhood still represents the same group of values and qualities that it represented in the nineteenth century, this greater certainty about identity between mother and daughter does nothing to relieve what was threatening about the suggestions of that identity for Dorothy and Brontë, but instead intensifies it enormously. "I see around me tombstones grey" presents an extreme case of earth as the devouring mother identified with death; the speaker cannot allow herself to imagine transcendence for herself after death, in spite of her dislike for the idea of a final mortality, because of her closing non-ironic acknowledgment that she is identified with that maternal earth. The figure of the mother in Dorothy's "Irregular Verses" ("To Julia Marshall—A Fragment") and the implicit figure of Mother Nature in other poems block her efforts and even her desire to become a poet. These maternal figures seem ominous enough; but compared with Sexton's and Plath's the nineteenth-century image permits at least an illusion of freedom. There is now no possibility of plausibly imagining an alternative transcendence.

Plath's late poem on the mother, "Medusa," uses with even greater intensity the same counterproductive or suicidal strategy that informs the poems about the father: the poem implicates the speaker herself in the attack on the mother, not because she must die in order to get rid of her, as in the case of the father, but because the two women are too much alike.

The mother's love is expressed as a grotesque sucking (she is pictured as having tentacles that grasp with suckers) that causes mother and child to exchange places. What the speaker is trying to deny is an identification with her mother that is mediated by the Christian myth of transubstantiation:

> Who do you think you are?
> A Communion wafer? Blubbery Mary?
> I shall take no bite of your body.

The refusal to identify with the mother also means a refusal of nourishment, past and present, so that to deny the mother is also to deny the self. The mother is identified with physical properties of motherhood that are seen here horrifically: "Fat and red, a placenta / Paralyzing the kicking lovers," "Bottle in which I live, / Ghastly Vatican"; and although these belong to the mother, the poem's concern with identity between daughter and mother implies the speaker's fear that they are hers too. The final line is ambiguous: "There is nothing between us" suggests both that the "Old barnacled umbilicus" has been severed and that there is nothing separating them.

Two of Sexton's farewells to her mother, written after her mother's death, endeavor to free themselves of the mother's presence, but both poems are weighted with the tug of origins back to death. The memory of the mother is at least restrictive, often fatal. In "The Division of Parts" the poet as daughter is loaded with guilt at her mother's death, so much so that she cannot "shed my daughterhood," and is haunted in sleep by her mother's image.[11] She is able to shift this burden somewhat, from herself as daughter to the more neutral position of "inheritor" (the occasion of the poem is the division of the mother's property between three sisters) by reducing the mother to an aspect of language. A torrent of words descriptively naming the mother closes with "my Lady of my first words," so that the inheritance is of language; this gift alone can be accepted without guilt. In "The Double Image" the portraits of mother and daughter hang opposite each other, so similar that they seem instead one portrait and its reflection in a mirror. The poet's closing guilty address to her own daughter, "I made you to find me," echoes the implied words of the poet's mother earlier in the poem, "I made you to kill me:"

> She turned from me, as if death were catching,
> as if death transferred,
> as if my dying had eaten inside of her.
> . . . .
> On the first of September she looked at me
> and said I gave her cancer.
> They carved her sweet hills out
> and still I couldn't answer.

In Plath's "Edge" one of the ways of figuring death is that the "perfected" woman has reincorporated her dead children back into her body. Sexton, making an even more explicit relation between death and maternity, makes pregnancy grotesquely the metaphor for her mother's death from cancer:

> That was the winter
> that my mother died,
> half mad on morphine,
> blown up, at last,
> like a pregnant pig.[12]

Later in the same poem she puns on the word "deliver," having it refer both to childbirth and to deliverance from suffering. If her mother gives birth to death, then the poet herself is death's twin. In "The Death Baby" the poet imagines her own babyhood as "an ice baby"; then, exactly repeating her mother, she pictures her death—assumed here to be a voluntary act—as the taking up of the death baby, "my stone child / with still eyes like marbles." When she holds the death baby, death itself "will be / that final rocking," where rocking also means turning into rock.[13]

"That final rocking:" Adrienne Rich ends *The Dream of a Common Language*, so far her most didactically feminist book, in a highly affirmative mood, with a woman who turns into a rock. "Transcendental Etude" (1977), the book's closing poem, bewilderingly celebrates a number of male visions of femininity that have always restricted women, both humanly and poetically, and yet this celebration is made in the name of a revolutionary feminism. To overturn Freud's views on femininity is the twentieth-century woman's equivalent for the nineteenth century's objections to patriarchal religion, and a poem of a year earlier, "Sibling Mysteries," introduces the grounds for anti-Freudian sentiment with textbook clarity:

> The daughters never were
> true brides of the father
>
> the daughters were to begin with
> brides of the mother
>
> then brides of each other
> under a different law[14]

"Transcendental Etude" enlarges experiential Lesbianism into an aesthetic project, at the same time enacting a program for recovering lost maternal origins. "A whole new poetry" will spring from the identity of self, lover, and mother, through the enlarging and consoling of the self:

> Birth stripped our birthright from us,
> tore us from a woman, from women, from ourselves
> so early on
> and the whole chorus throbbing at our ears
> like midges, told us nothing, nothing
> of origins, . . .
> . . . .
>
> Only: that it is unnatural,
> the homesickness for a woman, for ourselves,
> for that acute joy at the shadow her head and arms
> cast on a wall, her heavy or slender
> thighs on which we lay, flesh against flesh,
> . . . .
> *This is what she was to me, and this*

is how I can love myself—
as only a woman can love me.

The reader scarcely has a chance to consider whether this love
that obliterates difference can be productive poetically, be-
cause before going on the poem enacts the promised return to
the mother, in a final passage that is ostentatiously old-
fashioned both in its imagery and in its import for poetry.

Vision begins to happen in such a life
as if a woman quietly walked away
from the argument and jargon in a room
and sitting down in the kitchen, began turning in her lap
bits of yarn, calico and velvet scraps,
laying them out absently on the scrubbed boards
in the lamplight, . . .

More little objects, domestic and natural, all with traditional
feminine associations, are described for ten further lines. It is
implied that the woman is arranging them, but we see only
the objects, while she has faded from view. This description is
followed by a polemic against the traditional values of art:

Such a composition has nothing to do with eternity,
the striving for greatness, brilliance—
only with the musing of a mind
one with her body, . . .

The poems in *The Dream of a Common Language* are presum-
ably something more than this and it is misleading for the
poet to celebrate such absent musings as a paradigm for
poetry, even though the poem keeps on being seductively
lovely. The woman is passive and stereotypically lacking in
an identity of her own:

with no mere will to mastery,
only care for the many-lived, unending
forms in which she finds herself, . . .

She becomes both a dangerous object and the cure for the
wound it inflicts (the traditional types for the woman as

whore and as saint), becoming at last (but not finally, the poem suggests)

the stone foundation, rockshelf further
forming underneath everything that grows.

This ending may not be literally suicidal, as identity with the mother is for Sexton, but it is poetically terminal. Instead of "a whole new poetry beginning here," as promised, both poem and book end here with a return to the mother, to mothers of the past. Earlier the poem seemed to be proposing to take a detour into the past in order to reincorporate the past into the present, but the return never takes place. What happens in this poem is uncannily like the process of Dorothy's "A Winter's Ramble in Grasmere Vale," even to the point of the similarity of the closing images. Rich's "rockshelf" is uncomfortably close to the beautiful rock Dorothy encounters on a walk originally undertaken, as Rich's poem is, in a spirit of searching for newness; the rock is the emissary from Mother Nature that prevents her from continuing both her search and her poem. (Plath's mother in "Medusa" too may turn her into stone.) Rich's rock is an image of mother as nature, the cthonic feminine object whose existence as the valorized image of womanhood has impeded and continues to impede the ability of women to choose, among many other things, the vocation of poet. The great difference between Dorothy and Rich is that Rich is fully conscious of all the cultural implications of her exhortation, and willfully propounds this image when she could have chosen any other, whereas Dorothy can scarcely see around the impressive bulk of her brother's views. Dorothy has no polemical purpose; Rich knows her language is lovely enough to persuade us that she embraces inarticulateness, and that we should, too. Rich's lovely woman in the lamplight, turning her back on "argument and jargon," is as much a threat to the life of the female mind as Dickinson's Mother Nature, who "Wills Silence – Everywhere – ." The poem exhorts a twin impossibility; the literal in a poem, and this sort of woman as poet.

Two earlier poems in the same volume take a different position relative to the literal, and although Rich does not grant them the polemical force of standing last and of announcing themselves as models for a new poetry, they do suggest possibilities for poetry somewhere between total acquiescence to male paradigms of femininity and an unimaginable revolution in language. Like "Transcendental Etude" they look back at tradition, but not only do they avoid the trap of feminist literalism that that poem endorses, they also endeavor to find positive value in tradition. "To a Poet" (1974) is at once a critique of the poetics of the literal and a positive revision of Romantic egotism. Quoting, with significant changes, the first two lines of Keats' sonnet "When I have fears," Rich invites Keats to leave the solitude produced by his fear of mortality ("—then on the shore / Of the wide world I stand alone") and join a collectivity of poets. Gently correcting Keats' sorrowing inwardness, she carries Keats' special capacity for generous sympathy into this poem and beyond the point where Keats took it himself, to an actual address to other poets who might share Keats' own anxieties.[15] Here are Keats' lines:

> When I have fears that I may cease to be
> Before my pen has gleaned my teeming brain

and here is Rich's version:

> *and I have fears that you will cease to be*
> *before your pen has glean'd your teeming brain*

In addition to having Keats turn from addressing himself to addressing someone else, the poet fuses her "I" with his in an even subtler sympathy. The lines come in the middle of an address to a woman poet who is "dragged down" by the confining vocation of impoverished motherhood but for whom poetry is still somehow just possible:

> Language floats at the vanishing-point
> *incarnate*   breathes the fluorescent bulb

> *primary* states the scarred grain of the floor
> and on the ceiling in torn plaster laughs *imago*

The grand and abstract poetic language that this woman finds (in the traditional location of the sublime, "the vanishing-point") transcends her circumstances. The speaker then describes a different woman who lives

> where language floats and spins
> *abortion* in
> the bowl

At the opposite pole from the first woman's chance at a saving transcendence, for this woman word and object are one in a way that fully realizes the worst connotations of the closing of "Transcendental Etude." In a literalization of Keats' metaphor of the fertility of the mind, which he fears to lose, this woman must forgo her literal fertility and, because of this, any mental fertility she might have. This word that literally floats and then vanishes literalizes the transcendent language that figuratively floats at the vanishing-point for the first woman. Could this second woman write at all, she would be able only to repeat in a language close to literal a horrifying "female experience." While the poem corrects Keats in order to direct his and the poet's sympathy toward the suffering woman, it also endorses Keats as a way of correcting the idea of a reductive poetry of female literalism. Keats has already started the imaginative process he seeks when he chooses the word "gleaning" as a figure for writing poetry: layering Keats' poem with her own, Rich reminds us of the powerful transport figuration offers.

"To a Poet" makes its peace with tradition through a high degree of selectivity; Keats' sympathy and relative lack of self-centeredness are exceptional among the Romantics. "Phantasia for Elvira Shatayev" (1974) takes on, in order to revise, a much larger and more difficult portion of tradition. The poem admits and inserts itself into a dualistic system and makes its mark not by undermining it—as in Dickinson's more radical project—but by claiming to meet its challenge—to cross the various boundaries it sets up—through a feminist rhetoric. At the same time, the poem undermines the same literalism that "To a Poet" decries. It at once accepts and stretches beyond its limits the notion of a poetry of female experience: although the poem's pretext is an actual event, the deaths of the members of a women's mountain-climbing team, the experience is utterly unlike what is usually meant by "female experience," and the poem is in any case about transcending experience. The poem escapes the likelihood of its readers confusing its "I" with the author by having an overtly fictive persona, Elvira Shatayev imagined as speaking from beyond her death, but as when the poet fuses her own "I" with Keats' in "To a Poet," titling the poem "Phantasia for . . ." makes it clear that the poet is speaking here too. This layered persona is, furthermore, ready to take up other personae:

> If in this sleep I speak
> it's with a voice no longer personal
> (I want to say   *with voices*)

This collectivizing of the self is central to the poem's revision of Romantic egotism, and to its effort to find an explicitly feminist transcendence. Instead of a poet-hero solitary in his self-consciousness, the poem presents a group, heroic in its mutuality: "*I have never seen / my own forces so taken up and shared / and given back.*" The poem solves for itself the nineteenth-century women's fear that poetic power may be located only outside the self: poetic voice and power are here in an everywhere that is not other.

The poem asserts that transcendence need not belong exclusively to the masculine imagination. The poem's setting crowds it with memories of Romantic poetry's strivings after sublimity and of its assertions of imaginative power—Wordsworth's mountain visions in Books VI and XIV of *The Prelude*, Shelley's "Mont Blanc" and Promethean scenarios in Shelley and Byron—and of the Miltonic and Biblical mountains of vision that precede these. But having joined this company, the speaker and her companions, women of power and vision of their own, pass into the universal in a way that is overtly feminist. The poem harmoniously pairs what might be viewed as a traditionally masculine form of transcendence with a new and self-consciously feminist one:

> Every cell's core of heat   pulsed out of us
> into the thin air   of the universe
> the armature of rock beneath these snows
> this mountain   which has taken   the imprint of our minds
> through changes elemental and minute
> as those we underwent
> to bring each other here
> choosing ourselves   each other   and this life
> whose every breath   and grasp   and further foothold
> is somewhere   still enacted   and continuing

The first two lines of this passage represent a literal or physical transcendence of the body in death, which shifts imperceptibly into the major Romantic project of having the mind transcend its boundaries to imprint nature with its power. The last two lines reach another Romantic goal, to transcend the limits of death and find beyond it power and sublimity. Between these two Romantic projects and linking them syntactically is a transcendence of the individual self that identifies itself here and elsewhere as explicitly feminist. Not content simply to find for this feminist transcendence a place alongside them, the poem's extraordinary claim is that these Romantic projects are fulfilled only through it. It holds that the transcendence the Romantics sought was impossible under the conditions of Romantic egotism and is only possible through collectivity. The subordinate clauses that begin in the transitions between the pivotal lines, "changes elemental and minute / as those we underwent" and "this life / whose every breath . . . ," cause the first of the Romantic projects to be measured by and the second to be dependent upon the feminist project's achievement; only by first crediting the power of collectivity can the reader then enter into the feeling that neither the mountain nor death create insuperable barriers to consciousness. The passage makes these transcendences occur, and it makes them a totality.

The speaker's grieving husband is portrayed at first as finite and other, somewhat stereotypically and unfairly as women often are portrayed where the self is male. Climbing the mountain to bury her, his boots leave "their geometric bite / colossally embossed" on the snow; compared to the limitless women, he is enclosed in selfhood:

> You come (I know this)   with your love   your loss
> strapped to your body   with your tape-recorder   camera
> ice-pick

He will bury them "in the snow   and in your mind / While my body lies out here." The poem enters into the nineteenth-century problem of the woman dying into nature, but here it is the universe—"the possible," not cthonic nature—of which she has become a part, and death generates speech rather than curtailing it. The husband is put in the position of the male poet who gains his central speaking self from the silent otherness of the women he buries, but unlike Lucy and Margaret, these women cannot be buried in nature, nor can they be silenced:

> When you have buried us   told your story
> ours does not end   we stream
> into the unfinished   the unbegun
> the possible

But this man is engaged in a generous and loving action that atones for the speaker's memory of having "trailed" him on previous climbs when the old relations between the sexes still obtained. Through him, the poet forgives the male poets their limitations and accepts with grace what they have to offer; the poem is beyond anger.

Where "Transcendental Etude" foils its own feminist program by uncritically accepting what amounts to the male paradigm of the woman who merges with nature, "Phantasia" makes stronger claims for its feminism by revising and incorporating another traditional paradigm. Rather than the woman's becoming a rock, "the armature of rock" of the snow-covered mountain takes "the imprint of our minds." To imprint a rock is to re-engage a strategy like Dickinson's, to ask language's difference to reopen an apparent closure. By so beautifully having the dead climber speak, "Phantasia" performs (as do many of Dickinson's poems) one of the highest and most traditional imaginative functions: it calls the dead back to life. Having made outrageous claims for its fiction-making power, the poem closes with a final, powerful act of figuration:

> *What does love mean*
> *what does it mean   "to survive"*
> *A cable of blue fire ropes our bodies*
> *burning together in the snow   We will not live*
> *to settle for less   We have dreamed of this*
> *all of our lives*

Like Dickinson's "long, big shining fibre," this cable of blue fire is both infinitely suggestive, and irreducible and untranslatable. It joins the bodies together simultaneously as it joins them to sublime regions; and it makes the necessity for figuration inseparable from the necessity for collectivity and for transcendence.

"Phantasia for Elvira Shatayev" makes figuration necessary; "Transcendental Etude" ends by trying to make an end to figuration. The woman who becomes a rock begins her figurative life quite neutrally, as a metaphor for the manner in which vision takes place in the new life of women loving women: "Vision begins to happen in such a life / as if a woman quietly walked away . . . ." In other words, the poet can now write poetry that does not engage in abstract preludes to action, but that instead takes action itself. The woman is a figure for vision, or for poetry. But what begins to happen in such a poem is that the figure for vision becomes the vision itself; not only is this how vision occurs, but also this is the sort of vision that occurs. To prove that exhortations are over and that practice has begun, the poem stops using abstract terms like "spirit" and "poetry," and does something very practical: it gives us a concrete image. The image is at once tenor and vehicle, both a figure for vision and the vision itself. This collapse of the usual structure of rhetoric is repeated at the close of the passage, where it is said that the woman becomes the broken glass and the soothing leaf and the rockshelf, rather than, conventionally, that she is like these things. This is an undoing of rhetoric that can never be an undoing of language, in the manner of Dickinson's very different kind of undoing, because what it points toward is an impossible conflation of word and referent, of signifier and signified. This conflation is also the aim of that other tenet of contemporary women's poetry, to speak literally and to be true. A woman, fortunately, can be a rock only in a poem; language's difference saves this poetics from itself.

Notes

INTRODUCTION, PAGES 3-11

1. Hélène Cixous, "Sorties," in *La Jeune Née*, by Catherine Clement and Hélène Cixous (Paris: Union d'Editions, 1975), pp. 114-246.
2. Elaine Showalter, *A Literature of Their Own: English Women Novelists from Brontë to Lessing* (Princeton: Princeton University Press, 1977), p. 318.
3. Virginia Woolf, *A Room of One's Own* (London: Hogarth Press, 1929), p. 142.
4. Patricia Meyer Spacks, *The Female Imagination* (New York: Knopf, 1975).
5. But see, for one way of considering the ideological conditioning of poetry, Theodor W. Adorno, "Lyric Poetry and Society," *Telos*, 20 (1974), 56-71.
6. Major exceptions are the work of Suzanne Juhasz in *Naked and Fiery Forms: Modern American Poetry by Women, A New Tradition* (New York: Harper & Row, 1976), and the introduction by, and the essays collected by, Sandra M. Gilbert and Susan Gubar in *Shakespeare's Sisters: Feminist Essays on Women Poets* (Bloomington: Indiana University Press, 1979).
7. Rosalind Miles, *The Fiction of Sex: Themes and Functions of Sex Difference in the Modern Novel* (London: Vision Press, 1974), pp. 37-38.
8. Ellen Moers, *Literary Women* (New York: Doubleday, 1977).

CHAPTER I, PAGES 12-40

1. For an illuminating reading of Romantic images of women, see Irene Taylor and Gina Luria, "Gender and Genre: Women in British Romantic Literature," in *What Manner of Woman: Essays on English and American Life and Literature*, ed. Marlene Springer (New York: New York University Press, 1977), pp. 98-123; for more general accounts of literature's part in perpetuating a patriarchal culture that is oppressive to women, see, for example, Simone de Beauvoir, *The Second Sex*, trans. and ed. H. M. Parshley (French edition 1949; New York: Knopf, 1953), or Kate Millett, *Sexual Politics* (New York: Doubleday, 1970).
2. See Mary Daly, *The Church and the Second Sex* (1968; 2nd ed. New York: Harper & Row, 1975).

3. See also Northrop Frye's account of Wordsworthian Mother Nature in his *A Study of English Romanticism* (New York: Random House, 1968), pp. 16–20, in which he argues that this figure is a revival of the ancient mother goddess.

4. Harold Bloom, *The Anxiety of Influence* (New York: Oxford University Press, 1973).

5. A note on names: although it is condescending to refer to an adult and a writer by her first name, it is not quite possible to refer to Dorothy Wordsworth as "Wordsworth," even where William Wordsworth is not included in the discussion, and it is clumsy to use the full name. Dorothy Wordsworth will be Dorothy from here on. Dickinson is certainly Dickinson, and Emily Brontë may be able to claim Brontë, as least in the present context.

6. Carroll Smith-Rosenberg, "The Female World of Love and Ritual: Relations between Women in Nineteenth-Century America," *Signs*, 1, No. 1 (1975), 1–29.

7. Lynn Sukenick, "Feeling and Reason in Doris Lessing's Fiction," *Contemporary Literature*, 14 (1973), 519.

8. *The Standard Edition of the Complete Psychological Works of Sigmund Freud*, trans. and ed. James Strachey and Anna Freud (London: Hogarth Press and Institute of Psycho-Analysis, 1964), XXII, 119. Subsequent quotations from Freud are from this edition, cited as *SE* followed by volume and page numbers.

9. Karen Horney, "The Flight from Womanhood" (1926) and "The Dread of Woman" (1932), in *Feminine Psychology* (New York: Norton, 1967), pp. 54–70, 133–146.

10. Clara Thompson, "Penis Envy in Women," *Psychiatry*, 6 (1943), 123–125; rpt. in *Psychoanalysis and Women*, ed. Jean B. Miller (New York: Brunner, Mazel, 1973), pp. 43–47.

11. All quotations from Milton's *Paradise Lost* are from *John Milton: Complete Poems and Major Prose*, ed. Merritt Y. Hughes (New York: Bobbs-Merrill, 1957), cited hereafter as *PL* followed by book and line numbers.

12. Luce Irigaray, *Speculum de l'autre femme* (Paris: Éditions de Minuit, 1974). The first section of the book, "La Tache aveugle d'un vieux rêve de symétrie" (pp. 9–162), is devoted to a point-by-point critique of the path Freud charts for girls, particularly in the "Lecture on Femininity." If women are indeed not mirror images of men, then the Freudian scheme becomes groundless.

13. All quotations from Wordsworth are from *The Poetical Works of William Wordsworth*, 5 vols., ed. E. de Selincourt and H. Darbishire (London: The Clarendon Press of Oxford University Press, 1940–1949), cited hereafter (where necessary) as *PW* fol-

lowed by volume and page numbers; and from *The Prelude: Or Growth of a Poet's Mind*, ed. E. de Selincourt, 2nd ed. rev. H. Darbishire (London: The Clarendon Press of Oxford University Press, 1959). I quote from the 1805 version of *The Prelude*, rather than from the more familiar version of 1850 (except where otherwise noted), since most of my citations will pertain to Dorothy Wordsworth, and the 1805 version is the closer to the many versions she would have known.

14. Frances Ferguson, *Wordsworth: Language as Counter-Spirit* (New Haven: Yale University Press, 1977), pp. 173-194.

15. Jonathan Wordsworth, *The Music of Humanity: A Critical Study of Wordsworth's* Ruined Cottage, *Incorporating Texts from a Manuscript of 1799-1800* (London: Nelson, 1969), p. 102.

16. The lines including "faith" and "meditative sympathies" (952-955) were part of the experience of reading *The Excursion* only after 1845; up to that time, the reader would simply have found "Appeared an idle dream that could not live / Where meditation was. I turned away, . . . " Though the revision adds a note of explicit orthodoxy to the poem not present in "meditation," the effect of philosophic abstraction is about the same in the two versions.

17. The tradition that Lucy was Dorothy begins with Coleridge, who, quoting "A Slumber Did My Spirit Seal" in a letter of April 1799, guessed that it referred to Wordsworth's fear that his sister might die. Four of the five poems were written while Dorothy and William were isolated together in Germany. It is of course improbable that Lucy "was" anyone in particular.

18. Published under the title *George and Sarah Green: A Narrative*, ed. E. de Selincourt (London: The Clarendon Press of Oxford University Press, 1936). The quotation is from p. 86. Dorothy is misquoting and paraphrasing *The Excursion*, I, 777-780.

19. *The Complete Poems of Emily Jane Brontë*, ed. C. W. Hatfield (New York: Columbia University Press, 1941), p. 90.

20. Harold Bloom, *The Visionary Company: A Reading of English Romantic Poetry* (1961; rev. ed. Ithaca: Cornell University Press, 1971), pp. 217-218.

21. Sandra M. Gilbert discusses, from a slightly different point of view, this and other inhibiting effects of Milton on women writers, in "Patriarchal Poetry and Women Readers: Reflections on Milton's Bogey," *PMLA*, 93 (1978), 368-382.

22. See Elizabeth Gould Davis, *The First Sex* (1971; rpt. Harmondsworth, Middlesex: Penguin, 1976), pp. 143-144.

23. *Biographia Literaria*, Chapter 13. This and subsequent quotations are from the text edited by J. Shawcross (London: The Claren-

don Press of Oxford University Press, 1907); quotations from Coleridge's poetry are from *The Complete Poetical Works of Samuel Taylor Coleridge*, ed. Ernest Hartley Coleridge (London: The Clarendon Press of Oxford University Press, 1912).

24. Quotations from *Nature* and "Literary Ethics" are from *The Collected Works of Ralph Waldo Emerson*, vol. I ed. Alfred R. Ferguson and Robert R. Spiller (Cambridge: The Belknap Press of Harvard University Press, 1971), cited as *W*; quotations from other essays (including this one from "The Poet") are from the centenary edition, *The Complete Works of Ralph Waldo Emerson*, ed. Edward Waldo Emerson (Boston: Houghton Mifflin, 1903-1904), cited as *CW*.

25. It is important to exempt Keats at least in part from this generalization. "Negative capability" and a generous sympathy for others distinguish him, in thought and feeling if not always in poetic practice, from other poets for whom the self is central. Among the Romantics, Keats was also the poorest and came from the humblest origins, and he alone had no contact with classical education. It may be that certain aspects of women's experience as outsiders relative to the major literary tradition were shared by all the disenfranchised, regardless of gender. Though hardly an impediment poetically, that capacity for sympathy was quite literally fatal to him when translated into the traditionally feminine role that he adopted in nursing his dying brother Tom. Nonetheless, *Endymion* and "Lamia" chart as effectively as possible the extreme images of woman as other, from desired and elusive goddess to evil temptress.

26. *Journals of Dorothy Wordsworth*, ed. Mary Moorman (London: Oxford University Press, 1971), p. 113, entry for 21 April 1802.

27. Jacques Derrida, "The Purveyor of Truth," in *Graphesis, Yale French Studies*, 52 (1975), 31-113, p. 96, translated from "Le Facteur de la verité," *Poétique*, 21 (1975), 96-147. Derrida is conjoining Lacan's "phallocentrism" with his own "logocentrism." See Jacques Lacan, "La Signification du phallus" and "Propos directifs pour un Congrès sur la sexualité féminine," in *Écrits* (Paris: Le Seuil, 1966), pp. 685-695, 725-736. See also Jacques Derrida, *De la Grammatologie* (Paris: Éditions de Minuit, 1967), p. 23; translated as *Of Grammatology*, trans. Gayatri Chakravorty Spivak (Baltimore: Johns Hopkins University Press, 1976), pp. 10-11.

28. Jacques Derrida, "La Question du style," in *Nietzsche aujourd'hui?* (Paris: Centre Culturel de Cerisy-La-Salle, 1973), I, 235-287; also published in a four-language edition, translated into English as *Spurs*, trans. Barbara Harlow (Venice: Cobbo e Fiore, 1976).

29. *The Journals and Miscellaneous Notebooks of Ralph Waldo Emerson*, Vol. VIII 1841-1843 ed. William H. Gilman and J. E. Parsons (Cambridge: The Belknap Press of Harvard University Press, 1970), p. 87.

30. Gertrude Rachel Levy, *The Gate of Horn: A Study of the Religious Conceptions of the Stone Age, and Their Influence Upon European Thought* (London: Faber and Faber, 1948), pp. 83-88.

31. Joan Goulianos, ed., *by a Woman writt: Literature from Six Centuries by and about Women* (Indianapolis: Bobbs-Merrill, 1973), p. 363.

32. Florence Howe, Introduction, *No More Masks! An Anthology of Poems by Women*, ed. Florence Howe and Ellen Bass (New York: Doubleday, 1973), p. 33. The poem was published originally in Muriel Rukeyser, *The Speed of Darkness* (New York: Random House, 1968).

33. *The Poems of Anne Countess of Winchilsea*, ed. Myra Reynolds (Chicago: University of Chicago Press, 1903), pp. 20-23.

CHAPTER II, PAGES 41-103

1. Although parts or all of most of these poems have been printed in various places, there are reliable published texts only for those printed among Wordsworth's poems and subsequently to be found in *PW*, and for those published in Susan Levin and Robert Ready, "Unpublished Poems from Dorothy Wordsworth's Commonplace Book," *The Wordsworth Circle*, 9 (1978), 33-44. For poems not found in either of these places, my source is Dorothy Wordsworth's Commonplace Book, preserved in the Dove Cottage Library at Grasmere; there are other drafts and copies of Dorothy's poems in other manuscript sources, but this book, which contains entries dated 1826-1832, appears to contain the latest versions of the poems in question. (The Commonplace Book is Journal 21 in the collection of Dove Cottage bound xerographs in the Cornell University Library.) William Knight prints versions of several of Dorothy's poems (in addition to the five that are also printed in *PW*) in volume VIII of his edition of *Poetical Works of William Wordsworth* (London: Macmillan, 1896).

2. *The Letters of William and Dorothy Wordsworth: The Early Years 1787-1805*, ed. Ernest de Selincourt, 2nd ed. rev. Chester Shaver (London: The Clarendon Press of Oxford University Press, 1967), p. 2, late July 1787. References to the letters from this volume will be cited hereafter as *EY*, with page and date.

3. Full title: *A Narrative Concerning George & Sarah Green / of the Parish of Grasmere / addressed to a Friend*. Published as *George and*

Sarah Green: A Narrative, ed. E. de Selincourt (London: The Clarendon Press of Oxford University Press, 1936).

4. *The Letters of William and Dorothy Wordsworth: The Middle Years 1806-1820*, ed. E. de Selincourt, 2nd ed. rev. Mary Moorman (London: The Clarendon Press of Oxford University Press, 1969), I, 25, 20 April 1806.

5. See Richard Onorato, *The Character of the Poet: Wordsworth in The Prelude* (Princeton: Princeton University Press, 1971), pp. 164-205 and passim. Quotations from *The Prelude* are from the 1805 version, except where otherwise noted.

6. Although this poem was originally conceived as the conclusion of a longer poem (the last ten of 22 stanzas), to be discussed later in this chapter, what appears in the Commonplace Book to be the latest version divides the long poem (which in that form is titled "A Fragment") into three and gives separate descriptive titles to the resulting poems. The original long poem was written at some time before the fall of 1805. The manuscript of "A Winter's Ramble in Grasmere Vale" is on pp. 57-58 of the unpaged Cornell xerograph; the long poem, printed from an earlier manuscript, appears in Knight's edition of Wordsworth, VIII, 259-262; Mary Moorman prints "A Winter's Ramble in Grasmere Vale," omitting two stanzas, in an appendix to her edition of *Journals of Dorothy Wordsworth* (London: Oxford University Press, 1971).

7. For a fuller and more complex reading of "Nutting" as a working through of the poet's relations with "the feminine" in nature, see Michael G. Cooke, *Acts of Inclusion: Studies Bearing on an Elementary Theory of Romanticism* (New Haven: Yale University Press, 1979), pp. 137-146.

8. *PW*, II, 504-506. The passage was written during the summer before the winter in Germany when Wordsworth composed all but one of the Lucy poems. The passage includes a sequence of lines that Dorothy records as being a kind of leitmotif for the two of them and that Wordsworth finally used in the sequel to "Ode to Lycoris," a poem about Dorothy. F. W. Bateson takes this passage as conclusive evidence that the Lucy of the Lucy poems is Dorothy, in *Wordsworth: A Re-Interpretation* (London: Longmans, 1954), p. 152.

9. *Journals*, ed. Moorman, p. 15, entry for 14 May 1800. This edition comprises *The Alfoxden Journal* and *The Grasmere Journal*, and all citations from these texts are from this edition, cited hereafter as *AG*, with page number and date.

10. There are many examples of this restraint in *Alfoxden* and *Grasmere*; Rachel Brownstein, in "The Private Life," *MLQ*, 34 (1973), 52, cites the entry for 12 April 1802.

11. The poem is printed in Knight, VIII, 284-289; however, as Knight follows what appears to be the earlier of two texts in the Commonplace Book, I am following and quoting from the version that appears to incorporate Dorothy's latest revisions, found on pp. 35-36 and 43-47 of the Cornell xerograph.

12. Levin and Ready, pp. 36-38.

13. Levin and Ready read the sixth line of this passage as " 'Twill glance on one—and to reprove" (1. 75), but the manuscript that they transcribe (pp. 86-90 in the Cornell xerograph) appears to read, ". . . glance on me . . . ."

14. The same process of turning a description of the object world into a poem about subjectivity occurs in Wordsworth's derivation of "I wandered lonely as a cloud" from a *Grasmere* entry. For a reading of this process, with an emphasis different from mine, see Frederick A. Pottle, "The Eye and the Object in the Poetry of Wordsworth," *The Yale Review*, 40 (1950), 27-42; rpt. in *Romanticism and Consciousness: Essays in Criticism*, ed. Harold Bloom (New York: Norton, 1970), pp. 273-287.

15. See Geoffrey Hartman, "A Touching Compulsion: Wordsworth and the Problem of Literary Representation," *The Georgia Review*, 31 (1977), 358.

16. Levin and Ready, pp. 38-39. The poem was probably written in 1832: this poem and two others to be discussed later in this chapter are found in the Commonplace Book following what appears to have been intended as a kind of title page on which Dorothy writes, "Sick-bed Consolations—composed during the spring of the year 1832." Beginning in 1829 Dorothy was subject to periods of severe illness, which by 1835 caused her to be permanently bed-ridden.

17. Knight prints a version of the original long poem (see above, note 6) using the first line as title: "Peaceful Our Valley, Fair and Green." I am quoting here, from the four poems, from what appears to be the latest revision in the Commonplace Book. In some manuscripts "A Sketch" is copied out after the long poem, sometimes before, but it is always associated with the other Grasmere verses and in this latest version it appears first.

18. Although the original long poem was almost certainly originally written while Dorothy and William were still living in their own cottage in Grasmere vale, that she kept recopying and reworking this poem alone of the poems that she wrote during that period suggests that it retained for her a personal meaning long after they had moved away. The manuscript copy from which I quote (pp. 48-58 in the Cornell xerograph) was probably written in 1826 or 1827; at that time, the poem's sense of exclusion from a prized but inaccessible center would have had a very literal sig-

nificance for Dorothy, who still looked back on the Grasmere cottage as the happiest of homes.

19. Quotations from this poem are from the Commonplace Book, pp. 70–71. Knight prints the last five stanzas (VIII, 297) with the title "To My Niece Dora." Knight dates the poem 1827, although the first version in the Commonplace Book, which Dorothy was using in 1827 and from which she selected the verses for the fair copy from which Knight prints, is dated 1832. The poem is the first of the "Sick-bed Consolations" (see above, note 16).

20. The poem is printed in *PW*, IV, 162-163; though not dated individually, it is among the "Sick-bed Consolations," generally dated 1832. The original title in the Commonplace Book is "An incident in the schemes of Nature."

21. *Journals of Dorothy Wordsworth*, ed. E. de Selincourt, 2 vols. (London: Macmillan, 1959), cited hereafter as *J*, with volume and page. Vol. I contains the *Recollections of . . . Scotland*; vol. II contains the *Journal of a Tour on the Continent*, 1820. All quotations from the *Recollections* are from the section written in 1803, after Dorothy's return from the tour; the *Tour on the Continent* was written in 1821 from notes taken on the tour. (Because neither text was written at the time of the tour, I do not cite the dates given for the entries from which I quote.)

22. Geoffrey Hartman, *Wordsworth's Poetry 1787-1814* (New Haven: Yale University Press, 1964), pp. 60–65. I quote above and throughout from the 1805 *Prelude* because that is the version that Dorothy would have known, but the passage from Book VI was later revised to the more familiar "when the light of sense / Goes out, but with a flash that has revealed / The invisible world" (1850, VI, 600-602).

23. "Processions: Suggested on a Sabbath Morning in the Vale of Chamouny," *Memorials of a Tour on the Continent, 1820*, xxxii. Several of the *Memorials*, including this one, draw on Dorothy's *Journal* for subject matter and for wording.

24. William Coxe, *Sketches of the Natural, Civil, and Political State of Swisserland* (London, 1779), pp. 11-21.

25. *Collected Letters of Samuel Taylor Coleridge*, ed. E. L. Griggs (London: The Clarendon Press of Oxford University Press, 1956) I: 1785-1800, 330-331, 3 July 1797.

CHAPTER III, PAGES 104-161

1. Quoted in Elizabeth Gaskell, *The Life of Charlotte Brontë* (1857; Harmondsworth, Middlesex: Penguin, 1975), p. 230.

2. From the "Biographical Notice of Ellis and Acton Bell," written

for her 1850 edition of *Wuthering Heights* and *Agnes Grey*. All quotations from *Wuthering Heights* and Charlotte's prefatory material are from *Wuthering Heights*, ed. William M. Sale (New York: Norton, 1963), cited hereafter as *WH* with page numbers.

3. For accounts of Charlotte's misunderstanding of her sister's work, and the real harm it may have done, see Philip Henderson, Introd., *Emily Brontë: Poems Selected with an Introduction* (London: Lawson and Dunn, 1947), pp. ix-xii; and Robin Grove, " 'It Would Not Do': Emily Brontë as Poet," in *The Art of Emily Brontë*, ed. Anne Smith (London: Vision Press, 1976), pp. 34-39.

4. Carol Ohmann discusses the way critics trivialized *Wuthering Heights* once its author's identity had been revealed, in "Emily Brontë in the Hands of Male Critics," *College English*, 32 (1971), 906-913.

5. C. Day Lewis argues, on the biographical level, that Brontë was unconsciously frustrated at not being a man, and that her dissatisfaction with the world was a projection of this frustration. See "The Poetry of Emily Brontë," *Brontë Society Transactions*, 13 (1957), 94-97.

6. All quotations from Brontë's poetry are from *The Complete Poems of Emily Jane Brontë*, ed. C. W. Hatfield (New York: Columbia University Press, 1941), cited as P followed by the poem number assigned by Hatfield. In this edition, each of the poems in the non-Gondal notebook bears a number according to its position in the notebook (A 1 - A 31); these numbers, where applicable, will be cited as well as Hatfield's numbers, which are assigned chronologically.

7. Fannie E. Ratchford, *The Brontës' Web of Childhood* (New York: Columbia University Press, 1941), p. 12.

8. Grove, in Smith, pp. 42-46. Rosalind Miles, in an essay in the same collection, "A Baby God: The Creative Dynamism of Emily Brontë's Poetry," pp. 68-73, searching for autobiographical information, laments the absence of an authorial self.

9. A number of readers have noted the use of Byronic themes and stances in Brontë's poetry, for example Helen Brown, "The Influence of Byron on Emily Brontë," *Modern Language Review*, 34 (1939), 374-381; Dorothy J. Cooper, "The Romantics and Emily Brontë," *Brontë Society Transactions*, 12 (1952), 106-112; Alan Loxterman, "*Wuthering Heights* as Romantic Poem and Victorian Novel," in *A Festschrift for Prof. Marguerite Roberts*, ed. Frieda E. Penninger (Richmond, Va.: University of Richmond, 1976), pp. 91-92. Cooper also cites parallels between Brontë's poetry and gothic novels.

10. J. Hillis Miller discusses her ambivalent relation to her imagination in *The Disappearance of God: Five Nineteenth-Century Writers*

(Cambridge: The Belknap Press of Harvard University Press, 1963), pp. 158-159; Charles Morgan also sketches a theory of ambiguously received possession, in *Reflections in a Mirror* (London: Macmillan, 1944), pp. 142-145. My purpose is to expand and elaborate these suggestions.

11. Jonathan Wordsworth has suggested that the "I" is Julian throughout, and that the first three stanzas are the present-time frame for a recollection. If the figure at the window is Julian, then the Wanderer would be his beloved, Rochelle, in human or ghostly form. This reading would account for the erotic implications of the third stanza, but the voice in the first three stanzas differs too much from the voice we learn to recognize as Julian's for this reading to make sense. See "Wordsworth and the Poetry of Emily Brontë," *Brontë Society Transactions*, 16 (1972), 85-100.

12. See, among others: Margaret Willy, "Emily Brontë: Poet and Mystic," *English*, 6 (1946), 117-122; Muriel A. Dobson, "Was Emily Brontë a Mystic?," *Brontë Society Transactions*, 11 (1948), 166-175; Jacques Blondel, *Emily Brontë: Expérience spirituelle et création poétique* (Paris: Presses Universitaires de France, 1955), pp. 192-218.

13. Winifred Gérin, *Emily Brontë: A Biography* (London: The Clarendon Press of Oxford University Press, 1971), p. 154.

14. Barbara Hardy, "The Lyricism of Emily Brontë," in Smith, pp. 105-106.

15. Robert Kiely, *The Romantic Novel in England* (Cambridge: Harvard University Press, 1972), pp. 233-251, esp. pp. 237, 245.

16. Leo Bersani, *A Future for Astyanax: Character and Desire in Literature* (Boston: Little, Brown, 1976), pp. 197-223.

17. See Miller, p. 174.

18. For a fuller account of the figuration of nature in *Wuthering Heights*, see Margaret Homans, "Repression and Sublimation of Nature in *Wuthering Heights*," PMLA, 93 (1978), 9-19.

19. See, for example, Lawrence J. Starzyk, "Emily Brontë: Poetry in a Mingled Tone," *Criticism*, 14 (1972), 119-136; "The Faith of Emily Brontë's Immortality Creed," *Victorian Poetry*, 11 (1973), 295-305.

20. Seven French "devoirs" are published as an appendix to Gérin's *Biography*, pp. 266-274. "Le Papillon" is dated 11 Aug. 1842. Quotations are from *Five Essays Written in French by Emily Jane Brontë*, trans. Lorine W. Nagel (Austin: University of Texas Press, 1948), pp. 17-19.

21. Starzyk (1972), p. 124; Miller, p. 164.

22. Blondel, pp. 204-205; Morgan, pp. 142-145.

23. My translation; the original French is in Gérin's *Biography*, pp. 268-269.

24. The pertinent parts of Freud's discussion are in *Standard Edition*, XVIII, 36-43, 49-58. *A Future for Astyanax*, pp. 206-212.
25. Willy, p. 121; Dobson, pp. 171-172; Morgan, pp. 142-145.
26. Grove, in Smith, pp. 61-63.

CHAPTER IV, PAGES 162-214

1. See Joanne Feit Diehl's discussion of Dickinson's interest in her feminine predecessors, " 'Another Way to See': Dickinson and her English Romantic Precursors," Diss. Yale 1974, 24-25. See also Ellen Moers' discussion of Dickinson's references to Elizabeth Barrett Browning in *Literary Women*, pp. 84-91.
2. *The Letters of Emily Dickinson*, ed. Thomas H. Johnson and Theodora Ward (Cambridge: The Belknap Press of Harvard University Press, 1958), III, 700. Quotations from *Letters* are cited hereafter as *L*, followed by volume and page, and by date, where appropriate. Quotations from Dickinson's poems are from *The Poems of Emily Dickinson*, ed. Thomas H. Johnson (Cambridge: The Belknap Press of Harvard University Press, 1955), cited as P followed by the poem number assigned by Johnson.
3. Two articles describe affinities between Brontë's and Dickinson's styles and themes: Margaret Willy, "The Poetry of Emily Dickinson," *Essays and Studies*, 10 (1957), 91-104; David Drew, "Emily Brontë and Emily Dickinson as Mystic Poets," *Brontë Society Transactions*, 15 (1968), 227-232. Many other readers have noted in passing other similarities between the two poets.
4. It may be useful here briefly to review some of the work that has been done in this area. John Cody's *After Great Pain: The Inner Life of Emily Dickinson* (Cambridge: The Belknap Press of Harvard University Press, 1971) applies to the poems biographical information concerning Dickinson's femininity in a highly deterministic way; Lillian Faderman's "Emily Dickinson's Letters to Sue Gilbert," *The Massachusetts Review*, 18 (1977), 197-225, uses biographical information much more tactfully but it does not aim at a reading of the poems. Of those who have attempted to use a non-biographical or textually derived concept of femininity, Albert J. Gelpi and Joanne Feit Diehl have been the most successful in demonstrating the difference femininity makes for her identity as a poet, Gelpi in *Emily Dickinson: The Mind of the Poet* (Cambridge: Harvard University Press, 1966), pp. 109-127, by examining the array of feminine terms she uses about herself, such as bride and queen, Feit Diehl by analyzing Dickinson's way of characterizing various facets of poetic power as masculine, in the dissertation cited above and in " 'Come Slowly –

Eden': An Exploration of Women Poets and Their Muse," *Signs*, 3, No. 3 (1978), 572-587. Others have been less successful. Jean McClure Mudge's *Emily Dickinson and the Image of Home* (Amherst: University of Massachusetts Press, 1975) defines Dickinson's mind as innately feminine according to certain preconceived notions of "the feminine," for example Erikson's "inner space." Gelpi's more recent work on Dickinson, in *The Tenth Muse: The Psyche of the American Poet* (Cambridge: Harvard University Press, 1975), pp. 219-299, relies on a different but equally exterior system to show that Dickinson's term "circumference" is a feminine symbol; and other Jungian critics are similarly deterministic. Elsa Greene usefully challenges Dickinson's readers to remember the cultural prejudices about women that must have hindered her becoming a poet, but she ends her essay with an exhortation to read Dickinson's poems "as a woman's art based on female human experience," without indicating how to do so: "Emily Dickinson Was a Poetess," *College English*, 34 (1972), 70; see also the chapter on Dickinson in Suzanne Juhasz, *Naked and Fiery Forms: Modern American Poetry by Women, A New Tradition* (New York: Harper & Row, 1976), pp. 7-32. The difficulty with this approach is that Dickinson's "female human experience" (as a total recluse) has been shared by few other women.

5. See the account of her early worries about religion in Richard B. Sewall, *The Life of Emily Dickinson* (New York: Farrar, Straus and Giroux, 1974), II, 328, 356-361, 375-376, 380-383.

6. Edward Hitchcock, President of Amherst College and intellectual leader of Amherst Academy, which Dickinson attended between the ages of nine and sixteen, sermonized against the dangers of any poetry that did not serve orthodoxy. Sewall, pp. 352-353.

7. *CW*, III, 21. Joanne Feit Diehl emphasizes the proximity between Dickinson's poetic identity and Emerson's views in "The Poet," in "Emerson, Dickinson, and the Abyss," *ELH*, 44 (1977), 683-698; Elsa Greene points out the specifically masculine nature of Emerson's definition of the poet.

8. For a fuller reading of these texts, see Vivian Pollak, "Emily Dickinson's Valentines," *American Quarterly*, 26 (1974), 60-78.

9. Sewall, at the end of a discussion of Dickinson's early fondness for metaphors, reads this letter as the closest approximation in Dickinson to an announcement of the origin of poethood, *Life*, pp. 395-397.

10. John Cody reads the entire letter about the cold extensively, interpreting it exclusively as an expression of sexual anxiety, in *After Great Pain*, pp. 175-180.

11. See Thomas H. Johnson's introduction to *The Poems*, pp. xxx-xxxiii, for an account of the poem's publication and reception by the public.

12. Charles R. Anderson reads these poems without irony, in *Emily Dickinson's Poetry: Stairway of Surprise* (New York: Holt, Rinehart and Winston, 1960), pp. 191ff.

13. There is a discussion and catalogue of Dickinson's use of paradox and contrast in Brita Lindberg-Seyersted, *The Voice of the Poet: Aspects of Style in the Poetry of Emily Dickinson* (Cambridge: Harvard University Press, 1968), pp. 103-108, 204-207.

14. Others include poems numbered 364, 439, 571, 572, 801, 807, 838, 857, and 1057.

15. Anna Freud, *The Ego and the Mechanisms of Defense*, trans. Cecil Baines (New York: International Universities Press, 1946), p. 7.

16. See also Karen Horney's discussion of Freud's dualistic thinking, in *New Ways in Psychoanalysis* (New York: Norton, 1939), pp. 40-41.

17. Anderson, pp. 86-87; Inder Nath Kher, *The Landscape of Absence: Emily Dickinson's Poetry* (New Haven: Yale University Press, 1974), pp. 39-44.

18. Anderson, pp. 81-95. This is the major argument of his first chapter on Dickinson's poems about nature.

19. Anderson, p. 97, takes this poem to be mawkish and sentimental, as does Thomas H. Johnson, in *Emily Dickinson: An Interpretive Biography* (Cambridge: The Belknap Press of Harvard University Press, 1955), pp. 184-185.

20. John Emerson Todd discusses Dickinson's "ironic humility" (in relation to a different group of poems) in *Emily Dickinson's Use of the Persona* (The Hague: Mouton, 1973), pp. 9-10.

21. Gelpi, *The Tenth Muse*, p. 251.

22. David T. Porter cites this poem as an example of what he calls the "little spaniel" situation, in *The Art of Emily Dickinson's Early Poetry* (Cambridge: Harvard University Press, 1966), pp. 86-87.

23. There is an extensive discussion of Dickinson's mask of humility in the Master letters in Ruth Miller's *The Poetry of Emily Dickinson* (Middletown: Wesleyan University Press, 1968), pp. 173, 179-180.

24. Charlotte Brontë, *Jane Eyre* (Oxford: Shakespeare Head Press, 1931), II, 274.

25. Many feminists, as well as other critics, have pointed out this problem in Jung's thought. For a particularly salient critique, see Naomi Goldenberg, "A Feminist Critique of Jung," *Signs*, 2, No. 2 (1976), 443-449.

26. Anderson, pp. 42-43; Robert Weisbuch, *Emily Dickinson's Poetry* (Chicago: University of Chicago Press, 1975), p. 162.

CONCLUSION, PAGES 215-236

1. See, among others, Suzanne Juhasz, *Naked and Fiery Forms: Modern American Poetry by Women, A New Tradition* (New York: Harper & Row, 1976), pp. 3-5, 185, and passim; Florence Howe, Introduction, *No More Masks! An Anthology of Poems by Women*, ed. Florence Howe and Ellen Bass (New York: Doubleday, 1973), pp. 3-33.

2. *The World Split Open: Four Centuries of Women Poets in England and America, 1552-1950*, ed. Louise Bernikow (New York: Random House, 1974); the editor's introduction (pp. 3-47) makes many of the same arguments about women's poetry as those presented in the works cited above.

3. Luce Irigaray, *Ce Sexe qui n'en est pas un* (Paris: Éditions de Minuit, 1977), pp. 28, 77, 110-111 and passim; the author puts some of her suggestions for a new syntax into practice in *Speculum de l'autre femme*.

4. Adrienne Rich, *The Dream of a Common Language: Poems 1974-1977* (New York: Norton, 1978), p. 34; Alta, "Bitter Herbs," in *No More Masks!*, p. 294.

5. The rare "I" that does appear in Dorothy Wordsworth's journals is as close to literal as possible and might seem to be paradigmatic of the genuine self-presentation sought in these instances. But Dorothy achieves that effect by having refused to publish, while Rich and Alta claim, through the act of writing for publication, a universality for the "I" while it is also literally personal.

6. Irigaray's recent strategy for undermining dualism is a proposal for a structure of mind and of society based, like Dickinson's, on a non-hierarchical two or on multiplicity, rather than on "the privilege, the domination, the solipsism of *one*" (*Ce Sexe*, p. 207). Like the experience of reading Dickinson, this conception is extremely difficult for a reader conditioned by dualism to grasp; but like the non-dualistic language she begins to describe, it seems to offer a more challenging direction for feminist thinking to move in.

7. I am indebted here, for their persuasively positive readings of Plath, to Judith Kroll, *Chapters in a Mythology: The Poetry of Sylvia Plath* (New York: Harper & Row, 1976), and to Stacy Pies, "Coming Clear of the Shadow: The Poetry of Sylvia Plath," unpublished essay (Yale University, 1979).

8. All quotations from Sylvia Plath are from *Ariel* (New York: Harper & Row, 1966).

9. From *Live or Die* (Boston: Houghton Mifflin, 1966).

10. From *Diving into the Wreck: Poems 1971-1972* (New York: Norton, 1973).

11. This poem and "The Double Image" are from *To Bedlam and Part Way Back* (Boston: Houghton Mifflin, 1960).
12. "Flee on Your Donkey," from *Live or Die*.
13. "The Death Baby," from *The Death Notebooks* (Boston: Houghton Mifflin, 1974).
14. From *The Dream of a Common Language*. All subsequent quotations from Rich are from this volume.
15. Rich elsewhere expresses admiration for Keats and absorbs his "Negative Capability" into a discussion about Jung and "weak ego boundaries," "Three Conversations," in *Adrienne Rich's Poetry: Texts of the Poems, The Poet on Her Work, Reviews and Criticism*, ed. Barbara Charlesworth Gelpi and Albert Gelpi (New York: Norton, 1975), p. 115.

Index

Wordsworth, Dorothy, 5-6, 9, 18, 82, *41-103*, 238n-44n, 250n; life of, 14, 41-50 passim, 62; and religion, 32; and Coleridge, 34, 85-86, 88, 102-103; lack of poet's subjectivity, 36, 70-86, 88, 92-94, 103, 111, 129, 170, 211-12, 218; not a poet, 42, 48-49, 165-66; and maternal origins, maturation, and poetry, 43-70, 97-100, 156; and childhood, 46-57, 62-70; and feminized nature, 49-57, 70, 85-86, 95, 97-103, 152, 215, 221, 224, 229; as observer of autonomous nature, 71-75, 85-97, 100-103, 191-92; and EB, 104, 106-107, 111, 137, 150, 152, 156; and ED, 165-66, 170, 191, 194, 198, 200, 211-12

    works discussed: A Narrative Concerning George and Sarah Green, 27, 41-42, 48, 57-62, 149-50, 239n, 241n-42n; *Grasmere Journal*, 34, 41, 56-58, 72-73, 86-88, 242n-43n; poems (general), 41-42, 48-49, 241n; *Letters*, 41, 43-49, 57, 241n-42n; *Alfoxden Journal*, 41, 57, 71-75, 86-87, 242n; journals (general), 42-44, 49, 86; Holiday at Gwerndwffnant, 48, 62-70, 98-100, 112; A Winter's Ramble in Grasmere Vale, 50-53, 56, 60, 78, 82, 98, 106, 229, 242n; Irregular Verses—To Julia Marshall, 67-70, 98-100, 112, 160, 198, 224; Thoughts on My Sick-Bed, 75-78, 83, 85-86; Cottage poems, 78, 82-83, 85-86, 99-100, 102, 112, 137, 242n-43n (*see also* individual titles); A Cottage in Grasmere Vale, 78-81; After-recollections at the sight of the same cottage, 78, 81-82; A Sketch, 78-79; Lines intended for my Niece's Album,

82-83, 85, 98-100; Floating Island, 83-86, 244n; *Recollections of a Tour Made in Scotland, 1803*, 88-91, 94-95, 244n; *Journal of a Tour on the Continent*, 91-97, 160, 244n; Commonplace book, 241n-44n

Wordsworth, Dorothy and William Wordsworth, 41-46, 56-57, 75, 78, 81, 92, 95, 229, 241n-42n, 244n; WW's poems about DW, 25-26, 43, 46, 51-54, 101-103, 128, 239n, 242; WW's identification of DW with nature, 26-27, 85-86, 101-103, 104, 106, 152, 160; DW's use of WW's poems, 27, 59; DW's poems about WW and his poetry, 50-54, 65-67, 75-78, 81-83; WW's use of DW's journals, 73-75, 91-92, 243n-44n

Wordsworth, John, 44-46

Wordsworth, Jonathan, 239n, 246n

Wordsworth, Mary Hutchinson, 20, 58

Wordsworth, William, 6, 8, 111, 218, 238n-39n, 241n-42n; and feminine characterization of nature, 4, 13, 15, 17-23, 25-29, 49-57, 70, 85-86, 95, 101-103; and maturation and poetry, 20, 49-56, 65-67, 70; and imagination, 31, 33-34, 54-55, 65-67, 103, 118, 128

    works discussed: The Prelude, 18, 20-21, 24, 26, 33, 46, 49, 54-55, 64-65, 84-85, 89-90, 101-103, 160, 232, 244n; Ode: Intimations of Immortality, 18-20, 54-55, 66-67, 76, 80; Prospectus to *The Excursion*, 18-19; *The Excursion*, 20, 23-28, 59, 221, 234, 239n; Lines Composed a Few Miles Above Tintern Abbey, 20, 26-27, 54-55, 66, 76-78, 118, 128, 160; She was a Phantom of Delight, 20; Ruth, 20;

Library of Congress Cataloging in Publication Data

Homans, Margaret, 1952-
    Women writers and poetic identity.

    Includes bibliographical references and index.
        1.   English poetry—Women authors—History and
criticism.   2.   English poetry—19th century—History
and criticism.   3.   Women and literature.   4.   Words-
worth, Dorothy, 1771-1855—Poetic works.   5.   Brontë,
Emily Jane, 1818-1848—Poetic works.   6.   Dickinson,
Emily, 1830-1886—Criticism and interpretation.   I.   Ti-
tle.
PR589.W6H6   1980   821'.009'9287   80-7527
ISBN 0-691-06440-7